"I love America more than any other country in the world, and, exactly for this reason, I insist on the right to criticize her perpetually."

—James Baldwin

Of Thee I Sing

THE AMERICAN WAYS SERIES

General Editor: John David Smith
Charles H. Stone Distinguished Professor of American History
University of North Carolina at Charlotte

From the long arcs of America's history to the short timeframes that convey larger stories, American Ways provides concise, accessible topical histories informed by the latest scholarship and written by scholars who are both leading experts in their fields and polished writers.

Books in the series provide general readers and students with compel- ling introductions to America's social, cultural, political, and economic history, underscoring questions of class, gender, racial, and sectional diversity and inclusivity. The titles suggest the multiple ways that the past informs the present and shapes the future in often unforeseen ways.

CURRENT TITLES IN THE SERIES

How America Eats: A Social History of U.S. Food and Culture, by Jennifer Jensen Wallach

Popular Justice: A History of Lynching in America, by Manfred Berg

Bounds of Their Habitation: Race and Religion in American History, by Paul Harvey

National Pastime: U.S. History through Baseball, by Martin C. Babicz and Thomas W. Zeiler

Wartime America: The World War II Home Front, Second Edition, by John W. Jeffries

Enemies of the State: The Radical Right in America from FDR to Trump, by D. J. Mulloy

Hard Times: Economic Depressions in America, by Richard Striner

We the People: The 500-Year Battle Over Who Is American, by Ben Railton

Litigation Nation: How Lawsuits Represent Changing Ideas of Self, Business Practices, and Right and Wrong in American History, by Peter Charles Hoffer

Years of Rage: From the Klan to the Alt-Right, by D.J. Mulloy

All American Rebels: The American Left from the Wobblies to Today, by Robert C. Cottrell

Of Thee I Sing: The Contested History of American Patriotism, by Ben Railton

American Agriculture: From Farm Families to Agribusiness, by Mark V. Wetherington

Germans in America: A Concise History, by Walter D. Kamphoefner

American Exceptionalism, by Volker Depkat

Making America's Public Lands: The Contested History of Conservation on Federal Lands, by Adam Sowards

Hoops: A Cultural History of Basketball in America, by Thomas Aiello

To Reach the Nation's Ear: A History of African American Public Speaking, by Richard W. Leeman

How America Gets the News: A History of American Journalism, by Ford Risley and Ashley Walter

Of Thee I Sing

The Contested History of American Patriotism

Ben Railton

ROWMAN & LITTLEFIELD
Lanham • Boulder • New York • London

Published by Rowman & Littlefield
An imprint of The Rowman & Littlefield Publishing Group, Inc.
4501 Forbes Boulevard, Suite 200, Lanham, Maryland 20706
www.rowman.com

86-90 Paul Street, London EC2A 4NE

British Library Cataloguing in Publication Information Available

Library of Congress Cataloging-in-Publication Data

Names: Railton, Ben, 1977– author. | Rowman and Littlefield, Inc.
Title: Of thee I sing : the contested history of American patriotism / Ben Railton.
Description: Lanham : Rowman & Littlefield Publishers, 2020. | Includes bibliographical
    references and index.
Identifiers: LCCN 2020031260 (print) | LCCN 2020031261 (ebook) | ISBN
    9781538143421 (Cloth) | ISBN 9781538199916 (Paperback) | ISBN 9781538143438
    (ePub)
Subjects: LCSH: Patriotism—United States—History. | Political participation—United
    States—History. | National characteristics, American. | United States—Politics and
    government—History.
Classification: LCC JK1759 .R34 2020 (print) | LCC JK1759 (ebook) | DDC
    323.6/50973—dc23
LC record available at https://lccn.loc.gov/2020031260
LC ebook record available at https://lccn.loc.gov/2020031261

♾™ The paper used in this publication meets the minimum requirements of
American National Standard for Information Sciences—Permanence of Paper
for Printed Library Materials, ANSI/NISO Z39.48-1992.

Contents

Acknowledgments

This book was finished during the strangest and most stressful time I've ever lived through. That moment continues to unfold, and it's fair to say I have no idea into what late 2020 America and world *Of Thee I Sing* will be published. Anything I could say here about those subjects would feel incomplete and quite possibly irrelevant in a few months' time, so I'll focus here instead on a few of the many communities for which I'm profoundly grateful, now more than ever.

That starts with my professional homes for 15 years, Fitchburg State University and its English Studies Department and American Studies program. I've learned a great deal from all my colleagues there, especially DeMisty Bellinger-Delfeld, Judy Budz, Chola Chisunka, Katy Covino, Christine Dee, Steve Edwards, Lisa Gim, Sean Goodlett, Patrice Gray, Michael Hoberman, Aruna Krishnamurthy, Kate Jewell, Irene Martyniuk, Joe Moser, Tom Murray, Kisha Tracy, Diego Ubiera, Heather Urbanski, and Ian Williams. I've learned even more from the more than 3,500 students I've taught in that time; that includes far more particularly influential individuals than I could ever acknowledge in a sentence or two here.

My professional communities extend far beyond FSU, of course, as do the individuals for whom I'm especially grateful. With the New England American Studies Association, that includes Elif Armbruster, Akeia Benard, Nancy Caronia, M. M. Dawley, Luke Dietrich, Dan Graham, Sara Sikes, and Jonathan Silverman. With the Northeast MLA, it includes John Casey, Hilda Chacón, Maria DiFrancesco, Indigo Eriksen, Carine Mardorossian, Brandi So, and Claire Sommers. With the Scholars Strategy Network, it includes Ross Caputi, Tiffany Chenault, Dominik Doemer, Avi Green, Parastoo Massoumi, Ben Miyamoto, Danielle Mulligan, and Natasha Warikoo. My *Saturday Evening Post* column and work with Jen Bortel remain shining lights in my online writing life. I could genuinely acknowledge every single member of the #twitterstorians and broader Twitter scholarly communities, but will highlight just a fraction: Ariella Baker-Archer, Kassie Jo Baron, Danielle Cofer, Christina Proenza Coles, Robin Field, Dana Gavin, Sara Georgini, Rob Greene, Donna Harrington-Lueker, Erika Lee, Kevin Levin, Sheila Liming, John Edwin Mason, Keri Leigh Merritt, Meg Mulrooney, Megan Kate Nelson, Ashley Rattner, Heather Cox Richardson, Robin Jewel Smith, Greg Specter and the PALS crew, Jessica Thelen, Matthew Teutsch, Jana Tigchelaar, Kait Tonti, Laura Vrana, and Serena Zabin.

There's a reason why this is my second straight American Ways book, and third straight with Rowman & Littlefield. That reason is first and foremost Jon Sisk, but also includes Dina Guilak, Jessie McCleary, Chelsea Panin, Stephen Ryan, and John David Smith, along with everyone else with whom I've been fortunate to work with through R&L.

Steve and Ilene Railton, you know by now how much I owe to and have learned from both of you, but I'll never get tired of saying it here. Steve Peterson and Jeff Renye, ditto with your enduring and inspiring friendships. By far the best thing about my scholarly work over the last couple years has been my increasing ability to share it with Aidan and Kyle Railton. Indeed, I would argue that you two have really been co-contributors to this project at every stage and in every way, and it is infinitely better and stronger for your voices and ideas and perspectives and support, as am I.

Introduction

Competing Visions of Patriotism

On November 19th, 2019, Army Lt. Colonel and National Security Council (NSC) official Alexander Vindman testified before the House of Representatives' impeachment inquiry into President Donald Trump. Vindman, who had first-hand knowledge of the telephone call between Trump and the Ukrainian president, offered testimony that was highly damaging to the president, and so Trump's defenders and allies went on the attack against Vindman. They did so in large part by using his story as a Ukrainian American immigrant to directly impugn his patriotism and implicitly accuse him of treason: after Fox News host Laura Ingraham highlighted Vindman's background in relationship to his work as a Ukraine expert for the NSC, law professor and former Bush administration official John Yoo replied, "I find that astounding, and some people might call that espionage"; and the next morning CNN contributor and former Republican Congressman Sean Duffy went further, claiming, "I don't know that he's concerned about American policy, but his main mission was to make sure that the Ukraine got those weapons. . . . He's entitled to his opinion. He has an affinity for the Ukraine, he speaks Ukrainian, and he came from the country." Unstated but clearly present in these responses is the idea that Vindman's criticism of the president had marked him as unpatriotic and even un-American, opening up these broader questions about his affinities and allegiances.

Just over a century earlier, however, former president Teddy Roosevelt began his 1918 *Metropolitan* magazine article "Lincoln and Free Speech" with these lines: "Patriotism means to stand by the country. It does not mean to stand by the President or any other public official save exactly to the degree in which he himself stands by the country. . . . In either event it is unpatriotic not to tell the truth—whether about the President or anyone else." And in the prepared statement with which he began his testimony, Alexander Vindman expresses his own vision of patriotism clearly. "I have dedicated my entire professional life to the United States of America," he begins. "As a young man I decided that I wanted to spend my life serving the nation that gave my family refuge from authoritarian oppression, and for the last twenty years it has been an honor to represent and protect this great country." He contextualizes his ability to offer such honest public testimony as part of "the privilege of being an American citizen and public servant." And he ends with his father, whose "courageous decision" to leave the U.S.S.R. and move his family to the United States had, Vindman argues, "inspired a deep sense of gratitude in my brothers and myself and instilled in us a sense of duty and service." Addressing his father directly with his closing words, Vindman makes a moving and compelling case for Roosevelt's point about the essential patriotism of telling the truth: "Dad, my sitting here today . . . is proof that you made the right decision forty years ago to leave the Soviet Union and come here to the United States of America in search of a better life for our family. Do not worry, I will be fine for telling the truth."

Unfortunately, Vindman paid a significant price for his truth-telling—after Trump was acquitted by Senate Republicans in February 2020, he had both Vindman and his twin brother Yevgeny (a JAG officer and attorney on the NSC staff) removed from their positions and escorted out of the White House by security. While that action clearly constituted direct payback by Trump against a figure who had criticized him, it was applauded by Trump's supporters as a necessary step to remove figures who were not sufficiently patriotic to serve in such important national roles. As Tennessee Senator Marsha Blackburn Tweeted about Vindman, "how patriotic is it to badmouth and ridicule our great nation in front of Russia, America's greatest enemy?" Although the last phrase of Blackburn's Tweet jumps out, it is her contrast between "our great nation" on the one hand and "badmouth[ing] and ridicule" on the other that constitutes the core of her attack on Vindman's patriotism.

What underlies such attacks on Vindman's truth-telling as unpatriotic is a definition of patriotism that equates it with a celebration of the nation. Summed up by phrases like "my country, right or wrong" and "America: love it or leave it," this celebratory form of patriotism suggests that anything other than a full embrace of the nation, a vision of America as "the greatest country in the world," is unpatriotic. That celebratory patriotism is embodied in shared communal rituals: the singing of the national anthem with hat in hand and hand on heart; the recitation of the Pledge of Allegiance by schoolchildren at the start of each day; the closing of speeches with "God bless the United States of America." Out of such everyday rituals, scholar Michael Billig argues in his book *Banal Nationalism* (1995), a sense of national belonging and community is constructed. Those rituals and that community are at least potentially inclusive, able to be shared by all Americans, but in this form of patriotism they do require from their participants an endorsement of the celebratory vision of the nation.

The U.S. doesn't simply exist for celebration in the present moment, though—it has developed over centuries of complex history, much of which might seem difficult to celebrate. So a second, interconnected form of patriotism is the construction of mythologized narratives of the past, ones that allow for a concurrent embrace of the historical United States but that do so by excluding certain aspects of, and too often communities from, our history. 2020 has featured a striking example of this exclusionary mythologizing patriotism (which I'll call mythic patriotism for short) in *The Federalist* magazine's 1620 Project, a response to the *New York Times* magazine's 1619 Project that seeks to commemorate "the anniversary of the Pilgrims' arrival at Plymouth Rock." Given that Plymouth Rock itself is a myth, one constructed more than a century after the *Mayflower* reached the New England coast, that framing concisely illustrates how mythic patriotism imagines national histories which can then be celebrated as idealized American origin points and legacies—but which also require the exclusion and even the erasure of other histories and communities, such as the native cultures that were already present when the Pilgrims arrived.

Another element that both celebratory and mythic patriotisms share is that they often present patriotism as fundamentally passive, a participation in national community largely defined by acceptance and repetition of existing rituals and myths. On the other hand, one of American culture's most hotly debated recent events, NFL player Colin Kaepernick's controversial national anthem protests, have modeled a more active form of patriotism. Kaepernick's detractors have presented his actions as unpatriotic, as nothing short of attacks on American soldiers, the flag, and the nation itself; as fellow quarterback Drew Brees put it in a May 2020 interview, "I will never agree with anybody disrespecting the flag of the United States." Yet as illustrated by his decision to kneel rather than sit during the anthem after consulting former NFL player and Green Beret Nate Boyer over what action would be more respectful, Kaepernick clearly perceives his protest as a patriotic tribute to American ideals. But that tribute also embodies a form of activism, as this more active form of patriotism uses and challenges a communal moment of celebration like the anthem to advance an argument about how the nation both has fallen short of and needs to move closer to its ideals. As Kaepernick puts it, "To me this is something that has to change and when there's significant change and I feel like that flag represents what it's supposed to represent in this country, is representing the way that it's supposed to, I'll stand."

Kaepernick's anthem protests thus also embody a fourth vision of patriotism, a critical patriotic perspective that highlights the nation's shortcomings in order to move it closer to its ideals. An exemplary contemporary expression of such critical patriotism is the *New York Times* magazine's 1619 Project, a work of public scholarly journalism, created by journalist Nikole Hannah-Jones and written by a group of historians and artists, that defines the arrival of enslaved Africans as a national origin point in order to analyze the foundational and enduring histories and legacies not just of slavery, but also of African American protest and patriotism. As Hannah-Jones puts it in her Pulitzer Prize-winning introductory essay to the project, "It is black people who have been the perfecters of this democracy." The 1619 Project thus echoes and extends one of America's most succinct and moving expressions of critical patriotism, from the African American writer James Baldwin: "I love America more than any other country in the world and, exactly for this reason, I insist on the right to criticize her perpetually."

Both Kaepernick's protests and the 1619 Project have received significant and sustained backlash, attacks which reveal the potent challenge that these active and critical forms of patriotism present to the celebratory and mythic forms. These competing visions of American patriotism have never been more hotly contested, nor the stakes of how we define both patriotism and the nation clearer or higher, than they are in 2020.

In this book I trace the history and development of those four forms of American patriotism across nine of our most important moments and periods, from the Revolution and the Early Republic to the Civil War and Gilded Age, throughout the 20th century and into the 21st. Across these eras, these contested forms of patriotism have been consistently reflected in competing visions of American history, identity, and community, such as: the longstanding arguments over whether immigrant arrivals and communities need to take part in celebratory patriotic rituals if they are to become "Americanized," or whether such communities represent instead external threats to the nation's ideals; or the ongoing debates over whether Confederate and white supremacist images of America embody a mythic vision of the Founding or require active resistance from critical patriots in defense of national ideals. These and many other debates which I will highlight and analyze across my chapters illustrate the persistence, influence, and significance of competing patriotisms throughout American history.

Each of my four focal forms of patriotism can also be found in one of the four verses of Wellesley College English Professor Katharine Lee Bates' iconic lyrics for one of our most prominent national cultural works: "America the Beautiful." The song's most famous first verse, often the only one performed, illustrates an overtly celebratory embrace of America's beauties: "spacious skies," "amber waves of grain," "purple mountain majesties," "the fruited plain." Originally written as Bates traveled the United States by train in the early 1890s, these celebratory descriptions are based on actual elements of the landscape such as Colorado's Pike Peak, but are given heightened, idealized form through her poetic images and perspective. And like most examples of American celebratory patriotism, this one is potentially inclusive, able to be shared by all who are part of and appreciate this beautiful place.

Yet the idealized side to such celebratory patriotism can easily slip into propaganda, and too often our communal celebrations have been linked to the second, mythic form of patriotism. Bates' second verse illustrates such mythic patriotism, particularly through her image of "pilgrim feet, whose stern, impassioned stress/A thoroughfare for freedom beat across the wilderness!" While this myth does highlight certain aspects of what the Puritan arrivals brought to and experienced in America, it does so both by simplifying that community's own histories and by entirely excluding the histories of Native American cultures in New England and beyond; that exclusion was particularly ironic in the late 19th century Western United States, the time and place where Bates first composed the lyrics just a year before the Wounded Knee massacre. Idealizing a particular American history and community at the expense of others creates an exclusionary vision of the nation that makes it much harder for all Americans to share in this form of patriotism, making mythic patriotism far more divisive and even destructive than other celebratory forms.

Both celebratory and mythic patriotisms often foreground passive participation in shared communal rituals. In contrast, American history features many examples of a more active patriotic expression of commitment to and love of country, and Bates' third verse highlights a prominent such example: the service and sacrifice of Union soldiers during the Civil War. "O beautiful for heroes proved in liberating strife," she writes, "who more than self their country loved and mercy more than life!" Military service comprises one clear and consistent form of active patriotism, but American history provides examples of many others, from social activism and protest to political engagement, journalism, and cultural commentary to the creation of literary and artistic works. Like the best versions of celebratory patriotism, active patriotism represents an inclusive form in which all Americans can potentially take part, a communal vision of service through which all Americans can embody and extend our shared national identity and ideals.

At the same time, examples of active patriotism are often driven by a sense of wrongs that need righting, by a perspective that the nation needs to be moved forward from past or present failings toward a more perfect future. Bates' fourth and final verse offers a vision of this critical form of patriotism:

"O beautiful for patriot dream, that sees beyond the years/Thine alabaster cities gleam undimmed by human tears!" Written at the depths of Gilded Age inequalities, of the rise of Jim Crow and the lynching epidemic, of the culminating genocides of the "Indian Wars" and the nation's expansion into new imperial arenas, these lines implicitly but importantly contrast present "tears" with a "patriot dream" of a more beautiful future. That expression of critical patriotism can be linked to both historical and 21st century examples of that perspective, models of criticizing national flaws and failures in the hopes of moving the nation closer to its ideals and forward toward a more perfect union.

Of Thee I Sing's chapters and conclusion trace those four forms of patriotism across eight historical case studies and up to our present moment's examples and debates:

Chapter 1: The Revolution: Declaring and Constituting a Nation: The American Revolution originated and was sustained by expressions of celebratory patriotism, with Tom Paine, Benjamin Franklin, and other Revolutionary advocates creating and communicating foundational visions of an ideal America worth fighting for. Those views were turned by creative authors such as Phillis Wheatley and the Prospect Poets into a myth of history as all leading up to this glorious present and new nation. Yet Revolutionary War service itself, along with the efforts and debates of the Framers to construct that new nation, constituted a far more active form of patriotism. And the same years saw expressions of critical patriotism from Loyalists, feminists, and abolitionists: all those groups highlighted communities left out of Revolutionary celebrations, while the latter two sought to push the new nation toward a future that overcame those limiting discriminations.

Chapter 2: The Early Republic: Young, Expanding, and Divided: Throughout the early 19th century, celebratory national narratives coalesced around moments such as the War of 1812, the creation of the national anthem, and the 50th anniversary of the Revolution, and the development of collective memories of those events. The unfolding histories and images of national expansion, Manifest Destiny, and the xenophobia of the Know Nothing Party relied on a more overtly mythic vision of American history and identity. Yet new philosophical and social movements such as Transcendentalism and Young America made the case for more active forms of identity, civic engagement, and patriotism. And critical patriots such as Catharine Maria Sedgwick, William Apess, and David Walker highlighted the gaps in Early Republic myths and made the case for foregrounding women, Native Americans, and African Americans in a more inclusive vision of America.

Chapter 3: The Civil War: Testing Whether the Nation Could Endure: The Civil War tested all forms of American patriotism. Cultural support for the Union cause, including the works of Walt Whitman, Herman Melville, and Julia Ward Howe, expressed celebratory patriotism as a bulwark for the war's challenges and tragedies. The Confederacy and its supporters relied on myths of the Revolution and "states' rights" to connect their secession from the United States to patriotic histories. The war also featured numerous inspiring moments of active patriotism in service of American ideals, from Lincoln's philosophical ideas in "The Gettysburg Address" to the courageous efforts of United States Colored Troops, immigrant soldiers, and war nurses. And the critical patriotic voices of figures such as Frederick Douglass, Martin Delany, and Lucy Larcom wed the war to broader critiques of national shortcomings and arguments for how a more perfect union might arise out of the war's horrors.

Chapter 4: The Gilded Age: Wealth, Empire, and Resistance: The Gilded Age was bookended by two world's fairs that expressed and exemplified patriotic celebrations: the 1876 Centennial Exposition in Philadelphia and the 1893 Columbian Exposition in Chicago. Many of the era's excesses, from celebrations of extreme wealth and attacks on workers, to the anti-immigrant sentiments behind the Chinese Exclusion Act, to expansion and imperialism at home and abroad, were rationalized and supported by myths of American history and community. Yet in performances such as those of suffrage activists at the Centennial, August Spies at the Haymarket Trial, and Francis Bellamy's 1892 Pledge of Allegiance, the era featured overt and inspiring expressions of active patriotism. And authors and activists such as Helen Hunt Jackson, Standing Bear, Ida B. Wells, and the Anti-Imperialist League criticized Gilded Age excesses and horrors to make the case for a more unifying and inclusive American future.

Chapter 5: The Progressive Era: From Roosevelt and Reform to World War: The Progressive Era featured amplified forms of celebratory patriotism in a number of arenas, from Teddy Roosevelt's idealized status to the wartime deployment of the iconic national symbol known as Uncle Sam. Those celebrations were often closely tied to mythic patriotisms, whether in the Americanization movement's links to new immigration laws and restrictions, the anti-union "American Plan," or the post-World War I Red Scare. In contrast, a number of Progressive era movements embodied active patriotic efforts to push America closer to its ideals, from social reformers and women's suffrage activists to the Native American artists who achieved the passage of the 1924 Indian Citizenship Act. And other movements expressed more direct critical patriotic challenges to the nation's shortcomings, from anti-war pacifists to muckraking journalists to the founding of the NAACP.

Chapter 6: The Depression and World War II: Beyond the Greatest Generation: Long before the "Greatest Generation" narrative retroactively celebrated this era in American history, national battles against the Great Depression and World War II depended on celebratory images of collective solidarity and service. Yet those celebrations too easily gave way to mythic propaganda in support of social divisions and wartime restrictions, as exemplified by the Japanese internment policy. Communities of protest and service, such as the Depression-era Bonus Army and WWII Japanese American soldiers, embodied instead active patriotism's role in combating those crises. And authors such as Harlem Renaissance artists, political writers like John Dos Passos and John Steinbeck, and the Filipino American migrant worker and novelist Carlos Bulosan criticized the period's propaganda and myths and made the case for their own, alternative visions of America.

Chapter 7: The 1960s: Love It, Leave It, or Change It: Both the challenges of the Vietnam War and the prominence of 60s social and counter-cultural movements contributed to the rise of a new expression of celebratory patriotism, illustrated by the phrase "America: love it or leave it." That phrase itself expressed implicit national myths, a mythic patriotism given clearer expression in pop culture genres such as Westerns and war stories, many of which featured the larger-than-life presence of John Wayne. Both the Civil Rights and anti-war movements relied on concepts of active patriotism, of protest as a vital form of national participation and service. And paralleling but extending those movements were the critically patriotic examples of more radical artists such as James Baldwin and Nina Simone and communities such as the LGBT Rights and American Indian Movements.

Chapter 8: The 1980s: Morning and Mourning in America: The 1980s began (literally and figuratively) with one of nation's most overt expressions of celebratory patriotism: Ronald Reagan's campaign and his administration's slogan, "It's Morning in America." That political movement was closely linked to myths around wealth and work, as well as an idealized image of the '50s in responses to '60s social movements. The decade also featured models of active patriotism from the Vietnam veteran, anti-nuclear, and anti-Apartheid social movements. And counter-cultural communities such as AIDS activists and early rap artists expressed critiques of national failings in an effort to push America toward social and cultural justice and equality.

Conclusion: Patriotism in the Age of Trump: Donald Trump has expressed and relied upon celebratory patriotism more than any other American president, and we can likewise see contemporary examples of such celebratory patriotism in the backlash to the 1619 Project (such as the Woodson Center's 1776 Project). Trump's suggestion that his critics should "go back where they came from" comprises a concurrent form of mythic patriotism, as do the perspectives and actions of white supremacist terrorists like Jeremy Christian. The men who resisted Christian's violence offer one inspiring example of active patriotism, as do the countless protesters and whistleblowers who have stood up for our national ideals amidst our moment's outrages. And this era has produced numerous voices and texts that embody a critical patriotic perspective, from the intimate and angry works of Ta-Nehisi Coates and Gary Clark Jr. to The Killers' ironic and impassioned song "Land of the Free" to, most importantly and inspiringly, the ongoing protests against police brutality and racism that have themselves modeled a more inclusive and ideal American future.

Like many cultural works, the song "My Country 'Tis of Thee" took a long and winding road to becoming the popular schoolchildren's song we know today. The melody seems to have originated as an 18th century English hymn and subsequently evolved into that nation's "God Save the King"; before the 18th century was out it had likewise become the basis for national anthems in a number of other European nations, including Denmark's "A Song to be Sung by the Danish Subjects at the Fete of their King, to the Melody of the English Hymn" and Prussia's "Hail to Thee in the Victor's Wreath." The melody also made its way to the American colonies, and at George Washington's first presidential inauguration (in New York City in 1789) he was greeted with a version with new lyrics composed for the occasion, such as "Joy to our native land!/Let every heart expand/For Washington's at hand."

In 1831, the renowned Massachusetts organist and composer Lowell Mason worked with Samuel Francis Smith, a young man studying for the ministry at the Andover Theological Seminary, to compose the adaptation that became "My Country 'Tis of Thee." That version, also known simply as "America," was first performed by a children's choir at the July 4th celebrations at Boston's historic Park Street Church, where Mason was organist and choirmaster. Smith's lyrics feature the celebratory and mythic forms of patriotism as clearly as do Katharine Lee Bates', as in the lines "Sweet land of liberty" and "Land of the pilgrims' pride." But his most interesting line is "Of thee I sing," a self-referential acknowledgment not only of the song's existence as such, but also and most importantly of the role of such shared songs, of cultural works and their collective performances, in constructing both patriotism and through it the nation itself.

But there have always been competing visions of those constructions and of "My Country." In the same decade as that first 1831 performance of the song, Boston would also be the site for numerous moments and expressions of active and critical patriotism: the first issue of William Lloyd Garrison's abolitionist newspaper *The Liberator* was published in the city on January 1st, 1831; on January 25th, 1834, Garrison published an editorial in that paper expressing his support for the Mashpee Revolt, the Massachusetts rebellion through which the Cape Cod Native American community of Mashpee resisted white settler aggression and convinced the state legislature to name Mashpee a self-governing district; and on January 26th, 1836, one of the key figures in that successful Mashpee uprising, the Native American minister, orator, and author William Apess, delivered his fiery "Eulogy on King Philip" in Boston's Odeon lecture hall, making the case for the 17th century Wampanoag chief as a revolutionary American ancestor akin to and as deserving of commemoration as George Washington.

All these figures and communities likewise sang America, exemplifying active and critical perspectives on the work still to be done if that nation was to become a genuine land of liberty. As in 1830s Boston, every setting and period in American history has been defined by the presence of and conflicts between celebratory, mythic, active, and critical patriotisms. The history of competing American patriotisms is in many ways the history of America itself, a legacy that echoes ever more clearly and crucially into our own moment's debates and our shared future.

Chapter One

The Revolution

Declaring and Constituting a Nation

On March 23rd, 1775, a 38-year-old attorney, planter, and delegate to the Virginia House of Burgesses named Patrick Henry (1736–1799) rose to give a speech at the Second Virginia Convention. That convention, held from March 20th–23rd at St. John's Episcopal Church in Richmond in order to maintain distance from the colony's royal governor Dunmore and his administration in Williamsburg, was the second in a series of meetings of delegates and other civic leaders to debate the question of independence for Virginia and the colonies. Henry had proposed that the colonists raise a militia that would exist separate from the English army and government, and some of the convention's more moderate attendees had spoken out against that proposal as too belligerent and likely to increase the chances of war.

Henry's speech became famous, and a rallying cry for the incipient revolution, due to his closing line: "I know not what course others may take; but as for me, give me liberty or give me death!" But what's particularly striking about the speech is that Henry frames his revolutionary sentiments through an initial lens not of liberty but of patriotism. He opens by making his disagreement with his fellow delegates about precisely that topic, his vision of patriotism in response to theirs: "No man thinks more highly than I do of the patriotism, as well as abilities, of the very worthy gentlemen who have just addressed the House. But different men often see the same subject in different lights; and, therefore, I hope it will not be thought disrespectful to those gentlemen if, entertaining as I do, opinions of a character very opposite to theirs, I shall speak forth my sentiments freely, and without reserve."

Moreover, Henry makes clear that he sees his responsibility to offer such sentiments as itself an expression and exemplification of patriotism. "Should I keep back my opinions at such a time, through fear of giving offence," he admits, "I should consider myself as guilty of treason towards my country."

Given that Virginia (like all the colonies) was still part of England at this time, and Henry thus a subject of King George like every other Virginian, he here reframes the interconnected concepts of patriotism and treason in a particularly bold and crucial way. That is, while he goes on to argue that freedom is "the glorious object of our contest," he frames the battle to attain that freedom, "the noble struggle in which we have been so long engaged" and of which his own speech becomes a part, not just as an opposition to one nation, but also and especially as a patriotic embrace of another, new nation.

Henry's support for independence was one of many expressions of the American Revolution as an act of collective, celebratory patriotism toward the new United States. In framing documents like the Declaration of Independence, argumentative broadsheets like Tom Paine's pamphlets, and influential individual perspectives like Ben Franklin's, such celebratory patriotism became an integral element of the unfolding Revolution. Revolutionary celebratory patriotism also depended upon and deepened myths of America's history and identity, as illustrated by the poetic odes of Phillis Wheatley, Philip Freneau, and Joel Barlow. Yet the Revolutionary era also featured central examples of active patriotism, both in the war's courageous sacrifices and in the constitutive debates and documents that were its ultimate outcomes. And whether from Loyalists offering a distinct vision of Revolutionary patriotism or feminists and abolitionists fighting for those too often left out of the new nation's ideas and ideals, the era's histories and debates also modeled the presence and power of an alternative, critical form of American patriotism.

It stands to reason that in order for leaders of a colonial community to start a revolution to establish national independence, they would need to embrace celebratory patriotism, a vision of that new nation as truly worthy of such a bold action and the many costs and sacrifices it would necessarily entail. While the arguments for independence would certainly need to include the problems and failures of the colonies' current situation and relationship with England, they would also and especially have to feature a positive embrace of the new nation that could be created once that link was severed. The Declaration of Independence, the statement of the colonies' revolutionary intent drafted by Thomas Jefferson, revised by the delegates of the Second Continental Congress (1775–1776), and ratified and signed between July 2nd and 4th, 1776, embodies those multiple layers, delineating the colonists' many complaints against England and King George but framing them with a celebratory patriotic vision of America.

The first element of that celebratory patriotism is subtle but crucial, and is found before the famous words with which transcripts of the Declaration usually begin: "When in the course of human events . . ." The original signed document actually opens, "The unanimous Declaration of the thirteen United States of America"; for the broadside that was distributed to be read throughout the colonies, the phrase was revised to "A Declaration by the representatives of the United States of America, in general Congress assembled." The shift from "unanimous" to "representative" is an important one, illustrating that the delegates recognized the broadside as a document which would need to convince the broader American community of the cause of independence, rather than assume it was already agreed upon. But the two opening phrases nonetheless share a clear and crucial purpose: to define a unified new nation, replacing any vision of these communities as either English colonies or thirteen individual states with the concept of the "United States of America." Celebratory patriotism depends in the first place upon the construction of the imagined but instrumental community of a nation, and it was through phrases like this that the United States was so constructed.

After moving through those aforementioned complaints against the King, "a history of repeated injuries and usurpations," the Declaration's concluding paragraph returns to and amplifies that patriotic celebration of the new nation's identity and purpose. "We, therefore, the Representatives of the united States of America, in General Congress, Assembled, appealing to the Supreme Judge of the world for the rectitude of our intentions, do, in the Name, and by Authority of the good People of these Colonies, solemnly publish and declare, That these United Colonies are, and of Right ought to be Free and Independent States," the paragraph begins, reiterating that new national identity and linking it to a series of idealized defining concepts, from "rectitude" to the "Authority of the good People" to the "Right . . . to be Free and Independent." And the paragraph and the Declaration end with a clear, celebratory statement of just what the "united" in "United States" truly means: "And for the support of this Declaration, with a firm reliance on the protection of divine Providence, we mutually pledge to each other our Lives, our Fortunes and our sacred Honor."

The need for such mutual support and solidarity in the revolutionary fight for the new United States was summed up by a phrase associated, in the era and ever since, with the Second Continental Congress: "We must hang together, or we will surely hang separately." As with many historical quotes, it's possible that this one was apocryphal, or perhaps a paraphrase of that general sentiment of the necessity as well as the celebration of unity between the states at the outset of this revolutionary conflict. But the Congressional delegate to whom the quote was attributed, Pennsylvania's Benjamin Franklin (1706–1790), was more than just the gathering's elder statesman (at 70 years old he was by far the oldest delegate): he was also a figure whose own individual, evolving perspective on independence and America reflects the period's move toward celebratory patriotism.

On May 5th, 1775, as the delegates began to arrive in Philadelphia, a boat carrying Franklin and his grandson Temple back from England landed at the city's docks. By this time Franklin's relationship with England was already well-established and multi-layered: in 1756 he was made a Fellow of the Royal Society of London in honor of his ground-breaking experiments with electricity; and in the following year, 1757, he traveled to London for the first time and lived there for months, the start of a two-decade period when he would spend significantly more time in England than in Pennsylvania (he had been in England for more than a decade by 1775). As was the case with his 1775 negotiations, during all this time in England Franklin had served as an official representative of Pennsylvania, advocating for it and all the colonies in their evolving and, throughout this period, fraught relationship with England. Yet he did so as a friend to the Crown, so much so that when he was appointed to the Continental Congress William Bradford, a fellow Pennsylvania delegate, wrote privately to James Madison of a shared "great suspicion that Dr. Franklin came rather as a spy than as a friend, and that he means to discover our weak side and make his peace with the ministers."

Besides that long personal history with England, there was at least one other reason why Revolutionary-minded colonists might suspect Franklin's allegiance: his son William was in 1775 the Royal Governor of New Jersey and a devoted and outspoken Loyalist. But in fact it was in two private conversations with William that Franklin began to express openly his patriotic support for the Revolution and the United States. First, Franklin wrote a letter to his son while on that nautical journey home, detailing the failed negotiations and imploring William to resign his office and renounce the King. William did not do so, and not long after Franklin's return the two men met at a mutual friend's estate north of Philadelphia in an attempt to find common ground. As both men would subsequently describe the conversation, William argued that both the family and their respective colonies of Pennsylvania and New Jersey should maintain neutrality in the incipient conflict with England; the battles of Lexington and Concord had taken place a few weeks earlier. But Franklin vehemently disagreed, not only criticizing "the corruption and dissipation of the kingdom," but also and most importantly "declar[ing] in favor of measures for attaining to independence."

Franklin was never able to convert William to that cause, and their relationship was permanently and destructively altered as a result. But Franklin's own Revolutionary fervor and celebratory patriotism became only stronger, and much more publicly prominent, over the subsequent year leading up to the Declaration of Independence. He expressed that perspective, for example, in an impassioned July 1775 letter to an English friend and fellow printer, William Strahan, a document Franklin apparently never mailed but instead allowed to circulate in America. "You are a Member of Parliament, and one of that Majority which has doomed my country to destruction," Franklin writes, "You and I were long friends: You are now my enemy, and I am Yours." The respective associations of Strahan with England and Franklin with a new American nation, "my country," are clear and crucial.

Due to that publicized document as well as his statements and actions in the Continental Congress during that same period, Franklin's Revolutionary support and patriotism became not only beyond doubt, but also exemplary of the group's resolute mood and position overall. "The suspicions against Dr. Franklin have died away," William Bradford noted in another, July 1775 letter to James Madison. "Whatever was his design at coming over here, I believe he has now chosen his side and favors our cause." And John Adams wrote to his wife Abigail on July 23rd, 1775, that Franklin had "discovered a Disposition entirely American." He "does not hesitate at our boldest Measures, but rather seems to think us, too irresolute, and backward." Indeed, Adams admits that "the People of England, have thought that the Opposition in America was wholly owing to Dr. Franklin; and I suppose their scribblers will attribute the Temper, and Proceedings of this Congress to him."

Franklin's public embrace of the Revolutionary cause was certainly telling, but it was far from the only celebratory patriotic sentiment at the Congress or in the era. Perhaps the most aggressive statement of that sentiment was put forward by a young protégé of Franklin's, the English immigrant and journalist Thomas Paine (1737–1809), in his (initially) anonymous January 1776 pamphlet *Common Sense*. Franklin had met Paine during his last stay in London, and when Paine decided to immigrate to America in late 1774, Franklin helped him secure both passage and a job upon arrival with the Philadelphia printer Richard Bache. In January 1775, another local printer, Robert Aitken, started a new periodical, the *Pennsylvania Magazine*; Paine contributed two pieces to that first issue and in February Aitken hired him as editor. Paine would devote much of his work as both writer and editor for the magazine to the Revolutionary cause, since, as he wrote in one of those January 1775 articles, "every heart and hand seem to be engaged in the interesting struggle for *American Liberty*" (Paine's emphasis).

Paine's own greatest contribution to that struggle and expression of his impassioned American patriotism was *Common Sense*. The 47-page pamphlet, which sold more than 120,000 copies within the first few weeks of its Philadelphia publication and which some readers linked to Franklin before Paine's authorship became publicly known, based its arguments for the Revolution on a few key, interconnected ideas. The first, established in the pamphlet's opening lines and carried throughout, is a striking celebration of the Revolution and the new United States. "The cause of America is in a great measure the cause of all mankind," Paine writes in his introduction, adding later in the pamphlet that "The Sun never shined on a cause of greater worth." The essence of celebratory patriotism is not just that a nation deserves to exist—that "A government of our own is our natural right," as Paine argues—but also that there is something particularly special and important about the nation in question. Such an extreme embrace of the nation might be common sense for Paine, but it needs elaboration as an argument for an audience, and a second key element to Paine's patriotism is indeed his case for what makes America so deserving of not just independence but also celebration.

He makes that case most famously in his answer to the question, "where, say some, is the King of America?" He replies, "the world may know, that so far as we approve of monarchy, that in America the law is king." But while that alone does distinguish America from England, it is just one of many ways Paine makes the case for the new nation's uniqueness. He does so most fully in this passage: "Even the distance at which the Almighty hath placed England and America is a strong and natural proof that the authority of the one over the other, was never the design of Heaven. The time likewise at which the Continent was discovered, adds weight to the argument, and the manner in which it was peopled, increases the force of it. The Reformation was preceded by the discovery of America: As if the Almighty graciously meant to open a sanctuary to the persecuted in future years, when home should afford neither friendship nor safety." In this celebratory vision, every aspect of America, from its geography to its chronology to its community, have combined to yield a nation that not only needs independence from England, but is also quite literally a favorite of God.

A final key element of Paine's celebratory patriotism is the concurrent argument that opposition to the Revolution is both unpatriotic and villainous. "A line of distinction should be drawn between English soldiers taken in battle, and inhabitants of America taken in arms," Paine argues. "The first are prisoners, but the latter traitors. The one forfeits his liberty, the other his head." In the pamphlet's most impassioned passage, Paine goes further still, directly calling out those "men of passive tempers" who are resisting the Revolutionary cause. He presents that perspective as a failure to defend one's home and nation, asking them "whether you can hereafter love, honor, and faithfully serve the power that hath carried fire and sword into your land." And he closes this section with particular anger: "But if you say, you can still pass the violations over, then I ask, hath your house been burnt? Hath your property been destroyed before your face? Are your wife and children destitute of a bed to lie on, or bread to live on? Have you lost a parent or a child by their hands, and yourself the ruined and wretched survivor? If you have not, then are you not a judge of those who have. But if you have, and can still shake hands with the murderers, then are you unworthy the name of husband, father, friend, or lover, and whatever may be your rank or title in life, you have the heart of a coward, and the spirit of a sycophant." While Paine has harshly criticized England throughout the pamphlet, he reserves his strongest condemnation for these Loyalist Americans, defining those who do not share his celebratory patriotism as unpatriotic traitors to cause and country.

That absolute distinction between patriotism on the one hand and criticism of the Revolution and nation on the other is a limiting and exclusionary element to the celebratory patriotism exemplified by voices and texts like Paine's. But there's another mythic layer to such celebratory perspectives that was likewise central to many Revolutionary era arguments for America: the creation and deployment of idealized myths of the nation's past and identity. While such myths of an idealized American community go back at least to Puritan minister John Winthrop's "City on a Hill" image in his 1636 sermon aboard the *Arabella*, a trio of Revolutionary era poets illustrate how that mythic patriotism became a key element in the construction and celebration of the United States of America.

Two of those poets, Phillis Wheatley (1753–1784) and Philip Freneau (1752–1832), created their mythic images of America in works that helped make the literary case for the Revolution in the same years when the Virginia Conventions and Continental Congresses were debating the cause. Perhaps the most overt such literary argument for the Revolution was Wheatley's poem "To the Right Honorable William, Earl of Dartmouth" (1774), a work addressed directly to William Legge, the newly appointed English Secretary of State for the Colonies. As I discuss at length in my prior book in the American Ways series, *We the People*, in the third stanza of this multi-layered poem Wheatley engages more fully with her own experiences of enslavement than she does anywhere else in her published works, arguing that it is those experiences "from whence [her] love of freedom sprung." But she does so, importantly, after an opening two stanzas that use the concept of freedom to establish and argue for a profoundly mythic and celebratory vision of America.

Wheatley's opening stanzas personify Freedom as a Goddess who, "smiling like the morn," has risen "to adorn New-England" with "her genial ray." While Wheatley here references the particular region that is the only part of America she has known, Legge's role was to oversee all the American colonies, and both the ideals and the issues Wheatley highlights in her poem apply equally to them all. Indeed, Wheatley argues that thanks to this new American

rise of "Freedom's charms," "Each soul expands, each grateful bosom burns
. . . with pleasure." The threat of England's "wanton Tyranny" and "lawless
hand" have made Freedom "sick at the view" and left "America, in mournful
strain of wrongs," but in the poem's fourth and final stanza Wheatley reminds
Legge that it is "in thy pow'r" to redress those ills and help America become
once more this idealized community. And, crucially, she uses the concept of
patriotism to make that final appeal, arguing that if he supports the colonies
in their quest for freedom, "praise immortal crowns the patriot's name."

By 1775, Legge had been removed from power and the Revolution's first
battles had commenced, and Wheatley turned her arguments for that cause
and a mythic America to a telling new audience: General George Washington
(1732–1799). In her poem "To His Excellency, George Washington" (1775),
Wheatley once again creates an image of a uniquely American goddess of
freedom, this time calling her "Columbia," the "native of the skies" in service
of whose cause Wheatley's idealized Washington offers his "valor," his "virtues," his "guardian aid." Indeed, in the poem's final two stanzas, Wheatley
thoroughly links Washington to that mythic vision of America, imploring
that his "ev'ry action let the goddess guide" in his service to "the land of
freedom's heaven-defended race!" Such lines link all three of the poem's
idealized subjects—Washington, America, and the Revolution—into one
shared national mythology, all encompassed within that concept of Columbia.

Over the course of the Revolution's first year, Wheatley's poem became
an integral part of that conflict and cause. She sent a copy of it, along with a
brief prefatory note of introduction, to Washington's Cambridge headquarters in October 1775, and he responded with a February 1776 letter, praising
Wheatley's talents and inviting her to meet him "should [she] ever come to
Cambridge." The historical record is unclear on whether that meeting ever
took place, but the invitation itself reflects the striking connection between
Wheatley's literary images and arguments and the Revolution's military
leader in this crucial early period. And in any case, Washington also shared
the poem with his friend and fellow Continental Army officer Joseph Reed,
and Reed, a Philadelphian, passed the poem along to none other than Thomas
Paine. Paine would go on to publish the poem in the April 2nd, 1776 issue of
the *Pennsylvania Magazine*, making Wheatley's "George Washington" one
of the most prominent and influential literary arguments for that unfolding
Revolution.

It was not the only such Revolutionary poem, however, and a pair of 1775
works by Philip Freneau likewise make mythic images of America central to
their literary arguments for the new nation. Freneau was a prolific poet and
journalist with a number of striking connections to the Revolutionary era and
cause: he roomed with James Madison at Princeton University and became

lifelong friends with both him and Thomas Jefferson; studied navigation and served as a ship's captain with the New Jersey militia throughout the Revolution; and after the war established one of the new nation's first newspapers, the *National Gazette*. But it was poems like these two, "A Political Litany" and "American Liberty," that led Freneau to be known as the "Poet of the American Revolution."

The two poems are quite different in form and style: "Litany" a 25-line, sarcastic tirade against England that calls out particular figures by name; "Liberty" a 250-line, stirring depiction of the unfolding war that resembles a classical epic. But both nonetheless rely on mythic celebrations of America as central elements of their respective images and arguments. "Litany" does so in its opening and closing frames, opening with a direct appeal to God to "deliver us . . . from British dependence" in our battle for "freedom" and then, after a series of specific, sarcastic critiques of English political and military figures, coming back to that appeal and image in the closing: "We send up to heaven our wishes and prayers/That we, disunited, may freemen be still." These lofty framing lines might seem out of place in a satirical poem full of images like "the little fat man with his pretty white hair" and "a royal king Log, with his tooth-full of brains." But I would argue that they elevate what could otherwise feel like minor or petty critiques to a far more serious and patriotic level, one in which the unfolding conflict is between nothing short of freedom and tyranny, good and evil.

The epic "American Liberty," published later in 1775 after the battles of Lexington, Concord, and Bunker Hill, develops those mythic arguments for the Revolution in much more depth. It opens by once again explicitly linking the nation to idealized images of freedom: "What heart but bleeds to feel its country's wound?/For thee, blest freedom, to protect thy sway,/We rush undaunted to the bloody fray;/For thee, each province arms its vig'rous host,/Content to die, e'er freedom shall be lost." While recognizing the complex reality that those "provinces" (the thirteen colonies) possessed their own distinct militias, such as the New Jersey one that Freneau himself would soon join, Freneau nonetheless links them through their shared, patriotic defense of that collective national embrace of freedom. And he depicts the English opposition to the Revolution in similarly unifying and mythic terms: "Who plans her schemes to pull Columbia down?"

"Liberty" also adds two additional layers to these mythic images of Revolutionary America, similarly idealized narratives of both past and future that contextualize and amplify those arguments for the present cause. Freneau moves from his initial images of the Revolution's first battles to parallel, foundational historical conflicts, framing America's origin points as a similarly epic conflict between "Unnumber'd myriads of the savage foe" and the speaker's European ancestors who, "Tir'd of oppression," "Bravely resolv'd to leave their native shore/And some new world, they knew not where, explore." And after delineating that myth of the arrival and contact era, Freneau uses it to make another argument for the Revolutionary quest for freedom: "And should we now when spread thro' ev'ry shore,/Submit to that our fathers shunn'd before?" In this mythic vision of America's evolving history —one that overtly excludes indigenous communities from participation in that national project, and indeed frames them in direct opposition to it—the quest for liberty is a defining through-line that raises the stakes of the present Revolutionary conflict even higher still.

When Freneau's poem returns to that present conflict, it also and finally features an idealized vision of the future toward which that foundational and evolving national arc is trending. In the poem's concluding lines, Freneau links America's imagined geographic and economic dominance to the cause of freedom, envisioning a future "When Commerce shall extend her short'ned wing./And her free freights from every climate bring;/When mighty towns shall flourish free and great./Vast their dominion, opulent their state:/When one vast cultivated region teems,/From ocean's edge to Mississippi's streams." This is a particularly important element to the poem's mythic patriotism, as it illustrates that such a celebratory perspective is not at all limited to resisting English tyranny or establishing freedom for the existing colonies. Instead, this is an imagined America that, building on its mythic origins and through its Revolutionary efforts, will fulfill a genuinely exceptional national destiny. Or, as Freneau's final line puts it, "Such is the godlike glory to be free."

Linking celebrations of America's histories and the Revolution to such idealized imagined futures led Freneau and other contemporary writers to be called the "Prospect Poets." One other Prospect Poem that features those mythic elements is Joel Barlow's epic *The Vision of Columbus; A Poem in Nine Books*. Barlow (1754–1812) was in his early 20s and an ardent American patriot at the Revolution's outset, and began the poem while serving as a chaplain for the 4th Massachusetts Brigade. He first published *The Vision* in 1787 and would continue to revise and extend it for the rest of his life; its final form, *The Columbiad*, appeared in 1807 at nearly double the length of *The Vision* (8,350 lines compared to the original's 4,700). But *The Vision* reflects the essence of Barlow's mythic patriotism, and at its heart is an extended dialogue between an idealized Christopher Columbus and an angel. Barlow's Columbus envisions the entire Western Hemisphere but in the crucial Books V, VI, and VII focuses much more specifically, if for his turn of the 16th century moment anachronistically, on America's mythic past, Revolutionary present, and glorious future prospects.

Book VII's final stanza exemplifies those interconnected elements of a mythic patriotism. Barlow is writing there specifically about his fellow Prospect Poet (and one of George Washington's Revolutionary aides) David Humphreys (1752–1818), whose recent "Poem on the Happiness of America" (1786) had offered its own celebratory perspective. But Barlow's lines could just as easily refer to his own poetic project, and indeed to the American cause that all these Prospect Poets embraced and embodied. He notes that in Humphreys' works "in visions bright supernal joys are given,/And all the dread futurities of heaven./While freedom's cause his patriot bosom warms." He defines the national subject of such patriotic poetry: "His country's wrongs, her duties, dangers, praise,/Fire his full soul and animate his lays." And he makes clear the Revolutionary legacy that these poems carry forward: "Immortal Washington with joy shall own/So fond a favorite and so great a son." The mythic patriotism of poets like Humphreys, Barlow, Freneau, and Wheatley indeed both complemented and extended the celebratory patriotism of the Revolution's leaders and advocates.

The Revolutionary era's celebratory and mythic patriotisms were in at least one respect significantly different from many of the other examples of those forms that I'll highlight across this book's remaining chapters and time periods, however. Such celebratory and mythic patriotisms often feature, if they do not indeed require, a level of passive acceptance of and participation in shared communal rituals, such as standing with hand on heart and hat in hand while the national anthem is performed. Those passive and participatory forms of "banal nationalism," to reiterate my introduction's use of scholar Michael Billig's illuminating term for such rituals, become in this vision of patriotism essential ways through which both individuals and the community as a whole express the love of country on which this celebratory perspective depends.

The Revolutionary era's celebratory patriotisms, on the other hand, were significantly more active than passive. It's not just that such shared communal rituals had not yet been developed, although that was indeed generally the case. It's also, and more importantly, that in this period to celebrate the new nation in any way was to take a very definite and very dangerous action. After all, however much celebratory patriots like Patrick Henry and Thomas Paine sought to define American Loyalists as traitors to their cause, the reality was that unless and until the Revolution was successful, it was the Revolutionary colonists who were committing treason against England and the Crown. The "or we will surely hang separately" in that famous Continental Congress quote was quite literal, as after the Declaration the Congressional delegates, like most prominent Revolutionary leaders and advocates, faced the possibility if not the certainty of execution if their efforts came to naught.

Signing the Declaration of Independence was only one of many ways in which Revolutionary era Americans illustrated active patriotism. Certainly that was the case for every person who served in the Continental Army, fought with the various state militias, and took part in the war effort in any capacity, such as Mary Ludwig Hays, Margaret Corbin, and the many other women who brought water to the army on the battlefield and whose identities became collectively mythologized in the figure of Molly Pitcher. It would always be possible to describe military service as active patriotism, and there certainly have been examples in American history when that would be at best a fraught and at worst a blatantly inaccurate description, as I will argue was the case with Confederate military service. But given that these Revolutionary servicemen and women were risking their lives, both on and off the battlefield, to fight for the new United States, active patriotism seems in this case to be an entirely accurate frame.

Many of the era's other prominent moments and efforts in support of the Revolution could likewise be defined as examples of active patriotism. Groups of spies like the Culper Ring in 1778 New York City risked their lives—and even, in the case of figures like Nathan Hale, a spy executed in New York two years earlier, sacrificed their lives—to provide the Revolutionary army and leadership with vital strategic information. Figures like Paul Revere and William Dawes, the men who undertook a pair of desperate rides to warn their fellow patriotic colonists of impending British attack ahead of the April 1775 battles of Lexington and Concord, took similar risks. Even before the Revolution's battles officially began, organizations like the Sons of Liberty, the secretive Boston-based group who organized the December 1773 protest that came to be known as the Boston Tea Party, likewise embodied active patriotic opposition to England and support of the Revolutionary cause.

As the celebratory and mythic patriots made clear time and again, though, the Revolution comprised not just opposition to England (military and otherwise) but also and especially the envisioning and construction of a new nation, the United States of America. That process in no way ended with the September 1783 Treaty of Paris through which England surrendered and the Revolution's military conflict was concluded. While the following years featured many subsequent moments through which the United States continued to be envisioned and constructed, I would argue that one particularly significant such moment also represents another example of Revolutionary era active patriotism: the Constitutional Convention that between May and September of 1787 in Philadelphia's Pennsylvania State House drafted the United States Constitution.

The Convention and the Constitution have received as much attention and analysis as any American historical subjects, so I'll focus here on highlighting a couple ways to see them as examples of Revolutionary active patriotism. For one thing, their very existence reflects an optional, and thus an active, extension of the philosophical and political framing of the new nation begun in the Declaration and carried forward by the state constitutions drafted during the Revolution. After all, the United States already had such a unifying document, the Articles of Confederation, initially drafted near the outset of the Revolution (in 1777) and ratified before it concluded (in 1781). That historians have subsequently identified various flaws and weaknesses in the Articles which the Constitution was designed to correct offers a way to understand what took place but does not mean that it was inevitable that it would. Indeed, it would seem to me that a new nation coming out of decades of debate and conflict, first political and social and then military, might well resist moving back into that mode. That both the individual framers who came together in Philadelphia and the much larger communities who debated and ultimately ratified the Constitution were willing to do so in quest of a more perfect union represents an impressive example of active patriotism.

The document that they produced was complicated and in some ways deeply flawed, particularly when it came to the exclusion of enslaved African Americans from its construction of the national community. But in other ways the Constitution comprised an active and genuinely radical effort to codify the ideals of freedom and liberty for which the celebratory and mythic patriots had argued the Revolution stood. I would point in particular not just to the Constitution's creation of a government that featured no state religion, in contrast to every other constitutional republic at the time, but also to the one reference to religion anywhere in the Constitution's seven articles: the clause in Article VI which notes that, while elected and unelected government officials "shall be bound by Oath or Affirmation, to support this Constitution; . . . no religious Test shall ever be required as a Qualification to any Office or public Trust under the United States." When that clause was challenged during a July 1788 ratification debate in North Carolina, James Iredell, a Federalist and Constitutional advocate, argued, "how is it possible to exclude any set of men, without taking away that principle of religious freedom which we ourselves so warmly contend for?" That statement, like this radically inclusive element of the Constitution, represents an impressive and active embodiment of the era's patriotic celebrations of Revolutionary American freedom.

While the Revolutionary era's celebratory and mythic patriotisms were thus more active than has often been the case in American history, they nonetheless still too often shared another limiting quality: the tendency to exclude

American communities who did not fit their celebratory vision of the nation. Some of those communities, like American Loyalists who resisted the Revolution, were excluded because their perspectives and actions did not fall within the celebratory frame. Others, like women and enslaved African Americans fighting for their rights in the new nation, were excluded because their identities were not considered equal to those of other Americans. But all these communities were indeed part of Revolutionary America, and in distinct ways they all modeled a more critical form of patriotism, one that challenged the celebratory and mythic perspectives in an effort to both reflect and construct a more inclusive new nation.

I know there's something fundamentally counterintuitive about describing Revolutionary Loyalists—or Tories, as they were generally known in the language of the era—as American patriots of any kind. After all, this was a group who sided with an enemy during a time of war, an action that seems to fit quite clearly the definition of treason. Certainly a figure like Benedict Arnold, the Continental Army General and trusted aide to George Washington who in 1780 defected to the English side of the conflict, unquestionably committed an act of treason, and in so doing voluntarily chose to abandon any claim to an American identity and would as a result spend the rest of his life in Canada and then England. But Arnold is an extreme and unrepresentative case, not only because he was a military leader who sought to give the enemy a strategic advantage but also and relatedly because of his chosen abandonment of America and its future. For many Loyalists, the conflict was instead precisely over what was best for the American colonies that remained their home and community, at least until, in many cases, they were forced to leave it.

Every Loyalist story developed in its own complex way, and here I'll briefly highlight three that reflect distinct sides to the community's critical patriotism. Benjamin Franklin's son William (1730–1813) was an example of a Loyalist who sought to affect the debate through politics and paid a profound personal price for that perspective. Like his father, William was dedicated to civic service throughout his life, and in his case that service reflected the multi-layered connections between the colonies and England: in his teens he served for a year with a Pennsylvania militia during King George's War (1746–47); he studied law in Britain, becoming a fellow of the Royal Society of Edinburgh and working with his father to secure land grants for English immigrants to America; and in 1763 he was appointed Royal Governor of New Jersey, a role in which he served for more than a dozen years. At the outset of Revolutionary conflict he advocated publicly as well as privately with his father for maintaining that relationship with England, and for that stance he was imprisoned, first under house arrest and then for more than two years in a New Jersey prison after the Declaration of Independence. After his 1778 release as part of a prisoner transfer he moved to New York and attempted to organize a spy ring against the Revolutionaries; that period led to descriptions of him as a traitor and caused a permanent rift with both his father and his son Temple, but it could just as easily be seen as a final stage in a Loyalist's critically patriotic service toward the Anglo-American community he supported.

James Chalmers (1727–1806), a Scottish immigrant and landowner on Maryland's Eastern Shore, represented an even more active and direct Loyalist engagement with Revolutionary debates and conflicts. In March 1776, Chalmers authored and published anonymously (under the pseudonym Candidus) *Plain Truth*, an anti-Revolutionary pamphlet that challenged Paine's *Common Sense*. Chalmers frames his pamphlet with arguments that undermine the celebratory patriotic vision of the Revolution's goals, opening with an argument that Paine seeks "to cajole the people into the most abject slavery, under the delusive name of independence" and closing with the sentence, "INDEPENDENCE AND SLAVERY ARE SYNONYMOUS TERMS" (Chalmers' emphasis). In this critically patriotic vision, it is the disingenuous Revolutionary emphasis on liberty, the work of these "fabricators of Independency," which would curtail the rights of Americans and "very soon give way to a government imposed on us." When Chalmers' authorship of the pamphlet was discovered and he was driven from his home by a Revolutionary mob, he enlisted as an officer in the First Battalion of Maryland Loyalists, a regiment of American soldiers that fought alongside the English throughout the remainder of the war. Whatever our opinion of Chalmers' pamphlet and perspective, both that publication and his military service comprise active patriotism in support of his critical vision of the Revolution and his arguments for an alternative American future.

Native American political and military allies represent another distinct and significant critically patriotic contribution to the English cause during the Revolution. Every native tribe and nation had its own complex history and relationship with both the English and the colonists, and the Revolutionaries had a number of indigenous allies as well. But as illustrated by the young Mohawk Iroquois warrior and chief Joseph Brant (Thayendanegea; 1743–1807), Native Americans who allied with the English did so not because they were dependent on that nation, but rather because they perceived their own communal needs and future as best served by that alliance. Although Brant was only about 15 years old during the French and Indian War, he fought alongside the English in that conflict's Canadian theater, in defense of Iroquois land and rights; he and his family also had a multi-generational relationship with English political and business interests for the same purpose. When the Revolution began, Brant continued that alliance by organizing "Brant's Volunteers," a mixed regiment of both Mohawk warriors and Loyalists who fought against the Revolutionaries in a number of battles in New York state. His adversaries described heinous massacres and called him "Monster Brant," but historians have found most of those stories to be embellished if not entirely invented. If anything, the stories reflect a need to depict figures like Brant and the Volunteers as entirely hostile to America, rather than opposed to the Revolution yet representing another side to an American community and potential future.

I believe there is significant value in recognizing the critical patriotism of all three of these Loyalist opponents of the Revolution, not least because they were all part of that American community as of 1776 and can't be written out of history simply because their ideal collective future did not take place and instead the Revolution unfolded the way it did. Moreover, the fates of most Loyalists remind us that to challenge celebratory and mythic patriotisms is often to risk ostracism (if not far worse) at the hands of those patriotic forces. But at the same time, precisely because it was the Revolution which created the new nation of the United States of America, it wouldn't make sense to see these Loyalists as U.S. patriots, even if they were able to remain in that new nation; and most, including these three men, were not: Franklin and Chalmers ended their lives in England, Brant in Canada. Yet within the new United States there were also figures and communities who offered critically patriotic challenges of the Revolutionary celebrations and myths, and in so doing helped establish a legacy of critical patriotism as likewise part of that founding era.

Abigail Adams (1744–1818), wife and partner to one of the most prominent founders and framers, John Adams, expressed with particular clarity a feminist critical patriotic perspective on the Revolution. Abigail and John wrote back and forth throughout his contributions to the Revolution's documents and efforts, and on March 31st, 1776, she sent him a letter about his participation in the Second Continental Congress and the ongoing drafting of the Declaration of Independence. "By the way in the new Code of Laws which I suppose it will be necessary for you to make I desire you would Remember the Ladies," she wrote, "and be more generous and favorable to them than your ancestors. . . . If particular care and attention is not paid to the Ladies, we are determined to foment a Rebellion, and will not hold ourselves bound by any Laws in which we have no voice, or Representation." While it is the phrase "Remember the Ladies" that has received the most attention, by far the most striking aspect of this quote is Abigail's connection of the concept of "Rebellion" to the goal of creating a system of laws that better represent and give voice to this American community than has been the case in the past. She revises the celebratory patriotic emphases on independence and liberty in favor of a more critical view in which the Revolution and the new nation alike comprise an opportunity for a more egalitarian vision of who is part of America.

That feminist critical patriotic vision of the Revolutionary era was also embodied by figures and authors like Annis Boudinot Stockton, Hannah Griffiths, and Judith Sargent Murray. Stockton (1736–1801), the wife of another Continental Congress delegate (New Jersey's Richard Stockton), became well known for her courageous efforts in support of the Revolutionary cause: the only woman elected to the secretive American Whig Society, she safeguarded the group's papers during the Revolution at her Princeton estate. Stockton likewise encouraged the era's emerging community of women writers, helping found the Mid-Atlantic Writing Circle which featured a number of women, including Elizabeth Graeme Fergusson, Susanna Wright, Milcah Martha Moore, and Hannah Griffitts. And in her own creative works, as illustrated by her 1756 poem, "An Impromptu Answer," written in response to "A Sarcasm against the ladies in a newspaper," she boldly expressed revolutionary ideas of female empowerment and equality. That poem critiques not only the anonymous male writer's sarcastic sexism but also and most importantly an overly idealized, hierarchical vision of the world, particularly in its egalitarian final lines: "Although perfection's never found below/With them into a world of error thrown/And our erratas place against their own." While Stockton's poem was published two decades before the Declaration, it's easy to see Stockton's support for interconnected feminist and Revolutionary causes as part of a lifelong critical patriotic challenge to the American status quo.

Stockton's Mid-Atlantic Writing Circle colleague Hannah Griffitts (1727–1817), a Philadelphia Quaker who contributed dozens of poems to her cousin Milcah Martha Moore's voluminous commonplace book, linked feminism to incipient revolutionary patriotism even more clearly in her 1768 poem, "The Female Patriots." Griffitts opens with a complaint about the lack of patriotic activism from her community's men, who, "supinely asleep, & deprived of their Sight/Are stripped of their Freedom, and robbed of their Right." She then argues for the need for her titular female patriots to take up that cause: "If the Sons (so degenerate) the Blessing despise,/Let the Daughters of Liberty, nobly arise." She admits that in traditional political terms "we've no Voice," but makes the case for the boycotting of English goods as a key way these female patriots can nonetheless take action: "As American Patriots, our Taste we deny"; and so "rather than Freedom, we'll part with our Tea." And she ends by highlighting the broader revolutionary effects of not only such boycotts, but also her own poem and writing: "a motive more worthy our patriot Pen,/Thus acting—we point out their Duty to Men." By expressing and enacting their female patriotism, then, Griffitts and her peers likewise offer a feminist critical patriotic perspective on the frustrating, counter-productive absence of women from these public debates.

Perhaps the most radical late 18th century American voice for feminist critical patriotism began publishing in the years immediately following the Revolution. Unlike those of Adams and Stockton, Judith Sargent Murray's (1751–1820) Revolutionary era marriage nearly destroyed her life and ambitions: the daughter of a Gloucester (Massachusetts) merchant, she married local ship captain John Stevens, but his business failed during the war, and he fled to the Caribbean to escape debtor's prison, leaving Judith alone and responsible for his debts. In order to survive, Judith began anonymously publishing essays on women's rights and equality, with her first, "Desultory Thoughts upon the Utility of Encouraging a Degree of Self-Complacency, Especially in Female Bosoms," published in *Town and Country Magazine* in 1784. In 1788 she met and married a far more genuine partner, the Unitarian Universalist Reverend John Murray, with whom she would have a daughter, Julia, whose education became a central focus of her life. But her publishing career continued as well, and her 1790 *Massachusetts Magazine* essay "On the Equality of the Sexes" exemplifies her radical arguments for women's rights. That essay was literally and figuratively Revolutionary: she had been working on it since 1779; and its central arguments for women's liberty and independence and for education as a means to achieve them closely parallel the celebratory national ideals expressed by America's founding documents and Revolutionary advocates. Like Adams, Stockton, and Griffitts, and with even more public and rhetorical force, Murray makes the critical patriotic case that America will only truly be revolutionary when it extends those ideals to its female citizens.

A very similar case for extending the Revolution's ideals and effects to all Americans was made in this era by enslaved African Americans and their abolitionist allies. I wrote about this community at length in *We the People*, and here will close this chapter by highlighting two layers to the critical patriotism embodied by these inspiring Revolutionary Americans. Most overtly, these enslaved Americans highlighted the fundamental hypocrisy of a nation in which chattel slavery was legal (throughout its thirteen new states) celebrating liberty and independence as defining values, and used that critique to argue for their own freedom as a vital step toward moving the national community closer to those ideals. As early as January 13th, 1777, just six months after the Declaration of Independence, a group of Massachusetts slaves, aided by abolitionist allies, filed a petition for emancipation to that state's legislature, describing themselves as "a great number of blacks detained in a state of slavery in the bowels of a free and Christian country," and echoing the language of the Declaration to make the case for "a natural and unalienable right to that freedom which the Great Parent of the Universe hath bestowed equally on all mankind and which they have never forfeited by any compact or agreement whatever."

Their petition unfortunately went unanswered, and slavery remained legal in Revolutionary Massachusetts. Moreover, the state's groundbreaking 1780 Constitution reiterated and extended the hypocrisy of the nation's founding, celebratory ideals, as its framers began the document with as clear an echo of the Declaration of Independence as possible. The first section was entitled "A Declaration of the Rights of the Inhabitants of the Commonwealth of Massachusetts," and the opening Article I read in full: "All men are born free and equal, and have certain natural, essential, and unalienable rights; among which may be reckoned the right of enjoying and defending their lives and liberties; that of acquiring, possessing, and protecting property; in fine, that of seeking and obtaining their safety and happiness." While the Declaration of Independence was simply a statement of principles, the Massachusetts Constitution represented a legal framework for governance and society. As a result, this opening turned the Declaration's ideals of freedom and equality into legal rights that would form the basis for "The Frame of Government" that the Massachusetts Constitution's second section would further enumerate—rights that were denied every day to the state's more than five thousand enslaved residents.

In the aftermath of that Massachusetts Constitution's ratification, two of those enslaved residents, Elizabeth "Mumbet" Freeman (c. 1744–1829) and Quock Walker (c.1753–unknown), took up the critical patriotic legacy of the 1777 petitioners and wedded it to a profoundly active patriotism in support of their own and their community's freedom. In *We the People*, I trace at length the stories of these two inspiring Americans, each of whom worked with legal allies and used the 1780 Constitution's language to successfully win their freedom and push the state toward abolition. Freeman's first step toward those goals reflects a particularly striking example of active, critical patriotism in response to communal celebrations. In June 1780, she heard the newly ratified Massachusetts Constitution read aloud at a public gathering in her Western Massachusetts town of Sheffield, a ceremony intended to celebrate that Revolutionary document and its meanings for the state's residents. But it did not hold those meanings for Freeman and her community, and the next day she approached Theodore Sedgwick, a young Sheffield lawyer well known for his abolitionist views. According to the account provided by Sedgwick's daughter, the prominent 19th century novelist Catharine Maria Sedgwick, Freeman said to Theodore, "I heard that paper read yesterday, that says, all men are created equal, and that every man has a right to freedom. I'm not a dumb critter; won't the law give me my freedom?" Sedgwick took her case, and this powerful individual statement and moment of active, critical patriotism became the start of something far more communal and crucial still.

Ironically, both the town of Sheffield and the house in which Freeman was enslaved were also the site of one of America's first steps toward the Revolution's founding documents and its celebratory and mythic patriotisms. Freeman's slave-owner John Ashley (1709–1802) was a noted business and political leader in town, and it was in his home that eleven prominent community members signed the January 12th, 1773 Sheffield Resolves, a document also known as the Sheffield Declaration and printed publicly in the local paper *The Massachusetts Spy, or, Thomas's Boston Journal* on February 18th. That influential document, long seen as a direct predecessor to the Declaration of Independence, opened with a resolution that "Mankind in a state of nature are equal, free, and independent of each other, and have a right to the undisturbed enjoyment of their lives, their liberty and property." While that statement might seem universal, the Sheffield Resolves, like the Declaration and Revolution that they helped inspire, linked those shared rights overtly and centrally to the specific community and new nation emerging in America. This celebratory and mythic patriotism, expressed by voices like Patrick Henry, Ben Franklin, and Thomas Paine and extended by poets like Phillis Wheatley, Philip Freneau, and Joel Barlow, remains one of the Revolution's most significant legacies in American culture and community.

The Revolution's supporters and soldiers actively embodied and extended that celebratory patriotism, as in subsequent years did the Constitution's framers. But at the same time, other Revolutionary American communities took action in support of alternative, more critical visions of the nation and its future. From Loyalists who resisted the Revolution to feminists and abolitionists who highlighted and challenged the limits of its ideals, these American figures and communities established an enduring legacy of critical patriotism, one that we likewise can trace across the centuries and down to our contemporary moment's defining debates.

Chapter Two

The Early Republic
Young, Expanding, and Divided

In May 1831, a 25-year-old French diplomat and historian named Alexis Clérel (1805–1859), the Viscount de Tocqueville, arrived in New York with his friend Gustave de Beaumont. De Tocqueville's official mission was to study America's prison system in order to write a report for France's newly installed July Monarchy, but over the next nine months he and Beaumont traveled through much of the United States (as well as a brief August sojourn into Canada), observing and taking extensive notes on all that they saw and experienced there. After returning to France in February 1832, de Tocqueville quickly submitted his official report and began work on a much longer and more involved study of the United States, the result of which would be the two-volume book *De La Démocratie en Amérique*, usually translated as *Democracy in America*, with the first editions of the two volumes published in France in 1835 and 1840 respectively.

De Tocqueville's groundbreaking masterpiece covers numerous political, social, and economic topics, and does so with depth and nuance. But it is nonetheless framed and motivated by a profoundly celebratory perspective on the fledgling United States and its perfected version of the titular political and social system. As he writes in his introduction, "Amongst the novel objects that attracted my attention during my stay in the United States, nothing struck me more forcibly than the general equality of conditions. . . . The more I advanced in the study of American society, the more I perceived that the equality of conditions is the fundamental fact from which all others seem to be derived, and the central point at which all my observations constantly terminated." And he sums up not only that defining observation but also his own celebratory perspective in a telling pair of linked clauses from that same introduction: "I confess that in America I saw more than America; I saw the image of democracy itself."

De Tocqueville was not alone in perceiving or sharing such a celebratory vision of the United States in this Early Republic era. Indeed, it was in this period that some of the first communal celebrations and expressions of celebratory patriotism were created, including both Francis Scott Key's penning "The Star-Spangled Banner" during the War of 1812 and the numerous commemorations around the Revolution's 50th anniversary. Those celebrations were complemented by amplified mythic patriotisms, focused not only on American history but also on the nation's expanding geography (as illustrated by the concept of Manifest Destiny) and its Anglo-Saxon identity (as illustrated by policies like Indian Removal and movements like the Know Nothing Party). Yet other Early Republic philosophies and communities, including the Transcendentalist and Young America movements, espoused active patriotism in service of a more inclusive vision of the new nation. And in a number of impassioned and inspiring cultural and literary works, activist Early Republic figures like Catharine Maria Sedgwick, William Apess, and David Walker expressed critical patriotisms that challenged the era's celebrations and myths and offered images of and arguments for a more inclusive United States.

The dominant collective images of the War of 1812, both at the time and ever since, themselves reflect a celebratory and mythic perspective when it comes to the Early Republic United States. As with all wars, this conflict between the U.S. and England was caused by a number of distinct and complex factors, and one in particular—the English "impressment" of American sailors into their navy to take part in the ongoing Napoleonic Wars against France— represented an attack on U.S. interests to be sure. Those naval conflicts drew national attention as early as the 1807 battle off the coast of Virginia between the *USS Chesapeake* and the *HMS Leopard*. And they became part of a developing story of continued and increasing English aggression toward the United States, a lens through which the May 16th, 1811 fight near North Carolina between the aptly named *USS President* and the *HMS Little Belt* was seen as the first battle of the War of 1812.

Yet that patriotic story of the war's origins was partial at best, and left out a concurrent, unfolding history of U.S. aggression elsewhere in the Americas. Beginning with the 1787 Northwest Ordinance and ramping up after the 1803 Louisiana Purchase, the fledgling United States consistently sought to expand its territory into the "Northwest" (the area of modern-day Ohio, Michigan, and their neighbors). In so doing, U.S. settlers and military forces alike came into continued conflict with Native American nations such as the Shawnee, with whom the English allied both to resist U.S. expansion and to protect their own Canadian settlements and interests. A series of armed conflicts in

1810 and 1811 culminated in the November 7th, 1811 Battle of Tippecanoe, which represents another, quite distinct contender for the title of "first battle of the War of 1812." Moreover, once that war began in earnest, U.S. forces pushed even more aggressively into Canada, seeking not only military victories but further expansion of territory, an aggressive invasion exemplified by the May 25th–27th, 1813 destruction of the English settlement at Ontario's Fort George.

As part of that battle the American forces burned much of the Fort George settlement to the ground. But it was another, very different wartime fire, the August 24th, 1814 burning of Washington, DC by English forces, that became the dominant collective image of the War of 1812 in the United States. More specifically, images of the White House on fire—and of President James Madison and his wife Dolley fleeing that destruction—became the centerpiece of celebratory and mythic images of the war as an act of aggression against the new nation. Less than a month later, the English forces continued their attacks with the September 13th–14th, 1814 bombardment of Fort McHenry in Baltimore Harbor—and it was that bombardment, and more exactly the symbolic ability of both the fort and the United States to withstand such attacks and emerge victorious on the other side, which would become the linchpin of Francis Scott Key's celebratory poem and song, as well as the Early Republic national anthem they inspired.

Key's 1814 work was not his first such expression of wartime celebratory patriotism. The son of Revolutionary War officer and Early Republic lawyer and judge John Ross Key, Francis (1779–1843) likewise became a practicing lawyer in the Maryland and DC areas, working on the 1807 Aaron Burr conspiracy trial. But he was also an amateur poet and songwriter, and prior to the War of 1812 his best-known work was the celebratory "When the Warrior Returns" (1805), a poem that he set to the tune of English composer John Stafford Smith's popular "The Anacreontic Song" (also known as "To Anacreon in Heaven"). Written in honor of Stephen Decatur and Charles Stewart, two U.S. military officers returning home from the 1801–1805 First Barbary War in North Africa, "When the Warrior Returns" features many of the same celebratory patriotic images as Key's subsequent anthem, as illustrated by the phrase "By the light of the Star Spangled flag of our nation" as well as the song's closing couplet: "Mixed with the olive, the laurel shall wave/And form a bright wreath for the brows of the brave."

Key's more up-close and personal experience of the War of 1812 was due to his legal work: on the evening of September 13th, 1814, he was dining on board the *HMS Tonnant* in Baltimore Harbor, hoping to arrange an official prisoner exchange for a number of Maryland men, including the prominent local leader Dr. William Beanes. That night the English began their bombardment of Fort McHenry as part of a broader attack on Baltimore, and Key was held on board the *Tonnant* so he couldn't give away any of their plans. From the ship he witnessed both the overnight bombardment and the triumphant raising of the American flag the next morning, and over the next week he composed a four-stanza poem, initially entitled "Defense of Fort M'Henry," inspired by that experience. He first published that poem in Baltimore, both as a broadside and in the *American and Commercial Daily Advertiser* newspaper's September 21st edition. But he then took it to a Philadelphia publisher, Thomas Carr, who helped Key set the words once again to Smith's "Anacreontic Song." Re-titled "The Star Spangled Banner," that song would over the next few decades become a de facto national anthem, finally being officially designated as such with a President Woodrow Wilson Executive Order in 1916.

The first verse of "The Star-Spangled Banner" is the only one generally performed, and it already includes in its eight-line structure a striking illustration of celebratory patriotism. The first six lines focus on the experience of watching the overnight bombardment, but with a clear through-line of a patriotic embrace of "our flag," a celebration illustrated not just by the flag's resilience throughout the attack but also by Key's descriptive adverbs ("proudly," "gallantly") and adjectives ("broad stripes and bright stars" in particular). And the stanza's final two lines make plain the celebratory patriotic vision of both the flag and the United States implied by those descriptions, as the speaker connects the titular "star-spangled banner" to "the land of the free and the home of the brave." Those celebratory images of an idealized U.S. have over the centuries since become so ubiquitous as to make Key's work here seem perhaps less striking or influential, but if anything the opposite is true: it was through phrases and texts like Key's that such images of America were both constructed and solidified.

The song's less well-known latter three verses largely reiterate those focal points, including a repetition of "o'er the land of the free and the home of the brave" in each closing line. But the third and fourth verses in particular highlight a couple additional layers to the song's celebratory patriotism. The third verse depicts the nation's War of 1812 enemies not just as the English and their allies, but also as avowed enemies of the very existence of the United States: "that band who so vauntingly swore/That the havoc of war and the battle's confusion/A home and a Country should leave us no more." Moreover, Key implies that those enemies include not just the armies of a hostile foreign nation, but also adversaries within the U.S., specifically "the hireling and slave." That last word, coupled with Key's own status as a Maryland slave-owner, has contributed to Colin Kaepernick's 21st century connections of the anthem to histories and issues of race in America. But beyond that particular significant effect, the entire third verse also turns the War of 1812 into a second American Revolution, one in which this idealized new nation is pitted against domestic as well as foreign enemies whose victory would apparently mean no future for that nation.

The concluding fourth verse's opening lines extend that vision of the War of 1812, describing the American soldiers as "freemen . . . stand[ing] between their lov'd home and the war's desolation," and naming the (soon-to-be) victorious United States "the heav'n rescued land." And it is that latter image, of the United States as particularly favored by heaven, that Key's final verse most potently adds to the song and its constructions of American celebratory patriotism. It is that heavenly "power," Key argues, "that hath made and preserv'd us as a nation." And in the song's final new lines, before the aforementioned repeated closing line, Key adds one more telling phrase to that celebratory image: "Then conquer we must, when our cause it is just,/ And this be our motto—'In God is our trust.'" There's a reason why that latter phrase would half a century later be added to American currency (first appearing on the two-cent coin in 1864), as it provides a succinct summation of celebratory patriotic images of the United States as an idealized, even holy community. And a century later an anthemic song entitled "God Bless America" (1918) would bring renewed attention to that sentiment, a vision of the nation as heavenly favored that is delineated clearly by the final stanza of Francis Scott Key's "The Star-Spangled Banner."

Not long after the War of 1812 concluded with the December 1814 Treaty of Ghent—although news of the treaty took a while to travel to the Americas and the war's culminating Battle of New Orleans actually took place in January 1815—the United States began to celebrate the 50-year anniversaries of the events leading up to its first war with England, the American Revolution. Those events had never disappeared from collective memories or national narratives, not least because many of their central participants remained alive into the early 19th century. But by the 1820s the members of that generation were passing away, as exemplified by the famous paired deaths of John Adams and Thomas Jefferson on July 4th, 1826. Inspired both by that sense of personal and collective history being potentially lost and by the occasion of the 50th anniversaries of events like the Boston Massacre and the Boston Tea Party, Revolutionary commemorations throughout the decade and into the 1830s wedded tributes to the histories and figures from that founding era to expressions of celebratory patriotism in the present.

Exemplary of those celebratory commemorations was the early 1830s collective recovery and embrace of George Robert Twelves Hewes (1742–1840). As traced at length in historian Alfred Young's book, *The Shoemaker and the Tea Party: Memory and the American Revolution* (1999), the Bostonian Hewes was an active pre-Revolutionary protester and participant in both the

Boston Massacre and the Boston Tea Party who went on to serve in multiple roles in the Continental Army during the Revolution; two of his many sons likewise served in the Massachusetts militia during the War of 1812. Yet despite that multi-generational military service, and despite Hewes' frequent participation (usually while wearing his Continental Army uniform) in July 4th ceremonies in Boston during the early decades of the 19th century, as of 1830, the nearly 90-year-old Hewes lived in difficult circumstances, often relying on friends for housing and having to continue his lifelong work as a shoemaker in order to make ends meet.

The era's celebratory commemorations changed all that, however. That trend produced a continued collective thirst for more patriotic historical accounts, and in 1833 a writer named James Hawkes learned of Hewes' numerous Revolutionary era experiences and decided to tell his story, with a particular focus on the Boston Tea Party. The resulting book, *A Retrospect of the Boston Tea Party; with a Memoir of George R.T. Hewes* (1834), became a hit, and with its success Hewes became a celebrity. He went on speaking tours of New England to share his Revolutionary memories; served as a guest of honor at Boston's July 4th commemorations each year until his death in 1840; posed for artist Joseph Cole for his portrait *The Centenarian* (1835), which hangs to this day in Boston's Old State House; and was the subject of another popular book, Benjamin Bussey Thatcher's *Traits of the Tea Party: Being a Memoir of George R.T. Hewes* (1835).

Both Hawkes' and Thatcher's books are structured as memoirs, narrating much of Hewes' life from early childhood up through their 1830s moment. Yet from their titles on they thoroughly associate that individual life and identity with the Revolutionary events, not just the Tea Party but also (in their extended subtitles) the Boston Massacre, the 1775–76 English Siege of Boston, and other Revolutionary battles. Such links reflect one level of their celebratory patriotism: making this singular figure into an idealized representative of foundational American moments and collective memories. Concluding his description of Hewes' experience of the Tea Party, Thatcher writes that it "shows pretty clearly the spirit of the times. . . . Nothing can better illustrate the excitement of the day, than incidents and paragraphs like these." And while both Hewes and Thatcher acknowledge the controversial nature of such protests at the time, they argue in response for the protests' popular and patriotic qualities. As Thatcher puts it, "It will be noticed that the Boston movements are here generally described as *laudable*, and no exception is made even to the riotous character of the party of the 16th, such was its popularity. . . . [Its] necessity was at last unanimously acquiesced in by the American Party" (Thatcher's emphasis).

Hawkes, who refers to Hewes in his subtitle as *A Survivor of the Little Band of Patriots Who Drowned the Tea in Boston Harbor in 1773* and dedicates his book "To the Surviving Officers and Soldiers of the American War of the Revolution, as a Just Tribute of Respect and Gratitude," highlights one prominent additional layer to these 1830s celebratory patriotic images. As laid out with particular clarity in his Preface, he argues not just that the largely forgotten Hewes deserves better remembrance, but that it is only by celebrating him and his peers that we can reach a sufficient understanding of America's genuinely revolutionary qualities. As he puts it, "The single event of destroying a few thousand pounds of tea, by throwing it into the water, was of itself of inconsiderable importance in American history; but in its consequences, it was, doubtless, one in the series of events, destined to change, and probably improve the condition, not only of our posterity, but of mankind in all ages to come." The implicit and important argument here, one illustrated by both these books and the era's historic recollections overall, is that the Revolution's ideals require continued commemoration and celebration, that such collective expressions of celebratory patriotism, which would likewise include the creation and performance of a national anthem like "The Star-Spangled Banner," are necessary if we are to remember and carry forward those idealized American histories and qualities.

That celebratory perspective on the Revolution would certainly have to be described as idealized, particularly given the controversial and divisive sides to events such as the Boston Tea Party in their own era. Downplaying those controversies thus also meant depicting Revolutionary era Loyalists as not part of that vision of American identity, even in the pre-Revolution period when any potential future was still possible. But beyond that historical Loyalist community, in the present, early 19th century moment, this form of celebratory patriotism did have the potential to include all American communities. Yet at the same time, the Early Republic period featured concurrent mythic patriotisms, idealized stories of America's past and its collective identity which were used to justify both present oppressions and images of a national future of which certain communities were explicitly not part.

Many of those Early Republic mythic patriotisms were directly tied to one of the period's central trends: the westward expansion of the nation's geographic territory. That process of expansion began as early as the year of the Constitutional Convention, with the 1787 Northwest Ordinance which would play a significant role in the causes and campaigns of the War of 1812. It was greatly amplified by the 1803 Louisiana Purchase and the many subsequent explorations of, migrations into, and settlements in that newly acquired territory over the following few decades. And it reached a new level with the events leading up to and surrounding the Mexican American War, including the 1848 Treaty of Guadalupe Hidalgo, which not only concluded that war but in a single moment ceded much of the rest of the continent to the United States. Each of those histories was distinct and complex, but one element that they all shared was an underlying, mythic assumption that the United States had a natural and perhaps even inevitable claim to territory beyond its Revolutionary era starting points, and indeed to the continent as a whole.

That form of mythic patriotism was apparent throughout the Early Republic period, but was given an overt name by the lawyer and political journalist John L. O'Sullivan (1813–1895). O'Sullivan, whose father, John T. O'Sullivan, was an Irish American immigrant and U.S. Consul to the North African Barbary States, founded *The United States Magazine and Democratic Review* when he was only 24 years old, and as the magazine's editor for more than twenty years (1837–1859) used it to espouse a consistently celebratory perspective on American politics, democracy, culture, and literature. In a November 1839 editorial entitled "The Great Nation of Futurity," O'Sullivan wedded that celebratory perspective to mythic predictions of an ideal American future, a concept which he called there the nation's "divine destiny." Six years later, in a July-August 1845 editorial (entitled "Annexation") on the subject of what to do about the independent Texas Republic, he coined a more specific phrase for the idea of inevitable geographic expansion as part of that mythic future, calling it "our manifest destiny." And in a December 1845 article for the *New York Morning News*, he further developed the concept: "That claim [in this case to "the whole of Oregon" as part of an ongoing boundary dispute with England] is by the right of our manifest destiny to overspread and to possess the whole of the continent which Providence has given us for the development of the great experiment of liberty and federated self-government entrusted to us."

That final quote of O'Sullivan's succinctly sums up a number of layers to the mythic patriotism comprised by the concept of "manifest destiny." The concept depends on two of the central components of celebratory patriotism: an idealized definition of American identity, as captured in O'Sullivan's phrase "great experiment of liberty and self-government"; and a vision of that idealized nation as a favorite of heaven, as reflected in his "which Providence has given us." As with the celebratory patriotism of the era's Revolutionary commemorations, this concept likewise implies—indeed, it requires—that present and future Americans directly extend and amplify that celebratory legacy, as embodied in O'Sullivan's argument that the idealized identity has been "entrusted to us." And the concept puts all those celebratory patriotisms in service of a profoundly mythic view, not only of America's own "manifest destiny" but also and most troublingly of a continent that apparently exists and is waiting only to be "overspread" and "possess[ed]" by the United States. As with so many mythic patriotisms, this one elides numerous communities already present across that continent, from Native American tribes to existing European American settlements such as the Mexican American communities throughout the Southwest and West.

This myth of inevitable and righteous national expansion likewise featured and helped popularize a pair of complementary and equally mythic American ideals. At the heart of the Early Republic's myths of expansion was the image of the pioneer, an iconic frontier identity encapsulated in hugely prominent and popular figures like Daniel Boone (1734–1820) and Davy Crockett (1786–1836). As traced by scholarly biographies like John Mack Faragher's *Daniel Boone: The Life and Legend of an American Pioneer* (1992) and Richard Bruce Winders' *Davy Crockett: The Legend of the Wild Frontier* (2001), the frontier legends of pioneers like Boone and Crockett were not only constructed in their own era, but with the full participation, and indeed frequently the direction, of the men themselves. While the creation and propagation of those legends certainly contributed to the men's personal and professional successes, those processes also complemented and bolstered the myth of manifest destiny, imagining a new class of idealized American heroes who represented the spirit of that expanding Early Republic nation.

One of the earliest published versions of Boone's story exemplifies the links between the pioneer and American myths. In 1784, schoolteacher and surveyor John Filson published *The Discovery, Settlement, and Present State of Kentucke* [sic], considered the state's first written history. Filson knew Boone from their shared experiences in that state, and included as an appendix "The adventures of Colonel Daniel Boon [sic], formerly a hunter, containing a narrative of the wars of Kentucke." Ostensibly dictated by Boone himself, the appendix in any cases functions more as an origin point for frontier and national legends than a biographical or historical chronicle. As Filson's Boone puts it, "Here, . . . where wretched wigwams stood, the miserable abodes of savages, we behold the foundations of cities laid, that, in all probability, will equal the glory of the greatest upon earth. And we view Kentucky, . . . rising from obscurity to shine with splendor, equal to any other of the stars of the American hemisphere." And he ends the appendix on the same note: "This account of my adventures will inform the reader of the most remarkable events of this country. I now live in peace and safety, enjoying the sweets of liberty, and the bounties of Providence, with my once fellow-sufferers, in this delightful country . . . delighting in the prospect of its being, in a short time, one of the most opulent and powerful States on the continent of North America."

The mythic patriotism of manifest destiny depended upon and amplified such pioneer ideals, and the two myths functioned together as a justification for the Early Republic's national expansions. The figure of Andrew Jackson (1767–1845), who came to embody those interconnections and bring them to the nation's highest political office, also added one more mythic ideal to the mix: the image of the self-made man. That concept and its association with an idealized American identity went back at least to Ben Franklin, who helped create the myth in his autobiographical descriptions of his rise from rags to riches. But Jackson's life story included even more extreme such details: he was born in a log cabin in an unsurveyed area on the border between North and South Carolina, to a father who died before he was born and a mother he lost while he was still a child; he later volunteered for the Revolution at 13 and worked his way up through the military and political ranks from there. Jackson also linked the self-made man concept to the frontier, as he rose to prominence in Tennessee and became the first president not born in Virginia or Massachusetts. That 1828 presidential election result thus signaled the truly national dominance of the interconnected, Early Republic mythic patriotisms of Westward expansion, the pioneer, and the self-made man.

Another aspect of Jackson's rise to prominence reveals a more overtly exclusionary side to these interconnected mythic patriotisms, however. While Jackson's most substantive military command was of the American forces at the War of 1812's culminating Battle of New Orleans, forces that included Native American soldiers from a number of Louisiana tribes, much of his military career, both in that war and in the years after its conclusion, was spent fighting a series of brutal conflicts against Southeastern native nations (including the Muscogee and Seminole nations). His tactics in those conflicts were sufficiently, unnecessarily brutal that the Cherokee nicknamed him "Indian killer"; the Creek knew him as "Sharp Knife" for similar reasons. While each of those campaigns featured specific causes and contexts, an underlying factor across them and throughout the era was a conflict between the expansion of white settlers (and through them U.S. territory) and the Native American homelands against which those expansions were consistently directed.

When Jackson was elected president, his first proposed policy, Indian Removal, represented an attempt to forcibly resolve those conflicts and displace the native tribes who stood in the way of that goal of American expansion. As I discuss at length in my book *We the People*, Jackson's arguments for Indian Removal were based on his own mythic vision of Native Americans as fundamentally outside of both American identity and the nation's expanding future. As he put it in his December 3rd, 1833 annual address to Congress, after he had been re-elected to a second term in 1832,

That those tribes cannot exist surrounded by our settlements and in continual contact with our citizens is certain. They have neither the intelligence, the industry, the moral habits, nor the desire of improvement which are essential to any favorable change in their condition. Established in the midst of another and a superior race, and without appreciating the causes of their inferiority or seeking to control them, they must necessarily yield to the force of circumstances and ere long disappear.

While proponents of expansion and Manifest Destiny did not always express that exclusionary myth quite so bluntly, the simple fact is that if the continent was intended to be "overspread" and "possessed" by the United States, as O'Sullivan's influential, mythic patriotic vision detailed, that future would come at the expense of existing Native American nations, along with Mexican American communities through much of the Southwest and West.

The exclusion of those communities from the idealized frames of Manifest Destiny and expansion was one way in which the era's mythic patriotisms depended upon discriminatory visions of the nation, and the period's anti-immigrant sentiments were another. The connection of such xenophobia to images of patriotism and treason began with the Early Republic's most controversial laws, the 1798 Alien and Sedition Acts. Driven by fears that French diplomats and immigrants were spreading anti-American propaganda, in the broader context of the late 1790s "Quasi War" between the United States and France, those laws sought not only to criminalize criticism of the government but also to give the federal government significantly more power to discriminate against and deport immigrant Americans. Both those elements were tellingly defined through the concepts of patriotism and American identity: the "Act for the Punishment of Certain Crimes Against the United States" targeted those who "print, utter, or publish . . . any false, scandalous, and malicious writing" about the government; while the "Act Respecting Alien Enemies" created that new legal category for "all natives, citizens, denizens, or subjects of the hostile nation" during a period of war, giving the president the authoritarian power to "apprehend, restrain, secure, and remove" such immigrants based on this exclusionary vision of their still foreign and essentially un-American identity.

The Alien and Sedition Acts were sufficiently extreme and controversial that they received substantial political pushback, including from Thomas Jefferson and James Madison. Those founding American leaders and future presidents helped draft the 1798 and 1799 Kentucky and Virginia Resolutions, political and legal statements that challenged the Acts as unconstitutional and thus themselves un-American. After Jefferson's contested election to the presidency in 1800, and the concurrent transition in power from John Adams' Federalist Party to Jefferson's Democratic-Republican one, most of the Acts' provisions were allowed to expire, although elements of the Alien Enemies Act remained on the books and would become part of the legal context for the World War II discriminations against and internment of Japanese Americans. But in any case the broader connection of anti-immigrant sentiments to mythic patriotisms remained a force in Early Republic America, and found a particularly clear expression in the creation and platform of the political movement and party generally called the Know Nothings; the movement also went by the even more telling names the Native American Party and the American Party.

The Know Nothings, who first rose to political power in local elections throughout the 1840s, became a national force in the early 1850s, sweeping the 1854 Massachusetts elections and winning significant legislative victories and political offices in states across the nation. Although the movement came to be closely associated with anti-Catholic and anti-Irish sentiment, in truth its platforms and policies were much more broadly and comprehensively opposed to immigration, as the name "Native American Party" would suggest. They did so specifically, as illustrated by an 1854 San Francisco chapter's opposition to Chinese immigration (notwithstanding the fact that the Chinese community in that city predated the U.S. annexation of California) and advocacy for a state Supreme Court ruling that no Chinese American could testify in court against a white person. And they did so generally, as with proposed legislation in Massachusetts that would restrict voting and office-holding to men who had lived in the state for at least 21 years and that likewise called upon the U.S. Congress to change the requirement for naturalization as a citizen from 5 to 21 years. These actions and ideas went far beyond the wartime contexts of the Alien and Sedition Acts, and sought to make anti-immigrant sentiment a truly foundational feature of the national political landscape.

The 1856 national platform of the American Party, adopted at the party's February convention after it had rebranded itself under that telling new name, reflects the connection of mythic patriotisms to these anti-immigrant ideas. The platform begins with "An humble acknowledgement to the Supreme Being, for his protecting care vouchsafed to our fathers in their successful Revolutionary struggle, and hitherto manifested to us, their descendants, in the preservation of the liberties, the independence and the union of these States." Its first two stated goals are "The perpetuation of the Federal Union and Constitution" and that "Americans must rule America." And it calls "the present Administration's" replacement of "Americans" with "foreigners" in political offices one of the "existing evils" that, "to remedy . . . and prevent the disastrous consequences otherwise resulting therefrom, we would build up the 'American Party' upon the principles hereinbefore stated." Like the links between the myths of Manifest Destiny and self-made pioneers and the Jacksonian policy of Indian Removal, the Know Nothing/American Party exemplifies the exclusionary side to many of the Early Republic's mythic patriotisms.

Yet one of the same voices that advocated for those mythic patriotisms also expressed another, more active and much more potentially inclusive, form of Early Republic patriotism. In the Introduction to Volume 1, Number 1 (1837) of his newly created *United States Magazine and Democratic Review*, John L. O'Sullivan advances his arguments "for the advocacy of that high and holy DEMOCRATIC PRINCIPLE which was designed to be the fundamental element of the new social and political system created by the 'American experiment.'" O'Sullivan emphasizes in particular that experimental quality to both the American Revolution and its Early Republic identity, arguing that "The American revolution was the greatest of 'experiments,' . . . and the present is most emphatically an age of 'experiments.' The eye of man looks naturally *forward*; and as he is carried onward by the progress of time and truth, he is far more likely to stumble and stray if he turn his face backward, and keep his looks fixed on the thoughts and things of the past." And he defines that Revolutionary and contemporary American experiment alike as "the democratic cause" which "ought to engage the whole mind of the American nation, . . . to carry forward the noble mission entrusted to her, of going before the nations of the world as the representative of the democratic principle and as the constant living exemplar of its results" (O'Sullivan's emphases).

O'Sullivan's editorial became a foundational text for the Early Republic active patriotic community that came to call itself the Young America movement. Founded and led by O'Sullivan and a number of other significant political and cultural figures, including the English immigrant and radical reformer George Henry Evans, the Illinois Senator and future presidential candidate Stephen A. Douglas, and the New York financier August Belmont, the movement did feature some of the period's most prominent celebratory and mythic patriotisms: an idealized vision of the Revolution and through it American identity; expansion as a key element of the nation's future growth and promise. But as O'Sullivan's editorial indicates, Young America's emphasis was not on passively commemorating (much less venerating) historical ideals or figures, but on arguing for and modeling an active, experimental, democratic patriotism that would require ongoing contributions from all Americans, especially those in the current generation, to achieve such ideals.

Moreover, the Young America movement included a strong cultural component, a case for the role of artists and authors in actively constructing and propagating a uniquely American culture. O'Sullivan's fellow *U.S. Magazine* editor Evert Augustus Duyckinck (1816–1878) was a particular patron of the visual arts, and both supported the work of Hudson River School painters like

Thomas Cole and Asher Durand and linked their distinctly American subjects to Young America's ideas and ideals. Another member of O'Sullivan and Duyckinck's cohort, the journalist and playwright Cornelius Mathews (1817–1889), helped bring in fellow literary figures like William Cullen Bryant, William Gilmore Simms, and Nathaniel Hawthorne. In a June 30th, 1845 speech in his home city of New York, during the course of which he gave the movement its name, Mathews expressed this vision of active, cultural patriotism:

> Whatever that past generation of statesmen, law-givers and writers was capable of, we know. What they attained, what they failed to attain, we also know. Our duty and our destiny is another from theirs. Liking not at all its borrowed sound, we are yet (there is no better way to name it) the Young America of the people: a new generation.

Those sentiments, like the ideas in O'Sullivan's editorial, interestingly paralleled the guiding principles which over the same years, just over two hundred miles to the northeast in Concord (Massachusetts), launched another distinctively American social, cultural, and philosophical movement: Transcendentalism. Ralph Waldo Emerson's influential 1836 essay "Nature" is considered the foundational text for the Transcendental movement, and it opens with its own expression of the need for active, democratic experiment in the present: "Our age is retrospective. It builds the sepulchers of the fathers. It writes biographies, histories, and criticism. The foregoing generations beheld God and nature face to face; we, through their eyes. Why should not we also enjoy an original relation to the universe? Why should not we have a poetry and philosophy of insight and not of tradition, and a religion by revelation to us, and not the history of theirs? . . . There are new lands, new men, new thoughts. Let us demand our own works and laws and worship." If we demand and secure such an active relationship to our moment and world, he argues in the essay's concluding paragraph, "So shall we come to look at the world with new eyes."

In "Nature," Emerson (1803–1882) frames his arguments for such active participation in society in somewhat universal terms, but the following year, in his speech "The American Scholar" delivered to the Harvard graduating class of 1837, he developed a concurrent philosophy of active American patriotism. "Our day of dependence, our long apprenticeship to the learning of other lands, draws to a close," he begins, and then turns to his titular topic, "the American Scholar. Year by year we come up hither to read one more chapter of his biography. Let us inquire what new lights, new events, and more days have thrown on his character, his duties, and his hopes." After tracing at length the influences upon such scholars, their duties and responsibilities, and the topics and questions they might explore, he comes in his conclusion to his fullest association of that scholarly role with an idealized vision of the nation: "Mr. President and Gentlemen, this confidence in the unsearched might of man belongs, by all motives, by all prophecy, by all preparation, to the American Scholar. . . . A nation of men will for the first time exist, because each believes himself inspired by the Divine Soul which also inspires all men." As with the voices of the Young America movement, Emerson certainly still offers celebratory and mythic patriotisms, but here they are likewise intertwined with a vision of the necessary, democratizing, active work required of every American—for every American can be the Scholar Emerson envisions—if those ideals are to be achieved and passed on.

Two of the literary and cultural figures most directly inspired by Emerson and Transcendentalism extended that active, democratizing patriotism into their distinct genres and styles. When the journalist and poet Walt Whitman (1819–1892) self-published his first book, the collection *Leaves of Grass* (1855), he sent a copy to Emerson, along with a letter expressing his beliefs both that "swiftly, on limitless foundations, the United States too are founding a literature" and that "I say you have led The States there—have led Me there." And that 1855 edition of *Leaves* begins with a Preface in which Whitman lays out his visions of both celebratory and active patriotisms. On the first, he writes, "The Americans of all nations at any time upon the earth, have probably the fullest poetical nature. The United States themselves are essentially the greatest poem." And he defines the role of the poet as precisely that of an active patriot carrying forward and democratizing those ideals: "The American poets are to inclose [sic] old and new, for America is the race of races. The expression of the American poet is to be transcendent and new"; "An individual is as superb as a nation when he has the qualities which make a superb nation. The soul of the largest and wealthiest and proudest nation may well go half-way to meet that of its poets." This Preface, like the poems that follow it—especially the long opening poem named in subsequent editions "Song of Myself"—links Whitman's profound, Transcendental emphasis on the value and power of the individual soul to his concurrent celebration of the nation, and both require the active work of poets and all Americans to carry those legacies forward.

Emerson's Concord neighbor, friend, and protégé, the author and naturalist Henry David Thoreau (1817–1862), expressed in one of his most prominent actions and works a distinct and more critical form of active patriotism. In late July 1846, when he was about a year into what would be a two-year sojourn in his cabin at Walden Pond, Thoreau happened to meet Concord's tax collector, Sam Staples. Staples asked Thoreau to pay unpaid poll taxes, and he refused, citing his opposition to both the Mexican American War and the concurrent extension of slavery into new American territories, themselves two direct reflections of the violent and divisive effects of myths of Manifest Destiny and national expansion. Thoreau would spend a night in the Concord jail before a family member paid the tax against his wishes, and he turned that experience into the source for two interconnected texts: his January and February 1848 lecture series "The Rights and Duties of the Individual in Relation to Government," delivered at the Concord Lyceum; and his 1849 essay "Resistance to Civil Government," published by his fellow Transcendentalist and reformer Elizabeth Peabody in a May 1849 collection entitled *Aesthetic Papers* and posthumously re-published under its more well-known name "Civil Disobedience."

In that essay, Thoreau advances a clear argument about the active patriotic duty of each American if the nation is to move closer toward its ideals. "To speak practically, and as a citizen, . . . I ask for, not at once no government, but *at once* a better government. Let every man make known what kind of government would command his respect, and that will be one step toward obtaining it" (Thoreau's emphasis). He connects that argument to an alternative, still celebratory but more active account of the "Revolution of '75" and its legacies in his own moment, noting that "I think it is not too soon for honest men to rebel and revolutionize." And he ends with a critical patriotic vision of an American government and community that lives up to the founding celebrations of liberty and equality, writing, "I please myself with imagining a State at least which can afford to be just to all men." Thoreau's active patriotism, expressed in this essay and embodied throughout his tragically short life, weds the Transcendental emphases on the individual and the unfolding present to an argument that it is the expansion of justice and equality to all Americans, rather than the expansion of the nation's territory, which should be America's manifest destiny.

While Thoreau's active, critical patriotism offered an important challenge to the Early Republic's celebratory and mythic patriotisms, it was neither the only nor the first such critical patriotic perspective in the era. Indeed, a number of authors and activists expressed their own critical patriotic voices and arguments throughout the period, pushing back in particular on the exclusionary and discriminatory sides to the celebrations and myths and modeling the ways in which the nation could move closer toward its inclusive ideals. From creative writers like Catharine Maria Sedgwick to political writers and activists like William Apess and David Walker, these inspiring Americans carried forward the legacy of the Revolutionary era's critical voices and communities and ensured that this alternative form of American patriotism would remain part of the evolving nation.

The novelist Catharine Maria Sedgwick (1789–1867) had an inspiring personal connection to one of the Revolutionary era critical patriots. Sedgwick's father, Theodore, was the young Sheffield (Massachusetts) lawyer who took Elizabeth Freeman's case in 1780 and helped her win her freedom from slavery; after that court decision Freeman went to work for the Sedgwick family, where young Catharine, who was born a few years later and whom Freeman helped raise, came to know her as Mumbet. In an 1853 volume of the periodical *Bentley's Miscellany*, Sedgwick published a moving piece, entitled "Slavery in New England," in which she recounts Freeman's story and testifies to the influence Freeman had on Sedgwick's own development and perspective. From its title on, that piece itself embodies a critical patriotic perspective, one that seeks both to force New Englanders to grapple with the histories of slavery in the region, histories already under-remembered in the early 19th century, and to highlight and celebrate Freeman's exemplary American story and identity.

Nearly three decades before that piece appeared, Sedgwick's third novel, *Hope Leslie, or, Early Times in the Massachusetts* (1827), used the genre of the historical romance to offer a groundbreaking and compelling critical patriotic perspective on the state's and nation's 17th century origin points and communities. Writing in part in response to James Fenimore Cooper's popular novel *Last of the Mohicans* (1826), Sedgwick sought to create a quite distinct representation of those early American histories, and through them of Native American communities and perspectives. In her Preface, she addresses that revisionist goal directly, noting of Native American courage and resilience that, "These traits of their character will be viewed by an impartial observer, in a light very different from that in which they were regarded by our ancestors. In our histories, it was perhaps natural that they should be represented as 'surly dogs,' who preferred to die rather than live, from no other motives than a stupid or malignant obstinacy. Their own historians or poets, if they had such, would as naturally, and with more justice, have extolled their high-souled courage and patriotism." Just two years before Andrew Jackson would propose his Indian Removal policy, such an argument for Native American patriotism offered a striking challenge to many of the era's myths.

Hope Leslie includes many characters and plot threads, but it is in one potent early moment that the novel truly illustrates the potential effects of that critical patriotic perspective. One of Sedgwick's protagonists is Magawisca, a young Pequot girl (and daughter of a chief) who has been taken in as a ward by the Puritan Fletcher family after the horrors of the 1636 Pequot War. In the novel's Chapter IV, Magawisca recounts to the family's teenage son Everell her experiences of that war's Mystic Massacre, a brutal attack in which the English and their Narragansett allies burned a Pequot village and massacred its almost entirely civilian population. Everell has previously only heard the story of the war from the English perspective, and "this new version of an old story," which he recognizes as "putting the chisel into the hands of truth, and giving it to whom it belonged," affects him greatly: "Everell's imagination, touched by the wand of feeling, presented a very different picture" of

the massacre and these histories. Both Magawisca's and Sedgwick's goals
in creating that different picture exemplify critical patriotism: they aim not
only to force Anglo American audiences, in Everell's 1630s moment and
Sedgwick's 1820s one alike, to admit the truth of their actions toward the
Pequot people both in this massacre and throughout their shared histories; but
also and especially to imagine and work toward a collective future of which
Magawisca and all Native American communities can be part.

In 1829, just two years after Sedgwick published her novel and in the same
year that Jackson first proposed his exclusionary policy, the Pequot minister,
orator, activist, and author William Apess (1798–1839) began to share his
own critical patriotic perspective on American histories and images. He first
published his autobiography *A Son of the Forest* (1829), which detailed,
among other striking stories, his teenage military service with a New York
militia in the War of 1812. I wrote about Apess at length in my book *We the
People*, highlighting in particular his multi-layered efforts to challenge the
era's exclusions of Native Americans: locally and collectively, as part of the
1833–34 Mashpee Revolt that successfully defended and permanently established that native community on Cape Cod; and rhetorically and individually,
as in impassioned texts like the essay "An Indian's Looking-Glass for the
White Man" (1833). Here I'll focus on Apess' most overt expression of critical patriotism, as part of his final public performance: the bold and stunning
1836 oration "Eulogy on King Philip," delivered at Boston's Odeon lecture
hall, site of contemporary speeches by Ralph Waldo Emerson and many other
Transcendentalists and New England luminaries.

The existence and stated purpose of that speech themselves comprise
critical patriotic challenges to mythic histories. King Philip, a 17th century
Wampanoag chief to whom Apess was related on his mother's side, was best
known as the namesake of a brutal 1670s war that included the destruction of
the Puritan town of Lancaster. Yet Apess, speaking in the heart of Boston and
New England, seeks not only to eulogize this figure who had generally been
defined as an adversary, but also to make the case that he should be remembered and celebrated by all Americans as an iconic revolutionary leader and
patriot. He argues, "as the immortal Washington lives endeared and engraven
on the hearts of every white in America, never to be forgotten in time—even
such is the immortal Philip honored, as held in memory by the degraded but
yet grateful descendants who appreciate his character; so will every patriot,
especially in this enlightened age, respect the rude yet all accomplished son of
the forest, that died a martyr to his cause, though unsuccessful, yet as glorious
as the American Revolution."

Apess' appeals to his fellow patriots aren't solely intended to revise and
expand our collective histories, however. His concluding lines reflect the

concurrent, present and future orientation of his critical patriotism, his hopes that this perspective on America can help lead it toward a more perfect union. "You and I have to rejoice that we have not to answer for our fathers' crimes; neither shall we do right to charge them one to another. We can only regret it, and flee from it; and from henceforth, let peace and righteousness be written upon our hearts and hands forever, is the wish of a poor Indian." These lines closely echo the critical patriotic, and even more optimistic, final sentence of his "Indian's Looking-Glass" essay: "Do not get tired, ye noble-hearted— only think how many poor Indians want their wounds done up daily; the Lord will reward you, and pray you stop not till this tree of distinction shall be leveled to the earth, and the mantle of prejudice torn from every American heart—then shall peace pervade the Union." In these texts, as in every moment of his too short, profoundly inspiring life, William Apess embodied a critical patriotic challenge to the myths of the Indian Removal era.

In the same year that Apess published his autobiography, another young Bostonian firebrand launched his own critical patriotic broadside against American myths and exclusions. David Walker (1796–1830) was born in Wilmington, North Carolina to an enslaved father (who died before his birth) and a free mother, making him legally free but deeply tied to and affected by the system of slavery. As an adult he moved to Charleston, South Carolina and then Philadelphia, joining the groundbreaking African Methodist Episcopal (AME) Church in both cities, before settling in the mid-1820s in Boston's Beacon Hill neighborhood, a haven for free African Americans. He became over the next few years a leading voice, in that Bostonian community and throughout the North, for abolitionism, civil rights, and the development of a thriving commercial and social scene for the African American community, such as in his role as a contributor to the nation's first black-owned newspaper, *Freedom's Journal*. And in September 1829 he published a book, *Walker's Appeal, in Four Articles; Together with a Preamble, to the Colored Citizens of the World, but in Particular, and Very Expressly, to Those of the United States of America*.

As that long title indicates, Walker directly modeled his *Appeal* upon the U.S. Constitution, beginning with a Preamble and moving through four Articles. In many ways the book embodies the critical side of critical patriotism, laying out the case for Walker's opening assertion, offered to his "Dearly beloved Brethren and Fellow Citizens," that "we (colored people of the United States) are the most degraded, wretched, and abject set of beings that ever lived since the world began." The Articles trace four root causes of that state, four interconnected forms of oppression and exclusion that Walker demands that all Americans face head on; he does so in a style that combines passion, exemplified by his frequent capitalizations, italics, and exclamation points, with nuanced logic and argumentation. But the very creation of his text, as well as its direct parallels to the Constitution, embodies a critical patriotic challenge to the nation's celebratory and mythic ideals. And in his conclusion Walker takes that work one step further, quoting at length the opening of the Declaration of Independence and then exclaiming, "See your Declaration Americans!!! Do you understand your own language?"

For much of the Early Republic period, Americans seemed to understand those Revolutionary ideas and ideals in a celebratory and mythic way, commemorating them through newly constructed rituals like a national anthem and carrying them forward through myths like Manifest Destiny. But the active patriotism of movements like Young America and Transcendentalism challenged Americans not to passively accept those visions of the past, and instead to take action to embody the nation's ideals in the present. And through their critical patriotic writings and activisms, figures like Henry David Thoreau, Catharine Maria Sedgwick, William Apess, and David Walker directly challenged those celebrations and myths and worked to push the new nation toward a more just and inclusive future.

Chapter Three

The Civil War

Testing Whether the Nation Could Endure

On March 4th, 1865, President Abraham Lincoln (1809–1865) rose to deliver his Second Inaugural Address. With the Civil War about to enter its fifth year, having dragged on far longer and more horrifically than most Americans had likely expected, and having faced a serious challenge from both Democratic nominee and Union General George McClellan and from Radical Republicans within his own party, such as his own Secretary of the Treasury Salmon P. Chase, Lincoln's re-election to the presidency had in the course of the 1864 campaign been far from a sure thing. Although Lincoln ended up winning re-election with relative ease, receiving 55% of the popular vote and a 212–21 margin in the Electoral College, there was no doubt on that March morning that the nation remained deeply and painfully divided, not only between the Union and Confederacy but also throughout its states and communities. Lincoln would have been forgiven if he used the occasion of this prominent national speech to sound ominous, or at the very least concerned, notes.

But as was his wont throughout his presidency, and especially in his public addresses and statements, Lincoln instead offered that reeling nation a profoundly optimistic perspective, an expression of his "high hope for the future." In so doing he built on a famous line from his First Inaugural Address four years earlier, where he had offered a vision of celebratory and mythic patriotism as cause for optimism about America's ideals and future even as the war loomed: "The mystic chords of memory, stretching from every battlefield and patriot grave to every living heart and hearthstone all over this broad land, will yet swell the chorus of the Union, when again touched, as surely they will be, by the better angels of our nature." And he closed this Second Inaugural Address by envisioning the collective, active patriotic work that would be required if the nation were to embody and carry forward those better angels once more: "With malice toward none, with charity for all, with firmness in the right as God gives us to see the right, let us strive on to finish the work we are in, to bind up the nation's wounds, to care for him who shall have borne the battle and for his widow and his orphan, to do all which may achieve and cherish a just and lasting peace among ourselves and with all nations."

The Civil War presented Americans with one of history's most profound tests of their celebratory patriotic ideals. But like their beloved president, they nonetheless found ways to reiterate and extend such celebratory patriotism, as illustrated by cultural works like the war poems of Walt Whitman and Herman Melville and the wartime anthem composed by Julia Ward Howe. They did so in significant measure to counteract the mythic patriotism that underlay and bolstered the Confederacy's arguments for its existence and cause. And they supported their celebratory perspective with some of American history's most striking examples of active patriotism, framed by Lincoln in another famous speech, the Gettysburg Address, and embodied by communities like the United States Colored Troops, immigrant soldiers, and the thousands of women who worked as wartime nurses. Yet even (indeed, especially) at this time of crisis, the nation likewise needed critical patriotic perspectives on both its history and its present identity, and figures like Frederick Douglass, Martin Delany, and Lucy Larcom extended and deepened that legacy of American critical patriotism.

As the Revolutionary War and War of 1812 had both already illustrated, a nation at war often places a particular emphasis on celebratory patriotism, and on a concurrent vision of criticism of the nation at such times as unpatriotic and even potentially treasonous. In the Civil War, a conflict in which the Union soldiers, leaders, and supporters were fighting for the very survival and continued existence of the United States of America, that emphasis became even more pronounced still. Indeed, since the war was from its outset divisive and debated even within the states that remained in the Union and fought for that continued national future, expressions of celebratory patriotism became in many ways a corollary to the war's military campaigns and political strategies, another front in the battle to advocate for and preserve a whole, unified, idealized United States of America.

The wartime addition of the phrase "In God We Trust" to U.S. currency illustrates this connection of the war effort to celebratory patriotic images of an idealized American identity. The phrase had originated at least in part with another celebratory patriotic description of the nation: the line in the fourth verse of Francis Scott Key's "The Star-Spangled Banner" that concludes "And this be on our motto: 'In God is our Trust.'" In November 1861, a Pennsylvania Baptist minister named Mark Watkinson petitioned the

Treasury Department to feature "Almighty God in some form on our coins" in order to link the Union cause to such longstanding images of America as a nation blessed by God. This would, Watkinson argued, "place us openly under the Divine protection we have personally proclaimed." Treasury Secretary Salmon P. Chase liked the idea, and over the next few years worked with Director of the U.S. Mint James Pollock to find a legal mechanism to bring that form of celebratory patriotism to the nation's currency. The Congressional Coinage Act of 1864 granted the Secretary the power to add the phrase to coins of his choice, and Chase authorized its inscription on one- and two-cent coins.

Such official government actions and images, like Lincoln's speeches and public statements, comprised one consistent and important form of Civil War celebratory patriotism. But the contributions of authors and cultural figures offered another, complementary and exemplary expression of such celebratory visions of the nation's enduring ideals despite—indeed, through—this time of crisis. Not surprisingly, many of those celebratory cultural works came from the pen of Walt Whitman (1819–1892), the groundbreaking journalist and poet who had connected both his texts and his authorial role as an American bard to idealized images of the nation since the 1855 preface to *Leaves of Grass*. Whitman's younger brother George joined the Union Army in 1862, and through his concern for his brother as well as his commitment to the cause, Whitman ended up working for many years as a volunteer nurse in the military hospitals around Washington, DC. He turned those experiences into the material for his collection of wartime poems, *Drum-Taps* (1865).

Drum-Taps features 43 poems that depict an impressively wide range of subjects and emotions, and can't be reduced to a single perspective or emphasis. But a celebratory patriotic view of the war and its connection to American ideals nonetheless both frames and serves as a through-line within the collection. This starts with key lines and images in the book's opening two poems: "First O Songs for a Prelude," where Whitman's expresses "pride and joy in my city" (New York) for "how she led the rest to arms, how she gave the cue," the ways in which this iconic setting for so many of Whitman's American odes became a microcosm of the unified Union cause; and then "Eighteen Sixty-One," where Whitman directly addresses that opening "year of the struggle": "As I heard you shouting loud, your sonorous voice ringing across the continent." That latter image, of the war as a parallel to the Early Republic myths of national expansion and Manifest Destiny, becomes a concurrent, unifying thread to the book's celebratory patriotisms, a way for Whitman to imagine, as he does overtly in the fourth poem, "From Paumanok Starting I Fly like a Bird," "The idea of all, of the Western world one and inseparable,/And then the song of each member of these States."

Whitman likewise links his celebratory patriotism to both the American future and the past. Published in May 1865, a few weeks after the Confederate surrender at Appomattox, *Drum-Taps* concludes with images of an even more idealized national future now that the war has reached a successful conclusion, as in the closing lines of the penultimate poem "Turn O Libertad": "Then turn, and be not alarm'd O Libertad—turn your undying face,/ To where the future, greater than all the past,/Is swiftly, surely preparing for you." But it is the collection's most historical poem, "The Centenarian's Story," which truly exemplifies Whitman's embrace of celebratory patriotism. In that long poetic dialogue, a Revolutionary War veteran shares his memories of that conflict with a Union Army volunteer, in the process inextricably linking the two conflicts into one ongoing fight for liberty and nation. The veteran recalls key moments such as the inspiring reading of the Declaration and the patriotic resilience of iconic leaders like Washington when New York was lost to the English and the Revolutionary cause seemed endangered: "But when my General pass'd me,/As he stood in the boat and look'd toward the coming sun,/I saw something different from capitulation." And when the Centenarian's story is concluded, the young Civil War soldier notes that, "The two, the past and present, have interchanged,/I myself as connecter, as chansonnier of a great future." While the book's final poems will most directly celebrate that future, this crucial connecting text links both the future and the collection's consistently idealized images of the Civil War cause back to the Revolutionary's patriotic national origins.

Complementing and extending Whitman's celebratory patriotic Civil War poems are those of his close contemporary Herman Melville; the two men were both born in New York in mid-1819 and passed away within six months of one another in 1891–92. As illustrated by his novels *Moby Dick* (1851), *Pierre; or, the Ambiguities* (1852), and *The Confidence-Man* (1857), Melville's philosophical and literary perspectives were distinctly darker and often more pessimistic than Whitman's. Elements of that darkness did find their way into *Battle Pieces and Aspects of the War* (1866), the poetry collection inspired by Melville's 1864 tour of Virginia's Civil War battlefields and featuring poetic accounts of many of the war's battles from throughout its distinct theaters. But Melville dedicates that volume "To the Memory of the Three Hundred Thousand Who in the War for the Maintenance of the Union Fell Devotedly under the Flag of Their Fathers," and that dedication's celebratory patriotism toward both the war and its historical legacies reflects an idealized perspective that throughout the collection serves as a counter to those darker themes.

Melville makes the contrast between those two tones central to the collection's first two, framing poems. In "Misgivings (1860)," he describes the evils which led to the war, "my country's ills," as "The tempest bursting from the waste of Time,/On the world's fairest hope linked with man's foulest crime." That last line sums up quite succinctly how a celebratory vision of America could grapple with the horrific histories, of slavery most of all but also of the sectional debates and divisions caused by that system which had brought this inspiring nation to such a low point. And in the next poem, "The Conflict of Convictions (1860–1)," Melville delves further into that contrast and the march to war it produced. "Return, return, O eager Hope,/And face man's latter fall," he begins "Conflict," and later he notes overtly how that fallen state represents a break from the nation's idealized histories: "the Founders' dream shall flee," since "the poor old Past" has "perished." These framing poems present a far more conflicted vision of the war's origins than does Whitman's fully celebratory perspective on that period, but Melville still depicts those wartime conflicts as contrasts with and thus reiterations of an overarching, celebratory view of the nation.

As the collection moves through poems focused on specific details and images from across the war's battles and theaters, Melville consistently returns to images which reflect that celebratory perspective. In "Malvern Hill (July, 1862)," he creates a Civil War echo and extension of Key's "Star-Spangled Banner," describing "The battle-smoked flag, with stars eclipsed,/We followed (it never fell!)." In "Gettysburg. The Check. (July, 1863)," he depicts the war's most overt single turning point in favor of the Union, Pickett's Charge, as an embodiment of the war's larger contrast between national ideals and adversaries that seek to undermine and destroy them: "He charged, and in that charge condensed/His all of hate and all of fire,/He sought to blast us in his scorn,/And wither us in his ire. . . . Surged, but were met, and back they set:/Pride was repelled by sterner pride,/And Right is a strong-hold yet." And in "The Armies of the Wilderness (1863–64)," he complements specific battle descriptions with italicized commentaries on these broader ideals, an overarching perspective which explicitly links this present fight to its historical, Revolutionary foundations. With stanzas like "Did the Fathers feel mistrust/Can no final good be wrought?/Over and over, again and again/Must the fight for Right be fought?" and "Dust to dust, and blood for blood—/Passion and pangs! Has Time/Gone back? or is this the Age/of the world's great Prime?," Melville defines the stakes of such battles as nothing less than the legacy of American ideals.

In a final series of poems on the war's conclusions, Melville continues to recognize the war's tragedies and toll but even more fully expresses this celebratory patriotic perspective. Of "The Surrender at Appomatox (April, 1865)," he writes, "The hope and great event agree/In the sword that Grant received from Lee." In "A Canticle: Significant of the National Exaltation of

Enthusiasm at the Close of the War," he situates that joyous event in its historical and idealized national contexts: "The Generations pouring/From times
of endless date,/In their going, in their flowing/Ever form the steadfast State;/
And Humanity is growing/Toward the fullness of her fate." And all these
concluding poems build to the collection's four-part final work, "America,"
which uses once more the symbolic image of the national "Banner" to trace
the war's perils and promise. By the war's end, that flag and the nation it
represents have certainly changed, becoming "hope grown wise,/And youth
matured for age's seat." But in Melville's more realistic celebratory perspective, such challenges have been necessary ones, that "spake of pain,/But such
as purifies from stain—sharp pangs that never come again." And having defeated and transcended them, the nation looks toward an even more idealized
future, "Law on her brow and empire in her eyes."

While these poetry collections expressed celebratory visions of the war
just after its successful conclusion, a few years earlier a contemporary of
Whitman's and Melville's had composed a lyrical ballad which became a
new anthem for the wartime nation. Born in 1819 New York just four days
before Whitman, Julia Ward Howe (1819–1910) would become a prominent social activist for both abolitionism and the nascent women's suffrage
movement, which drew on many abolitionists. In November 1861 she and
her reformer husband Samuel Gridley Howe (founder of the groundbreaking
Perkins School for the Blind) visited President Lincoln at the White House,
and Julia was inspired to write a poem in support of Lincoln and the unfolding war. She set her words to the music of the existing abolitionist song "John
Brown's Body," originally composed by William Steffe, and published this
new text, "The Battle Hymn of the Republic," in the February 1862 edition
of the *Atlantic Monthly*. The song quickly became one of the war's most
popular and influential pro-Union works, and was for example re-published
in Philadelphia in 1863 by the Supervisory Committee for Recruiting Colored
Regiments.

Perhaps the most overtly celebratory patriotic element of Howe's song is
the relationship between the title and the lyrics. Those lyrics do not explicitly
mention America at all, focusing largely on religious references, such as the
famous opening line, "Mine eyes have seen the glory of the coming of the
Lord," interwoven with images of war that are both symbolic ("His terrible
swift sword") and specific ("the watch-fires of a hundred circling camps").
Yet the title links both war (Battle) and religion (Hymn) to that American Republic, and in so doing turns the entire song into a celebration of an idealized,
blessed nation. Because of that multi-layered link, the song's most repeated
phrase, "His truth is marching on," while certainly and centrally referring
to God, likewise describes the progress of the American cause in the Civil

War. Indeed, Howe envisions that national cause as nothing less than a holy text, as illustrated by the third verse's striking opening line, "I have read a fiery gospel writ in burnished rows of steel." Building on prior images like the Revolutionary era's Prospect Poems and the phrase "In God We Trust," Howe creates an even more multi-faceted, celebratory patriotic vision of American ideals as a spiritual revelation brought to life.

The song's final verse takes that spiritual, celebratory patriotism to its extreme but logical conclusion, directly linking Christ's meaning and sacrifice to America's historic and contemporary quest for liberty. "In the beauty of the lilies, Christ was born across the sea,/With a glory in His bosom that transfigures you and me," Howe begins this culminating moment. And then comes the line that exemplifies the association of Christian and American ideals: "As He died to make men holy, let us die to make men free." The Civil War was full of death and loss, a brutal conflict that threatened to destroy the nation and reveal the limits of its idealized community. Yet as defined by authors like Howe, Melville, and Whitman, the war instead became an extension and amplification of those ideals, and thus in this view support for the Union cause comprised a profound expression of the most celebratory form of patriotic embrace of that idealized nation.

Of course the Civil War pitted Americans against Americans, and those idealized images of both the conflict and the nation had to grapple with that fraught and painful reality. Many celebratory voices did so through telling collective metaphors: Lincoln's vision, in a speech during his 1858 campaign for the U.S. Senate, of "a house divided"; and the frequent descriptions of the war as dividing a family, pitting "brother against brother" and the like. These familial metaphors offered a way in which celebratory patriots could continue to advance images of a unified, idealized America while recognizing that roughly half of that nation had become wartime adversaries. But the contrast went even deeper still, as advocates and leaders of the Confederate States of America consistently constructed and depended upon their own myths of American history and identity, frames through which they sought to define themselves as the true heirs to such national ideals while overtly excluding African American members of their communities from those images.

Advocates for the Southern slave states in opposition to the power of the federal government, and implicitly to the United States as a whole, had by the start of the Civil War been relying upon such myths of American history and identity for decades. The 1828 South Carolina Exposition and Protest, written anonymously by John C. Calhoun as part of the evolving Nullification Crisis between South Carolina and both the John Quincy Adams and Andrew Jackson administrations, in both of which Calhoun served as Vice President, exemplified the mythic elements of this proto-Confederate perspective. Calhoun argues that the federal government's actions were unconstitutional, not just in terms of specific powers and limits but also and most importantly in relation to the Constitution's spirit and legacy: "The Constitution may be as grossly violated by acting against its meaning as against its letter." That framing implicitly defines South Carolina as the true heir to the Revolution's and Founding's meanings, and in the document's final sentence Calhoun drives home those associations and his mythic patriotic arguments for this cause: "If the present usurpations and the professed doctrines of the existing system be persevered in—after due forebearance on the part of the State—that it will be her sacred duty to interpose—a duty to herself—to the Union—to the present, and to future generations—and to the cause of liberty over the world, to arrest the progress of a usurpation which, if not arrested, must, in its consequences, corrupt the public morals and destroy the liberty of the country."

Three decades later, when South Carolina and the other states that would form the Confederacy began to secede from the United States, they often employed similarly mythic perspectives as central elements of their justifications. South Carolina was the first state to secede, and its December 20th, 1860 "Declaration of the Immediate Causes which Induce and Justify the Secession of South Carolina from the Federal Union" features as a main argument a particularly clear such myth. The document opens with an extended description of the Revolution, "a struggle for the right of self-government . . . which resulted, on the 4th of July 1776, in a Declaration, by the Colonies, that they are, and of right ought to be, FREE AND INDEPENDENT STATES." The secessionists link their own 1860 declaration directly to that historical one, noting of the Founders that "they further solemnly declared that whenever any 'form of government becomes destructive of the ends for which it was established, it is the right of the people to alter or abolish it, and to institute a new government.'" In case this analogy between South Carolina's secession and the American Revolution's ideals was not clear enough, the 1860 declaration goes on to create a second such mythic historical link, this time to the U.S. Constitution: connecting the necessity of secession to "the ends for which the Constitution was framed," since "We affirm that these ends for which this Government was instituted have been defeated"; and then opening the final section with "We, therefore, the People of South Carolina."

The ten states that followed South Carolina's lead and seceded between January 9th (Mississippi) and June 8th (Tennessee), 1861, likewise consistently invoked such myths of a Revolutionary and Constitutional legacy, while just as consistently noting the centrality of slavery to their Confederate cause and nation. Georgia's January 19th Ordinance of Secession notes that "The Constitution delegated no power to Congress to exclude" any state from exercising their liberties, and "therefore our right was good under the Constitution"; thus, they state, "we resume the powers which our fathers delegated to the Government of the United States, and henceforth will seek new safeguards for our liberty, equality, security, and tranquility." Virginia's April 17th Ordinance of Secession positions the secessionist cause as the true heir to the Revolution's populist ideals, "having declared that the powers granted under the said Constitution were derived from the people of the United States, and might be resumed whensoever the same should be perverted to their injury and oppression." And Alabama's February 12th Ordinance of Secession defines the Confederacy's "purpose" as precisely taking up the legacy of the Revolution's ideals and documents: "to frame a provisional as well as a permanent Government upon the principles of the Constitution of the United States."

As these individual states continued seceding from the United States, the new Confederate nation they were constituting did indeed begin to form its own such government. In February 1861, the newly created Confederate Congress appointed one of its elected members, the Georgia lawyer and politician Alexander Stephens (1812–1883), as the C.S.A.'s Vice President. And on March 21st, in Savannah, Georgia, Stephens delivered a prominent speech that expressed a number of defining principles of that Confederate nation. Stephens' speech has come to be called the Cornerstone Speech, due to its strikingly blunt statements about the Confederate government's emphases on slavery and racial oppression: "its foundations are laid, its corner-stone rests, upon the great truth that the negro is not equal to the white man; that slavery and subordination to the superior race is his natural and normal condition. This, our new government, is the first, in the history of the world, based upon this great physical, philosophical, and moral truth." The U.S. Constitution includes in its infamous 3/5s clause a definition of enslaved African Americans as less than a full person for purposes of representation; but nonetheless the document as a whole, like the Declaration of Independence and other founding American texts, did help formulate national ideals of equality from which, as Stephens notes bluntly, the Confederacy was overtly separating.

But while Stephens recognizes that aspect of the Confederate government as a deviation from American and world history, and indeed "one of the greatest revolutions in the annals of the world," he at the same time frames his speech with a description of the Confederacy as in other key ways the true heir to the American Revolution's ideals. "This new constitution or form of government," he notes, "constitutes the subject to which your attention will be partly invited. In reference to it, I make this first general remark: it amply secures all our ancient rights, franchises, and liberties. All the great principles of Magna Carta are retained in it. No citizen is deprived of life, liberty, or property, but by the judgment of his peers under the laws of the land. . . . All the essentials of the old constitution, which have endeared it to the hearts of the American people, have been preserved and perpetuated." And he seeks to complement that argument for Revolutionary continuity with the Confederacy's radical emphases on racial hierarchy and slavery, arguing that those latter changes "form great improvements upon the old constitution. So, taking the whole new constitution, I have no hesitancy in giving it as my judgment that it is decidedly better than the old."

Stephens' speech lays bare two elements of American mythic patriotisms that have been consistently present but too often under-emphasized. The more obvious is their exclusionary purposes: not just that these myths tend to exclude certain American communities (such as African Americans) from their visions of the nation, but also that the myths are created precisely to support those exclusions. The cornerstones of the Confederacy were slavery and racial oppression, and its self-descriptions as the Revolution's true heir were intended to bolster and validate those exclusionary practices and perspectives. But that doesn't mean that Stephens and his ilk didn't at the same time genuinely believe in that vision of the American Revolution and the nation it established, and that is the second and even more destructive element to this mythic form of patriotism. It presents clear and seemingly legitimate, if certainly idealized, views on the nation's history and identity, ones with which all patriotic Americans would presumably agree; hence Stephens' description of "All the essentials of the old constitution, which have endeared it to the hearts of the American people." But those views have through these myths been written back into history from the present and are entirely shaped by that present's political purposes, which both makes them much more likely to be historically inaccurate and concurrently makes it much more difficult for Americans to understand and engage our foundational histories (their ideals as well as their realities) in nuanced and meaningful ways.

While of course the mythic patriotisms expressed by Stephens and the secession declarations were in key ways specific to those particular texts and contexts, such exclusionary myths could and did exist in and have destructive effects on communities throughout the Civil War United States. One of the most horrific such events was the July 13th–16th, 1863 explosion of white supremacist violence in New York City that came to be known as the Draft Riots. That name highlights a proximate cause of the riots, the March 1863 Congressional Enrollment Act which created a Union Army draft to increase its depleted ranks; wealthier Americans could buy their way out of the draft, causing resentment among communities such as New York's white working class. When white New Yorkers erupted in a multi-day orgy of violence in mid-July, their riots were sometimes framed by those sympathetic to their cause as a revolutionary uprising against tyrannical power akin to the mythic vision of the Confederacy, as illustrated by the phrase "The Irish Civil War." But in truth, this uprising was driven by anti-black racism just as fully as were secession and the Civil War it caused, a focus made clear by the principal actions of the rioters: attacking African Americans throughout the city and lynching more than one hundred of them; burning down numerous homes and buildings in both the African American and abolitionist communities, including the Colored Orphan Asylum and Horace Greeley's residence; and forcing thousands of African American residents to flee the city. The New York riots thus reflected the destructive power exclusionary myths of American communities possessed on a national level.

Such mythic patriotisms did not only target African Americans, and indeed the Early Republic myths of expansion and Manifest Destiny remained in force during the Civil War, as illustrated by another horrific historical event: the December 26th, 1862 execution of 38 Dakota Sioux Native Americans in Mankota, Minnesota, the largest mass execution in American history. Throughout 1862, white settlers continued to pour into Minnesota (which had become a state in May 1858) and onto native lands, while the U.S. government violated treaties with multiple tribes and left many such communities starving after failing to deliver food in "payment" for that stolen land. In August, Dakota Sioux Chief Little Crow led a six-week uprising against these invaders, a revolt framed throughout the U.S. not as an echo of the American Revolution nor as an oppressed people's quest for liberty and justice, but as an illegal war against the expanding nation. When the uprising was put down more than three hundred Dakota men were sentenced to death by Governor Henry Hastings Sibley; while President Lincoln commuted a number of the sentences, many of those men nonetheless remained imprisoned for life, and 38 others were executed on Lincoln's orders. The Sioux and Winnebago nations were subsequently removed from the state to distant reservations, once again on Lincoln's authority. The era's mythic patriotisms did not just divide North from South, but continued to divide the expanding United States into those communities perceived as part of that idealized nation and those overtly and violently excluded from it.

Lincoln's prominent role in both that horrific mass execution and the subsequent extension of the Jacksonian Indian Removal policy reminds us that even Civil War era celebratory patriotisms which embraced the United States in opposition to the Confederacy could too easily be wedded to their own mythic patriotisms, with the same potential to discriminate and exclude. That's an important rejoinder to any attempt to entirely distinguish the period's Union and Confederate celebratory patriotisms. But at the same time, both Lincoln's opposition to the Confederacy's myths and his celebration of American ideals led him, in his famous and most eloquent speech, to articulate and advocate for a more active form of patriotism, one which offers a distinct and vital way to understand the wartime service and sacrifice of a number of important and inspiring American communities.

Lincoln's "Gettysburg Address," delivered at the November 19th, 1863 dedication of the cemetery on that Pennsylvania battlefield, was even shorter than his Second Inaugural Address would be, but it packs even more of a patriotic punch.[1] More exactly, in its 278 words, Lincoln's speech depicts two distinct but interconnected forms of Civil War active patriotism, two ways that the Union cause as he defines it here extended the legacy of the idealized "new nation, conceived in Liberty, and dedicated to the proposition that all men are created equal," that "four score and seven years ago our fathers brought forth on this continent." First, he depicts the Union war effort itself as a battle to validate and cement that legacy, "testing whether that nation, or any nation so conceived and so dedicated, can long endure." He argues that Union Army soldiers like those "brave men, living and dead, who struggled here" at Gettysburg represent the embodiment of such active patriotism, that "what they did here" exemplifies that idealized legacy and thus that it is their actions, service, and sacrifice which "dedicate," "consecrate," and "hallow this ground." This is more than the standard paean to fallen heroes we might expect at a cemetery dedication, and which had been provided at great length by the speaker preceding Lincoln, former Secretary of State Edward Everett. It's an argument that it is these soldiers who most potently embody the Revolutionary memory that comprises a patriotic embrace of American history and ideals. And in Lincoln's vision the soldiers embodied that patriotism not just through their identity and community, but also and especially through their actions, "what they did here."

Moreover, and even more crucially for his view of active patriotism, Lincoln then closes his speech by pivoting from those soldiers' patriotic actions to those that all Americans must likewise perform. "It is for us the living," he argues, "to be dedicated here to the unfinished work which they who fought here have thus far so nobly advanced, . . . to be here dedicated to the great task remaining before us." That task is most overtly to see the war to a successful conclusion, and when Lincoln speaks of the need to take "increased devotion to that cause for which they gave the last full measure of devotion," he might seem to be imploring his audience (both present and national) to commit to seeing that war through. But while that is certainly part of his point, in the speech's final and most potent phrases, Lincoln defines both the soldiers' cause and those concurrent collective actions in a more overarching and patriotic way still: "that this nation, under God, shall have a new birth of freedom—and that government of the people, by the people, for the people, shall not perish from the earth." Lincoln here offers a celebratory patriotic vision of American history, identity, and ideals, but one entirely wedded to both the need for and the role of active patriotism, of the vital opportunity to enact a second American Revolution, "a new birth of freedom," through the Civil War and its extension and amplification of those national narratives. And, just as importantly, this celebratory vision of America and "the people" who constitute it likewise offers an inclusive alternative to the Confederacy's exclusionary myths, making clear that the war's active patriotism is not simply about military service or shared sacrifice, but about how such actions can embody and extend truly collective and national ideals.

Those who fought for and supported the Union cause in the Civil War did so for a variety of reasons, and cannot be reduced to any one analysis. Yet if we start with Lincoln's frame for these two levels of active patriotism, military and collective service, we can see inspiring examples of them across a few communities of Union soldiers and supporters. One community of active patriotic soldiers are the nearly two hundred thousand African Americans who fought between 1863 and 1865 as part of the United State Colored Troops (USCT). As Frederick Douglass put it, "Once let the black man get upon his person the brass letter, U.S., let him get an eagle on his button, and a musket on his shoulder and bullets in his pocket, there is no power on earth that can deny that he has earned the right to citizenship." Douglass' point was partly about changing perceptions of African Americans, in contrast for example to the Supreme Court's 1857 *Dred Scott* decision, which had ruled that enslaved African Americans could not be citizens as they were legal property rather than persons. But it was also and even more importantly about expanding visions of American identity to better align them with the legacies of ideals like "All men are created equal." And, crucially, expanding them through action: "earning the right to citizenship" being a particularly clear embodiment of active patriotism.

Two of the most prominent accounts of African American regiments, written by men who led and served in them, capture that sense of collective active patriotism among those soldiers. Thomas Wentworth Higginson (1823–1911), the journalist, editor, and abolitionist who served as colonel for the First South Carolina Volunteers, wrote about those experiences in his book *Army Life in a Black Regiment* (1869). In that book's concluding chapter, he argues, "We who served with the black troops have this peculiar satisfaction, that, whatever dignity or sacredness the memories of the war may have to others, they have more to us. In that contest all the ordinary ties of patriotism were the same." He adds, "We had touched the pivot of the war. . . . Till the blacks were armed, there was no guaranty [sic] of their freedom. It was their demeanor under arms that shamed the nation into recognizing them as men." And throughout the book Higginson details both the men's every day and their extreme service and sacrifices that comprised the actions which contributed to those lasting national effects.

Half a century later, one of the last surviving USCT troops published a personal narrative of his own such service. William Henry Singleton (1843–1938) was born a slave in North Carolina but during the war, when he was only 20, escaped and helped form and lead one of the first African American units, the First North Carolina Colored Volunteers (later part of the 35th USCT regiment). He went on to a long life of church leadership across the Northern U.S., and in 1922 published his brief autobiography, *Recollections of My Slavery Days*, serially in a Peekskill (NY) newspaper. Despite the book's title, Singleton focuses much of his text on his Civil War service, service driven by his belief, stated in response to a peer's attitude that the war would be over before he can join the fight, that "The war will not be over until I have had a chance to spill my blood." His work forming the regiment led to a meeting with President Lincoln himself, at which, Singleton recounts, he told Lincoln "I have a thousand men. We want to help fight to free our race. We want to know if you will take us in the service?" And in his book's final paragraph Singleton drives home what that active patriotic service has meant for himself, his community, and the nation: "America has been very good to me. I am one of its citizens. There is no stain on the Flag now. I once fought under its banner."

The United States Colored Troops were one of the most exemplary active patriotic communities to serve under and help expand the meaning of that banner, but the same could certainly be said of other cohorts of Union soldiers. In my book *We the People* I highlighted two examples of Civil War service from immigrant communities and individuals that likewise more than qualify as expressions of active patriotism. Men from the century-old Filipino American fishing villages in southern Louisiana defied that state's Confederate allegiance to fight for the Union instead; as early 20th century historian Sixto Lopez puts it, "to their lasting credit be it said, they joined and fought with the soldiers of the Union in order to free the slave, and some of the blood that helped to wash the stain of slavery from 'Old Glory' was Filipino blood." A 21st century amateur historian, Nestor P. Enriguez, has identified by name at least four Filipino Americans who joined the Union Navy: Caystana Baltazar, Andrew Belino, Antonio Ducasin, and Sabas Pilisardo. Despite those small numbers, the act of joining the Union forces despite their location deep in Confederate Louisiana reflects an inspiring and impressive active patriotic commitment to America's future and fate.

In another chapter of *We the People*, I trace the life and influence of Yung Wing (1828–1912), the educator and diplomat who became a vital force for Chinese American interconnections and relationships. Yung, who immigrated to the United States in 1847, earned his citizenship in 1852, and became the first Chinese American college graduate when he completed a Yale degree in 1854, expressed his commitment to his new nation in many ways across more than half a century. But one particularly striking moment came in 1864, when, after attending his 10th reunion at Yale, Yung decided to travel to Washington, DC and volunteer for the Union Army. As he told the Volunteer Department's director, Brigadier-General James Barnes (the father of a Yale classmate of Yung's, William Barnes), Yung was "anxious to offer my services . . . as an evidence of my loyalty and patriotism to my adopted country." Indeed, he adds in his 1909 autobiography's account of this moment, "as a naturalized citizen of the United States, it was my bounden duty to" volunteer. Barnes was "quite interested and pleased" but turned down Yung's offer; Yung was disappointed but "felt that I had at least fulfilled my duty to my adopted country." He certainly had, and that sense of national duty embodies the active patriotism behind much Civil War service.

Such service did not take place only in the armed forces, and another vital community, that of Civil War nurses, offers another example of an active patriotic contribution to the cause. Thousands of women and some men, such as Walt Whitman who wrote movingly about the experience in his 1863 *New York Times* article "The Great Army of the Sick" as well as his 1875 book *Memoranda During the War*, offered their services as nurses both in hospitals and on battlefields. The community included such luminaries as Clara Barton, who in 1862 founded an agency to facilitate battlefield nursing that was a direct predecessor of the Red Cross; and Dorothea Dix, who in April 1861 led an activist contingent that demanded formal status for wartime nurses and was named superintendent of all Union Army nurses as a result. Perhaps the most prominent Civil War nurse was Louisa May Alcott (1832–1888), who in late 1862 and early 1863 volunteered as a nurse for six weeks at the Georgetown, DC Union Army hospital (she intended to stay much longer but contracted typhoid and had to return home to convalesce); her letters about the experience were collected and published as *Hospital Sketches* (1863), which was her first significant literary success.

As might be expected, creative writers like Whitman and Alcott were particularly good at expressing the deeper patriotic meanings of their nursing experiences. In "The Great Army of the Sick," Whitman sums up the lessons of his work as a nurse by noting that, "The army is very young—and so much more American than I supposed." That perspective became part of "The Wound-Dresser" and "Hymn of Dead Soldiers," poems in *Drum-Taps* which link Whitman's nursing service to that collection's celebratory patriotic visions of the war and the nation. Alcott likewise concludes *Hospital Sketches* with her own reflections on how much "one may live and learn in a month," for "though a hospital is a rough school, its lessons are both stern and salutary." Although as a woman she was unable to join the army and thus "could not lay my head on the altar of my country," she was proud to have found a parallel (and in her case nearly as fatal) way to perform such a patriotic act. And in the book's final sentence she envisions connecting that service to another form of Civil War active patriotism: "The next hospital I enter will, I hope, be one for the colored regiments, as they seem to be proving their right to the admiration and kind offices of their white relations, who owe them so large a debt, a little part of which I shall be so proud to pay."

Although Alcott's recovery from illness did not permit her to return to the war effort in that way, the fugitive slave turned nurse Susie King Taylor (1848–1912) embodied such a connection between multiple forms of active patriotism. Born into slavery in Savannah, Georgia, Taylor escaped during the war when she was only 14, and quickly attached herself to the First South Carolina Volunteers, Thomas Wentworth Higginson's regiment. She worked as a nurse with the regiment throughout the war, often in collaboration with Clara Barton, marrying one of the regiment's African American officers (Sergeant Edward King) along the way. After the war and King's tragic death in 1866, she moved to Boston and devoted her life to working with the Woman's Relief Corps, a national organization for former Civil War nurses which was instrumental in creating Memorial Day celebrations to carry forward post-war celebratory patriotisms. And in 1902 she published a memoir, *Reminiscences of My Life in Camp*, dedicated to Higginson and intended, as she wrote in the preface, to "show how much service and good we can do to each other, and what sacrifices we can make for our liberty and rights." Like all of the war's nurses, and all these inspiring cohorts of soldiers as well, Taylor embodied the inspiring, active patriotic service at the heart of the Union cause.

Because that cause offered a direct challenge to the Confederacy's mythic patriotisms, not only as a wartime adversary but in their respective images of the United States, it's certainly possible to also see these Civil War active patriotisms as a form of critical patriotism. Yet while they may have been critical of the Confederacy's myths, those who served as part of the Union cause were at the same time embodying, extending, and amplifying the kinds of celebratory patriotisms expressed by the war's leaders and supporters, including Lincoln, Whitman, Melville, and Howe. So it is important to identify those Civil War era voices who more explicitly and thoroughly expressed a critical patriotic perspective, those who in fact used the occasion of the war, and its defining causes and debates, to both highlight the ways in which the nation had fallen short of its ideals and make the case for this moment as an opportunity to move toward a stronger as well as a more unified American future.

Offering a particularly potent and passionate such critical patriotic expression, as he did throughout his hugely influential life, was Frederick Douglass (c. 1818–1895). Douglass was one of the most vocal advocates for the creation of the United States Colored Troops, and saw that form of Civil War service as reflecting a direct challenge to the exclusionary racism that permeated the Union just as fully as it did the Confederacy. Indeed, due in no small measure to that prejudice, Douglass saw African American regiments as necessary if the war were going to not just result in emancipation, but genuinely move the nation closer to its defining ideals of liberty and equality. "He who would be free must himself strike the blow," he argued in an impassioned March 2nd, 1863 speech entitled "Men of Color, To Arms!" which was subsequently turned into a recruitment broadside for the regiments. And in his speech "Should the Negro Enlist in the Union Army?," delivered on July 6th, 1863, at Philadelphia's National Hall, he made the case that such service would, in "the living present," become the precise vehicle through which both full African American citizenship and the Constitution's "more perfect union" would be achieved.

But while the USCT regiments represented a wartime extension of Douglass's critical patriotic perspective, it was in another speech from a decade earlier that he most powerfully expressed his critical patriotism. In July 1852, the Rochester Ladies' Anti-Slavery Society invited Douglass, by that time a prominent abolitionist and orator as well as a Rochester resident, to deliver an address in honor of July 4th. But in his speech, delivered on July 5th and later given the title "What to the Slave is the Fourth of July?," Douglass overtly questions and challenges that invitation and premise: "Fellow-citizens, pardon me, allow me to ask, why am I called upon to speak here today? What have I, or those I represent, to do with your national independence? Are the great principles of political freedom and of natural justice, embodied in that Declaration of Independence, extended to us?" Those might seem to be rhetorical questions, but Douglass lays out their answers nonetheless: "This Fourth of July is *yours*, not *mine*. *You* may rejoice, *I* must mourn. To drag a man in fetters into the grand illuminated temple of liberty, and call upon him to join you in joyous anthems, were inhuman mockery and sacrilegious irony. Do you mean, citizens, to mock me, by asking me to speak to-day?" (Douglass' emphasis). For most of the speech's second half, Douglass traces the horrors of slavery, and the entire nation's implication in them, to lay bare those ironic gaps between celebration and reality.

Those elements make Douglass's fiery speech profoundly and compellingly critical, but he weds them to two arguments which exemplify the patriotic purpose to which he hopes to put those righteous critiques. For one thing, while he highlights the Revolution's and founders' failures to extend their promises of liberty to all Americans, he nonetheless also praises those histories and figures and urges his contemporary Americans to extend their ideals to enslaved African Americans. Of the Revolution, he argues, "Pride and patriotism, not less than gratitude, prompt you to celebrate and to hold it in perpetual remembrance. I have said that the Declaration of Independence is the ring-bolt to the chain of your nation's destiny; so, indeed, I regard it. The principles contained in that instrument are saving principles. Stand by those principles, be true to them on all occasions, in all places, against all foes, and at whatever cost." Of the Constitution, he adds, "Now, take the Constitution according to its plain reading, and I defy the presentation of a single pro-slavery clause in it. On the other hand it will be found to contain principles and purposes, entirely hostile to the existence of slavery." And he makes clear that such idealized national narratives are ultimately not about history at all, but rather the inspiration for present activism, since "We have to do with the past only as we can make it useful to the present and to the future."

In service of that present moment, Douglass frames his impassioned critique as precisely the tone necessary to move the nation closer to those ideals. "At a time like this, scorching irony, not convincing argument, is needed. O! had I the ability, and could I reach the nation's ear, I would, today, pour out a fiery stream of biting ridicule, blasting reproach, withering sarcasm, and stern rebuke. For it is not light that is needed, but fire; it is not the gentle shower, but thunder. We need the storm, the whirlwind, and the earthquake. The feeling of the nation must be quickened; the conscience of the nation must be roused; the propriety of the nation must be startled; the hypocrisy of the nation must be exposed; and its crimes against God and man must be proclaimed and denounced." And he ends by wedding that righteous fury to a critical patriotic optimism about the national future: "I, therefore, leave off where I began, with hope. While drawing encouragement from the Declaration of Independence, the great principles it contains, and the genius of American Institutions, my spirit is also cheered by the obvious tendencies of the age. . . . Notwithstanding the dark picture I have this day presented of the state of the nation, I do not despair of this country. There are forces in operation, which must inevitably work the downfall of slavery."

Contemporaries of Douglass's took such Civil War era critical patriotism even further, as illustrated by his friend and publishing partner Martin Delany (1812–1885). Born in Virginia to an enslaved father and free mother (and thus himself legally free), Delany would go on to become one of the 19th century's most accomplished Americans in a number of fields: from medicine, as he was one of the first African Americans admitted to Harvard

Med School; to journalism, as he edited the *North Star* newspaper alongside Douglass; to political activism. Always unwilling to accept the pervasive racism he encountered in every part of American society—for example, he and his cohort were expelled from Harvard after just a few weeks due to violent protests from their white peers—Delany harbored a decades-long dream of establishing an African American community in West Africa, from which all of his grandparents had been captured as slaves. At the outset of the Civil War, he still held that goal, and made it an underlying element of his social protest novel *Blake; or the Huts of America*, which was serialized in the *Anglo-African Magazine* between 1859 and 1862. The protagonist of *Blake* is a radical black activist traveling through the South in the hopes of leading a mass slave uprising that will culminate in the establishment of a new African nation.

But the war convinced Delany of the need to turn that radical spirit toward the fight for an American future instead, and he became one of the chief advocates and recruiters for the United States Colored Troops regiments. Delany's vision of those regiments and their active patriotic service went beyond even that of his friend Douglass, as he believed it was crucial for African American commissioned officers to lead these soldiers. In a February 1865 meeting with President Lincoln himself, Delany successfully made that case, leading not only to the overall creation of such roles but also to Delany's own commission as a major, the highest rank achieved by any African American Civil War officer. With the war's successful conclusion, Delany made clear that this critical patriotic battle was in no way over, holding a rally in Charleston, South Carolina the day after Lincoln's April 1865 assassination in which Delany both praised the fallen leader and argued for the ongoing, crucial work of advancing African American rights and moving the reunified nation closer to its ideals. He would dedicate himself to those continued efforts throughout Reconstruction: working for the Freedmen's Bureau, helping organize the Colored Conventions Movement, supporting the Freedmen's Bank, and generally seeking to extend his critical patriotic vision of the Civil War as a battle for African American and national ideals of equality and justice.

African American leaders like Douglass and Delany had a particularly striking basis for their critical patriotic arguments and actions, but such critical patriotism has never been limited to one community or perspective. One final Civil War era text, Lucy Larcom's poem "Weaving" (1862), links an equally critical patriotic perspective to the world of female mill workers in the industrial North. When she was just 11 years old, Larcom (1824–1893) went to work in the Lowell (Massachusetts) Boott Mills, becoming part of the first community of "mill girls" in that industrializing moment. During her time in the mills, a group of workers founded *The Lowell Offering*, a short-lived but impressive and influential magazine entirely edited and written by female mill workers, and Larcom published a number of poems and essays in its pages. After a decade in the mills, Larcom followed an older sister to the prairies of Illinois and worked as a frontier schoolteacher, and when she returned to Massachusetts in the 1850s, she built on that career to become a successful educator, journalist, and author. But her perspective and her writing never abandoned that world of Lowell and the mills, and in the Civil War's early years she composed "Weaving," a poem which links that setting and community to a critical patriotic perspective on the war's causes and goals.

The speaker of "Weaving" is an unnamed mill worker, one who initially focuses on her own work and its value: "I weave, to be my mother's stay;/I weave, to win my daily food." But the sight of the Merrimack River out the mill window leads her thoughts downriver, to the enslaved African American women with whose very different work her own is inextricably interwoven. She wonders, "And how much of your wrong is mine,/Dark women slaving at the South?/ . . . The beam unwinds, but every thread/With blood of strangled souls is red." It is that "hideous tapestry," the fundamental dependence of the nation on slavery and its products, that in the speaker's tragic vision becomes "war's abhorrent sight," "the curse unsaid" that the nation nonetheless cannot avoid. But the poem's final lesson, for that speaker and its audience both, is of the distinct, truly unifying national narrative that must come from these insights: "But, weary weaver, not to you/Alone was war's stern message brought:/'Woman!' it knelled from heart to heart,/'Thy sister's keeper know thou art!'" Critical patriots like Larcom, Delany, and Douglass sought to ensure that the Civil War, and the active patriotic service and celebratory national perspectives it entailed, would, while overcoming the Confederacy's mythic patriotism, also produce a United States that could genuinely, inclusively extend its founding ideals to all Americans.

NOTES

1. There are five slightly different transcripts of Lincoln's speech, based on five handwritten copies he gave to friends. My analysis here is based on the most frequently reproduced version, known as the Bliss Copy since Lincoln gave it to Colonel Alexander Bliss in 1864.

Chapter Four

The Gilded Age

Wealth, Empire, and Resistance

On October 28th, 1886, the Statue of Liberty was unveiled and dedicated on Bedloe's Island (subsequently renamed Liberty Island) in New York Harbor. French sculptor Frédéric Auguste Bartholdi's statue, officially titled *Liberty Enlightening the World*, had been planned for more than two decades by that time, and the torch-bearing arm had been displayed as early as the 1876 Centennial Exposition in Philadelphia, and then from 1876 to 1882 in New York's Madison Square Park. But construction delays and funding issues with the pedestal—the portion for which the United States was paying, as France financed the statue itself—had delayed completion. So when the pedestal was finally completed and the statue, which had been shipped from France, was assembled atop it, the long-awaited dedication ceremony was a spectacular affair, featuring New York City's first ever ticker-tape parade, the first illumination of the statue, and a speech from President Grover Cleveland.

Cleveland's brief speech illustrates the celebratory patriotic vision of America to which the Statue of Liberty would be linked from that moment onward. He thanks France for recognizing with this gift "our efforts to commend to mankind the excellence of a government resting upon popular will." He calls the statue "our own deity keeping watch and ward before the open gates of America, and greater than all that have been celebrated in ancient song." And he concludes that "We will not forget that Liberty has here made her home," predicting an even more glorious future in which "a stream of light shall pierce the darkness of ignorance and man's oppression, until liberty enlightens the world." Ideas like Cleveland's, along with Emma Lazarus's famous poem "The New Colossus," originally written in 1883 to help with the fundraising efforts for the pedestal, firmly established the statue as part of a celebratory patriotic image of America. "I lift my lamp beside the golden door!," Lazarus's statue proclaims in her poem's final line, certainly an inclusive expression of what she calls the "world-wide welcome" of those "huddled masses yearning to breathe free," but likewise an exemplary idealized vision of the United States.

In order to create that particular celebratory emphasis, however, these voices largely elided the statue's original purpose and meaning. The initial idea for the statue came from Édouard René de Laboulaye, a French politician and president of the French Anti-Slavery Society who at a dinner party mourning the April 1865 assassination of Abraham Lincoln conceived of a statue that would celebrate the abolition of slavery in the United States as a key step in the progress of "freedom and democracy" in the nation and around the world. Although Laboulaye's friend Bertholdi ended up designing a statue that did not foreground those historical themes, he did include one important and often overlooked element: the broken chains around the statue's feet. Those chains would seem to indicate that the statue's subject was herself once enslaved, and that she thus reflects the history of slavery as well as the progress of liberty through the Civil War and abolition. That emphasis would make the statue an expression of a more critical patriotism, a view that acknowledges one of America's most significant failures while still celebrating the triumph over that history through which the nation had moved closer to its ideals of liberty.

Throughout the final quarter of the 19th century, the era that became known as the Gilded Age, the United States was defined by prominent, collective expressions of celebratory patriotism. Those celebratory moments included not just the Statue of Liberty dedication, but also and especially the two World's Fairs that framed this period: the 1876 Centennial Exposition in Philadelphia and the 1893 World's Columbian Exposition in Chicago. While those celebrations ostensibly included all Americans, they often closely paralleled the era's mythic patriotisms, visions of the nation that were used to support increasingly elitist, xenophobic, and imperialist policies. Yet the celebratory moments also featured prominent expressions of active patriotic challenges to such exclusions, from the women's suffrage activists who forced their way into the 1876 Exposition's July 4th celebration to the Christian Socialism that informed Francis Bellamy's 1893 creation of the Pledge of Allegiance. And a number of Gilded Age critical patriots offered their own challenges to national myths, including August Spies and Henry George, Helen Hunt Jackson and Standing Bear, Ida B. Wells, and the authors and activists who formed the Anti-Imperialist League.

The Centennial Exposition, which ran from May 10th to November 10th, 1876, in Philadelphia's Fairmount Park, represented a sort of perfect storm for American celebratory patriotism. The occasion itself, the 100th anniversary of the signing of the Declaration of Independence in that city, was of course an overtly celebratory patriotic moment. The exposition was also the first World's Fair to be hosted in the United States, and so offered a natural moment for the U.S. to highlight and share its most idealized qualities for a world audience, as more than 37 countries participated in the exposition and many of its 10 million visitors likewise came from abroad. Finally, in 1876 the nation was in the concluding moments of 15 years of overt division and conflict, as the post-Civil War period of Federal Reconstruction would end as a result of the contested presidential election that took place three days before the exposition closed. The exposition thus became a chance to demonstrate, for that world audience but also for Americans themselves, the kind of unified national identity emphasized by the celebratory patriotic perspective.

Those celebratory demonstrations began with the May 10th opening ceremonies. Attended by more than 185,000 people, the festivities began with a performance of "The Centennial Meditation of Columbia, 1776–1876," a cantata composed by poet and Confederate veteran Sidney Lanier. The very invitation of Lanier to write that opening song illustrated a celebratory emphasis on a once again unified United States, and Lanier's lyrics express those sentiments as well: he moves through an idealized account of the nation's historical stages, calling the Civil War a time when "wild brother-wars new-dark the Light," but hoping the nation could "Forgive, and kiss o'er, and replight"; and concludes with the celebratory lines, "long, dear Land of all my love,/Thy name shall shine, thy fame shall glow!" And the opening ceremonies culminated in a moment that even more overtly symbolized American power, literally as well as figuratively. The entire exposition grounds were to be run by a single massive Corliss Steam Engine, an expanded version of an engine invented by Rhode Island engineer George Corliss in 1849. As the assembled crowds looked on, President Ulysses S. Grant, accompanied by his honored guest Brazilian Emperor Dom Pedro, pressed the buttons which put that machine and the exposition into gear. Journalist and author William Dean Howells observed the engine's status as a microcosm of the nation's power, writing, "Yes, it is still in these things of iron and steel that the national genius most freely speaks."

From the grounds and the catalog that described them to an accompanying poetry collection, the exposition's official statements complemented and extended those celebratory patriotic perspectives. Hermann Schwarzmann, the German American engineer and architect who as Chief Engineer designed the fairgrounds as well as their two permanent buildings (Memorial Hall and the Horticultural Hall), visited with colleagues the prior world's fair, the Vienna International Exposition in 1873, and the experience convinced them to make the Philadelphia exposition into something more distinctly American. "While

we should endeavor to celebrate our nation's Centennial in a manner worthy
of our nation's dignity," they wrote from Vienna, "it is not necessary in order
to do so that we should attempt to imitate the grandeur and dazzling beauty of
the expositions of the old world, but rather desire to appear for what we really
are. . . . We ought," they added, "to produce an equal monumental effect, and
be much more true to the construction." And the exposition's official catalog,
J.S. Ingram's *The Centennial Exposition Described and Illustrated, being a
Concise and Graphic Description of This Grand Enterprise, Commemorative
of the First Centenary of American Independence*, echoes that celebratory
patriotic sentiment, arguing in its Publishers' Preface that since the exposition's greatness is "due in no small measure to the high civilization which our
glorious institutions secure, [the descriptions] will be specially memorable to
the American people"—descriptions, the publisher hastens to add, that will
"conform to a popular presentation of only those things possessing novel or
superior attractions."

The exposition's attractions found ways to turn even the nation's recent
divisive and destructive histories into part of those celebrations. Particularly
striking in that regard, during what would end up being the final year of Reconstruction, was the culinary establishment known as "The Southern Res-
taurant," or simply "The South," at which, as the official description put it,
diners would be entertained by "a band of old-time plantation 'darkies,' who
will sing their quaint melodies and strum the banjo before the visitors from
every clime." Similarly, the Smithsonian Institution collected and displayed
at the exposition a number of compelling representations of Native American culture and art, but did so with accompanying text that read in part, "the
monuments of the past and the savage tribes of man are rapidly disappearing
from our continent." Such simplified and stereotyping depictions of American communities and cultures were inextricably intertwined with the era's
overarching mythic patriotisms, and illustrated the exposition's attempts to
turn contested histories and contemporary issues alike into components of a
consistently celebratory tone and experience.

A trio of texts closely associated with the Centennial exemplify the construction of that celebratory patriotic tone and perspective throughout the year
and across distinct genres. The poet Kate Harrington, a pen name for journalist and author Rebecca Harrington Smith (1831–1917), published a collection
entitled *Centennial, and Other Poems* (1876). The book features tributes to
her father (the playwright and professor N. R. Smith) and her adopted home
state of Iowa, but at its heart is the titular poem, "Centennial." "Centennial"
tells the story of a symbolic "youth" who carries "a banner bearing high the
name, 'Centennial.'" Harrington's descriptions of that banner link that 1876
commemorative purpose to the American flag, as it has "stars . . . behind

those crimson bars." This resolute youthful American offers that banner and its magical word as an optimistic answer to a number of critiques raised by both past conflicts and present divisions, with each of the poem's seven stanzas ending with a spoken "'Centennial.'" And the final stanza links him to a broader national setting and community, "the golden streets, where patriots heard,/And softly breathed our Union-word,/'Centennial.'"

Those kinds of celebratory patriotic visions became even more pronounced around the July 4th Centennial anniversary itself. Speakers at both the exposition's ceremony and others around the country both honored the past's idealized grandeur, usually in the form of the Founding Fathers, and marveled at the heights of present success to which the nation had ascended over those subsequent hundred years. Exemplifying that celebratory patriotic combination was prominent Congregationalist minister and reformer Henry Ward Beecher's July 4th oration in Philadelphia, preceding a public reading of the Declaration of Independence. Beecher intoned, "What our fathers were we know. Their life was splendid; their history was registered." Yet, he went on to argue, "there never began to be in the early day such promise for physical vigor and enriched life as there is today upon this continent." Like the exposition's depictions of contemporary American material power and prowess, Beecher's speech offered less a commemoration of the founding histories (although it aligned with that perspective) than an argument that such histories provided idealized origin points for a nation that had only become more perfect over time.

A final Centennial year text illustrates that vision of perfection with particular clarity. Edited by former Yale College President Theodore Dwight Woolsey, and collecting the voices and expertise of numerous scholars and authors, *The First Century of the Republic: A Review of American Progress* (1876) provided 17 chapters that traced such an upward trajectory for a number of distinct subjects, from agriculture to humanitarianism to jurisprudence. Uniting all those topics was the goal, stated in the Publishers' Advertisement, of "connecting the present with the past, showing the beginnings of great enterprises, tracing through consecutive stages their development, and associating with the individual thought and labor by which they have been brought to perfection." Overall, the book, like the Centennial Exposition and so many of these related 1876 events and texts, sought to highlight less the year's ostensible historical focus and more what the book called "the part taken by the American people in the remarkable material progress of the last hundred years."

Those Centennial year celebratory patriotic trends became dominant national narratives across a number of Gilded Age moments and events, as illustrated by the focus and tone of the Statue of Liberty dedication a decade later. But they reached their peak at the next world's fair hosted in the United States, the 1893 World's Columbian Exposition, which ran from May 1st to October 30th in Chicago. The Exposition was originally intended to commemorate the 400th anniversary of Christopher Columbus's 1492 first voyage from Spain to the Americas, although the opening was pushed back a year because its spectacular fairgrounds, and especially the elaborate centerpiece known as The White City, required more construction time. And in any case the Columbian Exposition set aside its ostensible historical subject even more fully than had the 1876 Centennial Exposition, becoming instead an explicit and extreme celebration of the United States, one that built upon a number of elements of that prior fair but took them to new heights of Gilded Age excess.

The Columbian Exposition's May 1st opening ceremonies illustrated that trend, echoing but extending key aspects of the Centennial's opening. As described by historian Thomas J. Schlereth, President Grover Cleveland once again set the exposition in motion, "pressing a gilded button sending electricity pulsating through the fair site"; this time the presidential action not only powered the entire fairgrounds but also produced a strikingly symbolic moment of celebratory patriotism: "banners and flags unfurled from atop twelve major exhibit halls" and "a shroud fell from [sculptor] Daniel Chester French's giant (seventy-five foot), gilded Statue of the Republic." The author of the 1893 exposition's official welcoming poem likewise paralleled but amplified Sidney Lanier's 1876 role: this poet, James D. Lynch, was a Confederate veteran and a lawyer in Reconstruction era Mississippi who had developed his literary reputation through neo-Confederate texts such as the epic poems *Robert E. Lee, or, Heroes of the South* (1876) and *Redpath, or, the Ku Klux Tribunal* (1877). So when he wrote on behalf of the United States, in his 1893 welcoming poem "Columbia Saluting the Nations," of the need to "Catch the head-light of the ages, leave the darkening past behind," both his invited presence and his words reflected a particularly mythic celebratory patriotic perspective at the exposition's opening ceremonies.

Perhaps the 1893 exposition's most explicit and extreme such celebratory patriotic perspective was offered in another opening text, one likewise authored by a former Confederate. That man, Virginia politician and judge J. T. Harris, was the Chairman of the National Commission which had planned the Columbian Exposition, and in his May 1893 introductory address he overtly laid out the idealized and mythic vision of American history and identity at the heart of the exposition. Beginning with Columbus's initial arrival in the Americas, Harris then argues, "It remained for the Saxon race to people this new land, to redeem it from Barbarism, to dedicate its virgin soil to freedom, and in less than four centuries to make of it the most powerful and prosperous country on which God's sunshine falls." Harris here echoes but once again ratchets up the two key elements of the celebratory patriotism of a text like Henry Ward Beecher's July 4th, 1876 oration: honoring the foundational past glories to which the occasion is ostensibly dedicated, a historical view that in Harris's case features a far more overt and discriminatory dismissal of Native American cultures; while at the same time constructing an image of the nation's unequaled present perfection. Across all these prominent public Gilded Age moments and events, we find such celebrations of an idealized, ever more perfected America.

As the depiction of Native Americans in Harris's speech illustrates, the celebratory patriotisms expressed at both of these Gilded Age expositions often featured, if they did not indeed rely upon, a complementary form of mythic patriotism. In order to create their unifying, idealized visions of the United States, that is, these celebratory commemorations too often either wrote challenging histories and the American communities to which they connect out of the story or constructed simplistic and stereotypical roles for them to play in those celebrations. Whether the "plantation darkies" of 1876 or the entirely absent African Americans of 1893, the vanishing Native Americans of 1876's Smithsonian exhibits or the conquered "Barbarism" of Harris's 1893 speech, or the invitation to neo-Confederate poets to become national voices of welcome at the opening ceremonies in both years, these mythic patriotisms permeated the grounds and texts of the expositions. They also, and more destructively still, can be found at the center of a number of Gilded Age America's most prominent and pervasive national issues and trends.

Many of the most prominent such trends centered on themes of wealth and work. When it came to the era's ideals of extreme wealth and elite status, a particular national myth served to buttress those ideals: the concept of the "self-made man." That longstanding concept had for at least a century helped turn individual historical figures like Ben Franklin, Daniel Boone, and Andrew Jackson into exemplary American stories and lives. In a September 1859 speech to the Wisconsin State Agricultural Society, Abraham Lincoln summed up both that concept and its connection to an idealized vision of American society: "The prudent, penniless beginner in the world, labors for wages awhile, saves a surplus with which to buy tools or land for himself, then labors on his own account for awhile, and at length hires another new beginner to help him. This is a just, and generous, and prosperous system; which opens the way to all—gives hope to all, and consequent energy and progress, and improvement of conditions to all." But it was in the Gilded Age that this specific image of one type of idealized American story became a much more widespread and dominant national myth.

One particularly successful cultural voice played a key role in advancing that myth: the novelist Horatio Alger (1832–1899). Between 1864 and the end of his life, Alger published more than one hundred young adult novels, along with biographies of figures like Lincoln, James Garfield, and Daniel Webster, all of which depicted variations upon the same stories of self-made young men (generally orphans or otherwise on their own) advancing from "rags to riches" and achieving their American dreams. Alger's fourth novel and first bestseller, *Ragged Dick; or, Street Life in New York with the Boot-Blacks* (1868), lays out that idealized American story with particular clarity in its closing paragraphs. Thanks to his sterling character, the orphaned street urchin Dick is by this time well on his way to professional and financial success which, as the narrator notes, "was indeed a bright prospect for a boy who, only a year before, could neither read nor write, and depended for a night's lodging upon the chance hospitality of an alley-way or old wagon." He is now "Ragged Dick no longer," but instead "Richard Hunter, Esq., . . . a young gentleman on his way to fame and fortune" who "has taken a step upward, and is determined to mount still higher." By making that idealized identity and story the centerpiece of so many similar and similarly successful books across the last few decades of the 19th century, Alger not only constructed his own consistent myth, but illustrated its pervasive presence and influence in Gilded Age America.

That myth came to be associated with a number of prominent Gilded Age Americans, but none more so than the steel magnate and philanthropist Andrew Carnegie (1835–1919). Carnegie's family immigrated from Scotland to Pennsylvania when he was 12 and within a few months both he and his father began work at the same Pittsburgh cotton mill; while his father quit after a few months to attempt to make a living as an independent weaver, Carnegie remained on the job, gradually working his way up to become one of the nation's leading industrialists. In his last decades of life, Carnegie spoke and wrote again and again, in speeches to schools and youth groups, in didactic essays like 1889's "Wealth" (later retitled "The Gospel of Wealth"), and in his posthumously published *Autobiography* (1920), about his life as a model for young Americans to emulate. But he also and crucially tied that exemplary individual story to idealized images of the nation, as illustrated by his 1886 book *Triumphant Democracy: Fifty Years' March of the Republic.* Carnegie dedicates that work "to the BELOVED REPUBLIC under whose equal laws I am made the peer of any man," doing so "with an intensity of gratitude and admiration which the native-born citizen can neither feel nor understand." Perhaps they cannot, but as he describes his mythic patriotic purpose in his preface, he does hope the book will "incline the American to regard with reverence and affection the great parent people from whom he has sprung, from whose sacrifices in the cause of civil and religious liberty he has reaped so rich a harvest, and to whom he owes a debt of gratitude which can never be adequately repaid."

Since those idealized images of wealth and work became closely associated with national mythic patriotisms in this era, it stands to reason that proponents of those myths would likewise seek to define criticisms of wealth and capitalism as fundamentally un- or even anti-American. They did so in particular through attacks on the late 19th century's burgeoning labor movement, and especially on that movement's association and interconnections with other movements and ideas often defined as "foreign" to the United States, including anarchism and communism. Many members as well as leaders of all those American movements were indeed immigrants or the children of immigrants, but in an era of unprecedented, massive waves of immigration, the demographics of the movements simply paralleled those of the growing national community. And in any case, the attacks on the movements didn't just highlight such demographics, which as always said nothing one way or another about a community's patriotism—they overtly contrasted them with exclusionary myths of American identity in order to depict the movements and communities themselves as un-American and unpatriotic.

Exemplifying those depictions were the arguments deployed against the eight accused Haymarket Square bombers during their trial. A May Day 1886 parade and labor protest in Chicago, part of a national strike, had turned violent, with a homemade bomb thrown at police officers and a subsequent firefight between police and protesters, all of which left eight officers and numerous civilians dead. In the aftermath authorities arrested eight prominent Chicago labor leaders, journalists, and anarchists, ostensibly because of possible connections to the riot and bombing but more so because of the kinds of sentiments expressed in a *Chicago Times* editorial: the nation, the *Times* argued, had become "the cess-pool of Europe under the pretense that it is the asylum of the poor"; and the editorial urged, "Let us whip these slavic wolves back to the European dens from which they issue, or in some way exterminate them." In his August 1886 closing argument at the trial, the state's attorney Julius Grinnell used similar language, arguing that an acquittal would mean "a lot of rats and vermin" on the city's streets. The jury was convinced and convicted all eight defendants, with seven sentenced to death; four men were eventually executed, one committed suicide in prison, and two along with the other defendant were pardoned by Illinois Governor John Altgeld. For Gilded Age America's myths of wealth and work, these radical perspectives represented nothing less than a fundamental threat to the nation itself.

The Haymarket Trial and these anti-labor movement arguments were far from Gilded Age America's only prominent anti-immigrant sentiments. And in the development, extension, and support for the first national immigration laws (which were also the first national immigration restrictions), those leading up to, including, and following the 1882 Chinese Exclusion Act, we see a similar deployment of mythic patriotism. Through such moments as the 1790s Alien and Sedition Acts and the 1840s rise of the Know Nothing/American Party, anti-immigrant sentiments have been tied to both myths of American identity and exclusionary attacks on existing American communities since the earliest post-Revolutionary debates. But the anti-Chinese American myths that became the basis for the Exclusion Act and its aftermaths took that trend further still, targeting a longstanding, multi-generational, and sizeable American community—there were over one hundred thousand Chinese Americans identified on the 1880 census—with a depiction of their fundamental foreignness to and inability to become part of an idealized American identity.

That myth of Chinese Americans and national identity was voiced by many figures and movements throughout the era, but with particular and telling clarity by none other than a Supreme Court Justice, John Marshall Harlan (1833–1911). In a series of late 1880s and early 1890s cases, the Court upheld the Chinese Exclusion Act and its legal aftermath as Constitutional, despite the entire absence of immigration or immigration law from the Constitution's elucidation of governmental powers and purview. In two other texts from that period, Justice Harlan expressed the mythic rationale behind such anti-Chinese American sentiments. In his otherwise inspiring dissent to the Court's *Plessy v. Ferguson* decision (1896) and its support for racial segregation, Harlan contrasted African Americans with Chinese Americans, calling the latter "a race so different from our own that we do not permit those belonging to it to become citizens of the United States." And in a public lecture delivered two years later, Harlan would take that perspective one step further, arguing that "this is a race utterly foreign to us and [that] never will assimilate with us." Harlan's rhetoric is most obvious and most troubling for its definitions of and discriminations against this "foreign race"; hundreds of thousands of whom, to repeat, were part of America and had been for generations. But the logic of his statements depends just as fully on constructing an mythic definition of that "us," of "the United States" as comprising its own "race" that determines which cultures and communities can and cannot become citizens of that nation.

Those anti-Chinese American prejudices specifically spurred the creation of the first national immigration laws, but they were also part of a larger pattern of Gilded Age anti-immigrant sentiments tied to mythic patriotisms. The period beginning around 1880 saw the largest and most sustained waves of immigrant arrivals in the nation's history, proportional to the U.S. population at the time; many of those arrivals came from Eastern and Southern European nations and Jewish communities that collectively challenged mythic images of a fundamentally Anglo-Saxon or Northern European American identity. In response, in 1894 a trio of young Harvard alumni, the lawyers Charles Warren and Prescott F. Hall and the scientist Robert DeCourcy Ward (all class of 1899), founded the Immigration Restriction League (IRL), an organization which sought, in the words of its founding constitution, to "arouse public opinion to the necessity of a further exclusion of elements undesirable for citizenship or injurious to our national character." MIT President Francis Walker, an IRL member, went further in his characterization of these immigrants, specifically defining their past as both outside of and entirely distinct from American history: "These people have no history behind them which is of a nature to give encouragement. They have none of the inherited instincts and tendencies which made it comparatively easy to deal with the immigration of olden time. They are beaten men from beaten races." And in seeking to define the threat posed by these immigrants, Prescott F. Hall contrasted them with an idealized, foundational "American" race, asking, "Is there, indeed, a danger that the race which has made our country great will pass away, and that the ideals and institutions which it has cherished will also pass?"

At the same time that xenophobes like Hall were relying upon one Gilded Age form of mythic patriotism to buttress their arguments, another form was deployed to support America's continued imperial expansions, across the continent and beyond its borders. Both the exclusionary policy of Indian Removal and the myth of Manifest Destiny continued throughout the period, now complemented by even more frequent violent wars against those Native American tribes that did not consent to removal. In this era the federal government also added another kind of removal policy into the mix: the removal of younger Native Americans from their homes and families into a system of residential schools that sought to "Americanize" them. Despite the seemingly inclusive nature of that goal, the schools nonetheless comprised an extension of mythic patriotism by other means, as they defined every aspect of native identity and community as entirely outside of American identity. Captain Richard H. Pratt, the founder of one such school, the Carlisle (Pennsylvania) Indian School, began an 1892 speech on the school's mission by expressing that exclusionary perspective quite succinctly: "A great general has said that the only good Indian is a dead one, and that high sanction of his destruction has been an enormous factor in promoting Indian massacres. In a sense, I agree with the sentiment, but only in this: that all the Indian there is in the race should be dead. Kill the Indian in him, and save the man."

Native American cultures were not the only longstanding communities with which U.S. expansion throughout the West was met—much of the region also included Mexican American communities that had existed for a century or more, first as part of New Spain and then as part of Mexico after it gained independence. The 1848 Treaty of Guadalupe Hidalgo that ended the Mexican American War and ceded much of that territory to the United States promised that inhabitants of those Mexican communities could "acquire the title and rights of citizens of the United States" if they chose to stay, and indeed that if they did stay they "shall be considered to have elected to become citizens." But despite those protections, the widespread practice of squatting by newly arrived American settlers, supported by federal laws such as the California Land Act of 1851 as well as by the power of both the U.S. military and the justice system, pushed many Mexican landowners and communities off their land. Parallel exclusionary laws like California's Anti-Vagrancy Act of 1855, which specifically targeted "Greasers" (defined as "the issue of Spanish and Indian blood"), likewise defined these Mexican American communities as fundamentally outside of an expanding America. And where such legal measures did not suffice to expel these communities, mob violence targeted them throughout the era: historians William D. Carrigan and Clive Webb, in their landmark 2003 study of anti-Mexican violence in the West and Southwest, estimate that between 1848 and 1928 at least 597 Mexican Americans were lynched.

All those territorial expansions and accompanying exclusionary actions could be defined as the behavior of an empire. Indeed, in the first half of his magisterial book *How to Hide an Empire: A History of the Greater United States* (2019), historian Daniel Immerwahr both defines continental expansion in those terms and links that expansion to many other imperial ventures throughout the 19th century. Immerwahr dedicates his book "to the uncounted," which along with the word "hide" in his title reflects his argument that many of these imperialist expansions were both at the time and since minimized in, if not entirely absent from, American histories. As Immerwahr puts it, those imperial territories tend to undermine unifying, mythic patriotic images of "the United States [as] as a politically uniform space: a union, voluntarily entered into, of states standing on equal footing with one another." In many of these ventures, then, the United States sought to become a larger nation without altering the national narratives on which its celebratory and mythic patriotisms frequently depended.

The nation's late 1890s imperial expansions, however, were far more difficult to minimize or ignore. These included the 1898 annexation of Hawaii, a sovereign nation whose Queen Lili'uokalani U.S. Marines forced out at gunpoint so that the United States could take control of the islands; and the late 1898 and early 1899 post-Spanish American War U.S. occupation of multiple Spanish colonial territories, including the Caribbean islands of Puerto Rico and Cuba (although the latter was soon granted independence) and the Pacific islands of Guam and the Philippines. While the contexts and unfolding histories and relationships in each of those cases were distinct, one central means through which proponents of both imperial expansion and mythic patriotism sought to hold those positions simultaneously was to argue that the inhabitants of these various territories were, not unlike Chinese, Native, and Mexican Americans, simply too foreign from and lesser than "Americans" to become genuinely part of our national identity. Exemplifying that perspective was a March 5th, 1899 *Boston Sunday Globe* political cartoon entitled "Expansion, Before and After," which used caricatured, bigoted imagery to satirically contrast "savage" native Filipinos with transformed Filipino Americans who could, in the cartoon's visual logic and accompanying sarcastic text, never truly "exchange the war club for the baseball bat."

Throughout the Gilded Age the United States was expanding in every sense: geographically, across the continent and into these imperial territories; economically, through the explosions of wealth and industrialization; and on the world's stage, as the 1876 and 1893 expositions illustrated. Yet the mythic patriotism that too often accompanied those expansions consistently reinforced definitions of American identity that left out both existing American communities and immigrant and international ones, contradicting the Statue of Liberty's imagery and rhetoric and instead linking the era's celebratory patriotisms to these exclusionary national myths.

As has so often been the case in American history, however, many of the exact same moments and events likewise featured challenges to those exclusionary myths: examples of alternative, active forms of patriotism that envisioned, expressed, and embodied distinct and more inclusive national ideals. Whether a July 4th, 1876 counter-ceremony for political and human rights, an 1892 patriotic performance of communal solidarity, or a voice of righteous protest at the culmination of an 1886 show trial, these moments and figures constructed and modeled Gilded Age active patriotisms that celebrated the nation's ideals while challenging it to live up to them more consistently and fully.

In one highly visible way, the 1876 Centennial Exposition included women to a degree not seen at any prior world's fair. The Exposition for the first time featured a Women's Pavilion, a building dedicated entirely to women's "artistic and industrial pursuits"; it was planned, financed, and constructed by an all-female Women's Centennial Executive Committee, led by President Elizabeth Duane Gillespie, a prominent Philadelphia philanthropist and Ben Franklin's great-granddaughter. While much of the Pavilion focused on women's domestic work and crafts, it did also feature examples of fine arts and cultural works that reflected the period's expanding professional and personal opportunities for women, in America and around the world. But one topic not represented at all in the Women's Pavilion was the subject of the era's most significant social and political movement for women's rights: the ongoing fight for women's suffrage.

Five leaders of the National Women's Suffrage Association (NWSA)— Susan B. Anthony, Matilda Joslyn Gage, Sara Andrews Spencer, Lillie Devereux Blake, and Phoebe W. Couzins—sought to rectify that omission at the exposition's most visible moment. They gained platform passes to be on the stage for the July 4th commemoration, and Anthony wrote to Centennial Commission President Joseph Hawley to ask if they could at that occasion present President Ulysses S. Grant with a copy of their "Declaration of Rights of Women of the United States." Hawley refused, writing back that, "If granted, it would be the event of the day." Many NWSA members responded to that frustrating refusal by boycotting the ceremony entirely, holding their national convention elsewhere in the city. But the five leaders attended the commemoration, and after a reading of the Declaration of Independence, they took action: formally descending from the stage, giving a copy of their own Declaration to the ceremony's official U.S. government representative (Michigan Senator Thomas Ferry), handing out many more copies to interested audience members, and then occupying a nearby, vacant platform to deliver a counter-speech on their movement and goals.

Susan B. Anthony's remarks from that protest platform embodied both the moment's and the suffrage movement's active patriotism. She notes that the event's July 4th timing was not ironic, as America's women "do rejoice in the success, thus far, of our experiment of self-government. Our faith is firm and unwavering in the broad principles of human rights proclaimed in 1776, not only as abstract truths but as the cornerstones of a republic. Yet we cannot forget, even in this glad hour, that while all men of every race and clime and condition, have been invested with the full rights of citizenship under our hospitable flag, all women still suffer the degradation of disfranchisement." And she closes by highlighting the movement's profoundly American demands: "We ask of our rulers, at this hour, no special favors, no special privileges, no special legislation. We ask justice, we ask equality. We ask that all the civil and political rights that belong to citizens of the United States, be guaranteed to us and our daughters forever." It is this counter-event and the suffrage movement, Anthony argues, that truly take up the legacy of the Revolution and its ideals, wedding that celebratory patriotic story to an active patriotism in search of equality and rights of which the Declaration's framers would be proud.

The commemorations surrounding the 1893 Columbian Exposition featured their own prominent expression of active patriotism, one that produced an enduring American patriotic performance: the creation of the Pledge of

Allegiance. In 1891, traveling Baptist minister and activist Francis Bellamy (1855–1931) was hired by publisher Daniel Sharp Ford to work at his magazine, *The Youth's Companion*, on an initiative called the Columbian Public School Celebration. This initiative sought to connect the in-development 1892 commemorations to a broader effort to get American flags into every public schoolhouse. Ford and Bellamy created the idea of a flag salute, to be debuted at public schools as part of the recently created Columbus Day holiday's national celebrations. Bellamy chaired a commission of educators tasked with planning and implementing the salute, and in the September 8th, 1892 issue of *The Youth's Companion*, he shared the Pledge of Allegiance he had written for the occasion: "I pledge allegiance to my Flag and to the Republic for which it stands, one nation, indivisible, with liberty and justice for all."

Both in that particular commemorative context and in its continued use as a ritual for schoolchildren, the Pledge might seem to be an example of celebratory patriotism, and indeed a relatively unthinking and even rote one at that. But if we engage with Bellamy's identity and perspective, we can see it instead as an expression of and opportunity for more active patriotism. Throughout his life, Bellamy preached and practiced the ideals of Christian socialism, seeking to wed his spirituality and ministry to radical arguments and activisms that challenged many Gilded Age American realities and worked to move the nation closer to its founding ideals of liberty and equality. He was forced to leave a ministry in Boston after he "preached against the evils of capitalism" (as his biographer Susan Jacoby describes it), and later voluntarily left a church in Florida because it endorsed racial segregation. In the years immediately leading up to his work on the Pledge, he helped found (in 1889), served as vice president of, and wrote a number of articles for the Boston-based Society of Christian Socialists, an organization dedicated to advancing those egalitarian principles.

Bellamy's reflections on writing the Pledge, composed as part of an autobiographical piece later in his life, make clear how much he saw it as an expression of that perspective and those ideals. He writes, "It began as an intensive communing with salient points of our national history, from the Declaration of Independence onwards; with the makings of the Constitution . . . with the meaning of the Civil War; with the aspirations of the people." He weds that historical account to an idealized vision of the nation itself: "And what does that last thing, the Republic mean? It is the concise political word for the Nation—the One Nation which the Civil War was fought to prove. To make that One Nation idea clear, we must specify that it is indivisible." And he concludes by considering "Its future? Just here arose the temptation of the historic slogan of the French Revolution which meant so much to Jefferson and his friends, 'Liberty, equality, fraternity.' No, that would be too fanciful, too many thousands of years off in realization. But we as a nation do stand square on the doctrine of liberty and justice for all." Both the act of turning those ideals into a Pledge and the act of reciting such a Pledge can thus be seen as genuine expressions of active patriotism, of a commitment to remembering, embodying, and carrying forward those national ideals.

On the issue of immigration Bellamy unfortunately endorsed instead the era's myths, writing in an 1897 editorial for *The Illustrated American* that "there are other races, which we cannot assimilate without lowering our racial standard, which should be as sacred to us as the sanctity of our homes." Too often, even those figures who envision and embody active patriotism in support of certain progressive ideals fail to extend those principles to other American communities. But one of the Gilded Age's most powerful expressions of active patriotism was voiced by an immigrant targeted by precisely such exclusionary prejudice: the German American upholsterer, newspaper editor, and labor activist August Spies (1855–1887). Spies was one of the eight defendants at the 1886 Haymarket trial and one of the four executed for his alleged crimes; and on one of the trial's last days, October 7th, he responded to the opportunity to speak on his own behalf with one of the period's most impassioned and impressive speeches.

For much of that speech, Spies both convincingly argues for his innocence of the specific charges levied against him and his peers and lays out the radical principles that have motivated their collective labor and political activism. But in his closing, he quotes the Declaration of Independence to make the case that it is he who embodies the Revolution's ideals, and his activisms that comprise active patriotic extensions of those principles, in direct opposition to Gilded Age attempts "to establish an oligarchy in this country so strong and powerful and monstrous as never before has existed in any country." And he concludes, "I can well understand why that man [State's Attorney] Grinnell did not urge upon the grand jury to charge us with treason. I can well understand it. You cannot try and convict a man for treason who has upheld the Constitution against those who trample it under their feet." As Spies stood in that docket, just as the suffrage activists stood on their 1876 stage and children reciting the Pledge stood for an expression of egalitarian ideals, he embodied a Gilded Age active patriotism that continued to fight for those founding national narratives.

In his condemnation of Gilded Age America's moves toward oligarchy, Spies likewise offered a bracing critique of what the nation risked becoming, and perhaps had already become, in this pivotal period. He wasn't alone in that expression of critical patriotism, as indeed a number of prominent and inspiring Gilded Age American authors and activists voiced their own critical patriotic perspectives, challenging not only seemingly fundamental elements of the nation's late 19th century identity, but also the too often foundational gaps between its ideals and realities—and in the process modeling alternatives which could bring America closer to those ideals.

A figure who extended and deepened Spies' critiques of Gilded Age American economic realities was the political economist and reformer Henry George (1839–1897). George was best known for his radical ideas about collective land ownership, and he also served as an inspiration for a number of Progressive Era reforms, including the secret ballot, accessible and affordable urban public transportation, and bankruptcy protections. But it was his groundbreaking book *Progress and Poverty* (1879) that reflected most clearly his critical patriotic perspective on American ideals. In it, George directly challenges the era's celebrations of American material progress, asking, "Where do we find the deepest poverty, the hardest struggle for existence, the greatest enforced idleness? Why, wherever material progress is most advanced." He recognizes that this perspective might likewise counter foundational American ideals about progress and the pursuit of happiness, but implores that, "If the conclusions we reach run counter to our prejudices, let us not flinch. If they challenge institutions that have long been regarded as wise and natural, let us not turn back." And he concludes the book with a patriotic argument for the more genuine and truly collective progress that could result from his proposed economic and political remedies: "While there is still time, we may turn to justice. If we do, the dangers that threaten us will disappear. With want destroyed and greed transformed, equality will take the place of jealousy and fear. . . . Who can presume the heights to which our civilization may soar?"

Native Americans comprised another American community that suffered quite directly as a result of Gilded Age myths of progress, and two advocates for that community offered their own critical patriotic perspectives. The author Helen Hunt Jackson (1830–1885) had been publishing poetry and novels since the 1860s, but in the late 1870s she learned more about the histories and current plight of Native Americans, and dedicated the remainder of her tragically short life to writing and activism on their behalf. She did so most potently in her 1881 book, *A Century of Dishonor*, which traces the foundational and unfolding histories of broken treaties, land theft, and genocidal wars directed by the U.S. government against native communities. But she documents those dishonorable histories, she writes in her Author's Note, out of an overtly patriotic sense of American ideals and how they might shape a more just future: "my object, which has been simply to show our causes for national shame in the matter of our treatment of the Indians. It is a shame which the American nation ought not to lie under, for the American people, as a people, are not at heart unjust. If there be one thing which they believe in more than any other, and mean that every man on this continent shall have, it is 'fair play.' And as soon as they fairly understand how cruelly it has been denied to the Indian, they will rise up and demand it for him."

Jackson experienced her own version of that shift in understanding toward justice for Native Americans, as she was brought into the cause after hearing a speech by the Ponca chief-turned-civil rights activist Standing Bear (Mant-cunanjin; c. 1829–1908). Standing Bear's Ponca tribe had been removed from their Nebraska homeland to "Indian Territory" (modern-day Oklahoma) in 1877, after decades of conflicts with white settlers and the U.S. army; when Standing Bear attempted to return to that homeland in order to bury his son, who had passed away from starvation in that hostile new setting, he was arrested by General George Crook for having left the reservation. With the help of Susette LaFlesche, an Omaha Native American interpreter, and her husband Thomas Tibbles, a journalist and reformer, Standing Bear sued for a writ of habeas corpus. The *Standing Bear v. Crook* (1879) trial represented the first time a Native American was allowed to advocate for his rights in a court of law, and Standing Bear took advantage of the opportunity, delivering a critical patriotic final speech in which he both defined himself as part of a national community and appealed directly to the judge's commitment to American ideals: "[My] hand is not the color of yours, but if I prick it, the blood will flow, and I shall feel pain. The blood is of the same color as yours. God made me, and I am a man. . . . I see the light of the world and of liberty just ahead. . . . But in the center of the path there stands a man. . . . If that man gives me the permission, I may pass on to life and liberty. If he refuses, I must go back and sink beneath the flood. . . . You are that man." Judge Dundy ruled in Standing Bear's favor, establishing as precedent that Native Americans were entitled to full legal personhood and thus civil rights under the law; in his decision the judge also symbolically and crucially linked Native Americans to founding American ideals, writing that they "have the inalienable right to life, liberty, and the pursuit of happiness." It was a crucial victory, and one that, like Standing Bear's voice and advocacy, would for years to come shift American conversations as well as influence activists like Jackson.

The three Reconstruction era Constitutional amendments had for the first time extended similar legal protections and rights to all African Americans, especially through the 14th Amendment, which guaranteed them both citizenship and "due process of law." But throughout the Gilded Age a variety of unfolding, exclusionary histories threatened that American community as well. One of the most horrific such histories was the lynching epidemic, the consistent threat of mob violence targeting African American individuals and communities across the nation. In response to that epidemic of violence, the pioneering journalist, author, and activist Ida B. Wells (1862–1931) offered her own critical patriotic challenges to collective myths as well as compelling arguments for justice. She published her first anti-lynching book, *Southern Horrors: Lynch Law in All Its Phases* (1892), not long after one such mob of racial terrorists burned down her Memphis newspaper office, and opens that book by directly invoking the attack as requiring her courageous response: "Since my business has been destroyed and I am an exile from home . . . the issue has been forced, and as the writer of it I feel that the race and the public generally should have a statement of the facts as they exist." And she defines that project as a critical patriotic one, an effort to extend the legacy of American ideals of equality and justice to this community for whom they continue to be denied: "If this work can contribute in any way toward proving this, and at the same time arouse the conscience of the American people to a demand for justice to every citizen, . . . I shall feel I have done my race a service."

Wells and a group of African American colleagues—including her husband, the attorney and activist Ferdinand Barnett (1852–1936), and Frederick Douglass—offered another such critical patriotic service in response to the 1893 Columbian Exposition's exclusion of African Americans. While a few African nations had exhibits at the exposition, the only representation of African Americans there was one constructed by the R. T. Davis Milling Company, which hired former slave Nancy Green to perform as the stereotypical character Aunt Jemima next to the "world's largest flour barrel." In protest, Wells and her peers authored *The Reason Why the Colored American is Not in the World's Columbian Exposition: The Afro-American's Contribution to Columbian Literature*, a pamphlet that they handed out to fairgoers. In the pamphlet's final chapter, "The Reason Why," Barnett advances their critical patriotic case most directly, in response to the exposition's "one all absorbing question . . . 'How shall America best present its greatness to the civilized world?'" In answer, Barnett writes that the titular "colored American . . . knew that the achievements of his country would interest the world, since no event of the century occurred in the life of any nation, of greater importance than the freedom and enfranchisement of the American slaves. He was anxious to respond to this interest by showing to the world, not only what America has done for the Negro, but what the Negro has done for himself." Although unfortunately that perspective and community were not included at the exposition, Barnett's essay and the pamphlet end with the critical patriotic hope that they "will so inspire the Nation that in another great National endeavor the Colored American shall not plead for a place in vain."

The world didn't just come to America during the Gilded Age, however—through the period's imperial ventures, America expanded in complicated and too often mythic ways into the world. In response to those imperial trends, a group of authors, politicians, and activists offered another expression of critical patriotism. As the U.S. concluded the Spanish American War and debated whether to annex and occupy the Philippines (among other territories), a number of prominent figures, including Jane Addams, Andrew Carnegie, Grover Cleveland, John Dewey, Henry and William James, and Mark Twain, formed an organization called the American Anti-Imperialist League. In a February 10th, 1899 "Address adopted by the Anti-Imperialist League," one of many broadsides they published and distributed widely, the organization linked its critical opposition to both the Filipino annexation and the concurrent war of occupation to patriotic national ideals, including among their overarching goals a desire "to agitate for the revival in the land of the spirit of Washington and Lincoln, . . . and to assert the vital truths of the Declaration of Independence embodied in the Constitution and indissolubly connected with the welfare of this Republic."

Throughout the Gilded Age, the legacy and status of those founding American truths was very much in dispute. Celebratory patriotisms, like those created at the 1876 and 1893 expositions and through the newly dedicated Statue of Liberty, emphasized American progress and greatness, but too often in ways directly tied to the era's mythic patriotisms around wealth and work, race and immigration, and expansion and imperialism. But in response, active and critical patriots modeled and embodied alternative national narratives, arguing that the work of extending the legacy of American ideals was at the end of the 19th century very much ongoing.

Chapter Five

The Progressive Era

From Roosevelt and Reform to World War

A pair of 1903 events revolutionized the worlds of transportation and technology and reflected a rapidly progressing early 20th century America. On June 16th, engineer and entrepreneur Henry Ford (1863–1947), along with his partner Alexander Malcomson and other investors such as the brothers John and Horace Dodge, incorporated the Ford Motor Company. Just over six months later, on January 12th, 1904, Ford would set a new land speed record on the frozen ice of Michigan's Lake St. Clair behind the wheel of his model "999," an innovative vehicle that became the inspiration for 1908's groundbreaking Model T. And on December 17th, 1903, in the Kill Devil Hills south of Kitty Hawk, North Carolina, the inventors Orville (1871–1948) and Wilbur Wright (1867–1912) made history's first recorded successful powered and manned flight in their pioneering aircraft the *Wright Flyer*; they would return to Kitty Hawk many times over the next two years, testing their *Wright Flyer II* and *Wright Flyer III* aircraft which began to illustrate the true potential for human air travel.

While each of these moments and unfolding stories was distinct and complex, they together helped embody a nation that seemed in the century's first decade to be taking on the personality and perspective of its president, Theodore "Teddy" Roosevelt (1858–1919). In his 1899 speech, "The Strenuous Life," delivered shortly before he was chosen by William McKinley as his new vice presidential running mate, Roosevelt had argued, "Far better it is to dare mighty things, to win glorious triumphs, even though checkered by failure." And in 1910, just after he completed his two-term presidency, he would proclaim in another speech that "It is not the critic who counts; not the man who points out how the strong man stumbles, or where the doer of deeds could have done them better. The credit belongs to the man who is actually in the arena, whose face is marred by dust and sweat and blood; who strives valiantly; who errs, who comes short again and again, because there is no effort without error and shortcoming; but who does actually strive to do the deeds; who knows great enthusiasms, the great devotions; who spends himself in a worthy cause." Both Roosevelt's own enthusiasms and those of these iconic inventors embodied a celebratory patriotic perspective on America's possibilities and promise at the start of the new century.

Yet over the next few decades, both of these transportation innovations would likewise become intertwined with mythic patriotisms. Around 1920, Henry Ford began to publish a series of overtly antisemitic articles, first in his weekly newspaper *The Dearborn Independent* and then in a four-volume work (published in Germany) entitled *The International Jew, the World's Foremost Problem*. Ford's antisemitic views were also part of his and the period's broader emphasis on the need for "Americanization," as reflected in the "American Melting Pot" ceremonies he held for workers at the Ford Motor Company. Similarly, one of the greatest pioneers in the world of aviation, aviator and inventor Charles Lindbergh, would become closely associated with both antisemitism and the German Nazi Party, particularly in an August 1939 radio address in which Lindbergh argued that "We must ask who owns and influences the newspaper, the news picture, and the radio station. . . . If our people know the truth, our country is not likely to enter the war." Lindbergh linked these sentiments to the period's America First Movement and its embodiment of mythic patriotism.

The Progressive Era featured amplified celebratory patriotisms in a number of arenas, from Roosevelt's idealized status and parallel overarching images of American accomplishment and promise to the wartime deployment of the iconic national symbol known as Uncle Sam. But those celebrations were often closely tied to mythic patriotisms, whether in the Americanization movement's links to new immigration laws and restrictions, the anti-union "American Plan," or the post-World War I Red Scare. In contrast, a number of Progressive era movements embodied active patriotic efforts to push America closer to its ideals, from social reformers and women's suffrage activists to the Native American artists and communities who achieved the passage of the 1924 Indian Citizenship Act. And other social and political movements expressed more direct critical patriotic challenges to the nation's shortcomings, from anti-war pacifists to muckraking journalists to the founding of the groundbreaking NAACP.

Teddy Roosevelt was of course far from the first president to be closely associated with celebratory patriotic images of the United States. I have traced a number of other such connections, from George Washington and Revolutionary American ideals to Andrew Jackson and the myth of the "self-made man" to Abraham Lincoln's consistently celebratory perspective on the nation even at one of its darkest and most divided moments. The collective celebrations of Teddy Roosevelt extended each of those legacies in some key ways: the legends of his wartime exploits with the Spanish American War's "Rough Riders" echoing both Washington and Jackson's military backgrounds; the stories of his defining, rugged experiences in the American West, after a childhood marked by often debilitating illnesses, turning this privileged son of an elite New York family into a self-made man of sorts; and the consistent quotations and celebrations of Roosevelt's speeches and rhetoric, from both before and during his time as president, creating an emphasis on his own celebratory voice and perspective that had among prior presidents been the case only for Lincoln.

In other ways the celebrations of Roosevelt added new layers onto those existing legacies, however. Many had to do with the West, and specifically with the relatively new celebratory patriotism that closely associated American ideals with "the frontier." Early in his life Roosevelt contributed a foundational text to that developing concept with his four-volume history, *The Winning of the West* (1889), in which he strove to live up to another historian of the frontier, Francis Parkman, "to whom Americans who feel a pride in the pioneer history of their country are so greatly indebted." In a new foreword included in a 1900 "Presidential Edition" of the book, published while Roosevelt was serving as McKinley's Vice President, Roosevelt makes the case for this celebratory patriotic vision of the West even more overtly, writing, "The whole western movement of our people was simply the most vital part of that great movement of expansion which has been the central and all-important feature of our history—a feature far more important than any other since we became a nation, save only the preservation of the Union itself. It was expansion which made us a great power." And he likewise equates criticisms of expansion, such as the arguments made by the era's Anti-Imperialist League, with anti-American sentiments: "The same forces, the same types of men, stood for and against the cause of national growth, of national greatness, at the end of the century as at the beginning."

Roosevelt also came to be closely linked to another of the period's amplified celebratory patriotic emphases: on American military prowess as a key feature of its international reputation and relationships. In a September 2nd, 1901 speech at the Minnesota State Fair, Vice President Roosevelt shared one of his favorite aphorisms and perhaps one he coined himself, although he called it a "West African proverb": "Speak softly and carry a big stick—you will go far." As president, he turned that concept into the basis for foreign policy (especially in the Western Hemisphere) and a significant increase in the size and strength of the military, both of which were exemplified by the famous "Great White Fleet." On Roosevelt's orders, that armada of 16 battle-ships circumnavigated the globe between December 16th, 1907, and February 22nd, 1909, a period that, perhaps not coincidentally, encompassed the 1908 election in which Roosevelt's friend and current Secretary of War William Howard Taft was elected president. While the ships' hulls were painted white, giving the fleet its nickname, each also featured an elaborate red, white, and blue banner on its bow, symbolizing quite literally the fleet's celebratory patriotic representation of American prowess. In his 1913 *Autobiography*, Roosevelt reflects on what the fleet had contributed to images of American power as a global force not to be challenged: "When I left the Presidency I finished seven and a half years of administration, during which not one shot had been fired against a foreign foe. We were at absolute peace, and there was no nation in the world with whom a war cloud threatened, no nation in the world whom we had wronged, or from whom we had anything to fear. The cruise of the battle fleet was not the least of the causes which ensured so peaceful an outlook." Not unlike the era's other transportation and techno-logical advances, these military expansions echoed and amplified Gilded Age ideals of American material prowess, now brought fully to the world stage.

While Teddy Roosevelt expressed and embodied those celebrations of an expanding, increasingly powerful nation, a far different Progressive Era figure expressed a distinct but parallel idealized vision of America as "the promised land." That concept has been present at each stage of American history, with the Revolutionary era's Prospect Poems illustrating the close re-lationship between those idealized images and other founding American ide-als. But the unprecedented waves of immigrant arrivals between about 1880 and 1920 brought with them renewed visions of America as a promised land, and not just in the way that the nation might be so imagined by any would-be immigrant. Of the more than 20 million immigrant arrivals over those four decades, more than two million were Jewish, many fleeing the antisemitic prejudice and pogroms devastating Europe in this era. From the earliest re-corded Jewish stories, the concept of a promised land had comprised an inte-gral element to the community's spiritual and philosophical ideals. And while Jerusalem and Israel continued to occupy that imagined, idealized space most consistently for Jews around the world, for many of these late 19th and early 20th century Jewish immigrants, the United States came to be seen as another iteration of "the promised land."

One of those immigrant arrivals, Maryashe "Mary" Antin (1881–1949), expressed that celebratory patriotic perspective with particular clarity and passion. Antin was born in the Russian village of Polotzk (in modern-day Belarus), and when she was 13 immigrated with her mother and five siblings to the Boston area to join her father, who had come three years earlier and was operating a grocery store in the city's South End. She had a lifelong passion and talent for education, attending the prestigious Girls' Latin School (the predecessor to today's Boston Latin Academy) and then moving to New York to attend Columbia University's Teacher College and Barnard College, during which time she also married Columbia Geology Professor Amadeus William Grabau. Those educational experiences would also become a central focus of the triumphant story of immigration, Americanization, and the idealized opportunities available in the United States that she constructed in her first and most popular book, her autobiography *The Promised Land* (1912).

From an early moment in her book Antin creates the titular image of the United States. Describing Passover services during a period of intense antisemitic violence in Russia, she writes, "But what said some of us at the end of the long service? Not 'May we be next year in Jerusalem,' but 'Next year—in America!' So there was our promised land, and many faces were turned towards the West." She adds, "My father was inspired by a vision. He saw something—he promised us something. It was this 'America.' And 'America' became my dream." When she finally gets to experience that promised land, it more than meets her ideals, and the primary factors are the myths of national history and identity that she encounters in school: "I am glad that American history runs, chapter for chapter, the way it does; for thus America came to be the country I love so dearly. I am glad, most of all, that the Americans began by being Englishmen, for thus did I come to inherit this beautiful language in which I think." Or, as she puts it at the start of the book's most celebratory patriotic chapter, "My Country," "The public school has done its best for us foreigners, and for the country, when it has made us into good Americans. I am glad it is mine to tell how the miracle was wrought in one case. You should be glad to hear of it, you born Americans; for it is the story of the growth of your country; of the flocking of your brothers and sisters from the far ends of the earth to the flag you love; of the recruiting of your armies of workers, thinkers, and leaders. And you will be glad to hear of it, my comrades in adoption; for it is a rehearsal of your own experience, the thrill and wonder of which your own hearts have felt."

Antin's book thus certainly celebrates immigrant communities, as long as they become as "Americanized" as she has. But she also and most consistently emphasizes America's unique and historic greatness, an ideal identity that she as an immigrant is particularly positioned to appreciate and celebrate. As she writes in the book's concluding paragraph, "The past was only my cradle, and now it cannot hold me, because I am grown too big; just as the little house in Polotzk, once my home, has now become a toy of memory, as I move about at will in the wide spaces of this splendid palace, whose shadow covers acres. No! it is not I that belong to the past, but the past that belongs to me. America is the youngest of the nations, and inherits all that went before in history. And I am the youngest of America's children, and into my hands is given all her priceless heritage." Such moments echo the Revolutionary era's Prospect Poems in their celebratory patriotic depiction of America as the culmination of world history, but add the compelling parallel of immigrant individual, familial, and communal histories that have likewise led to this idealized place. Antin's last sentence is "Mine is the whole majestic past, and mine is the shining future," and she refers in equal measure to her own story and that of her adopted nation.

Just two years after Antin published her autobiography, a series of June and July 1914 events plunged Europe and eventually much of the world into The Great War (now known as World War I), significantly darkening that shining future. For many years the United States, coming out of a long era of what Teddy Roosevelt called in his 1913 autobiography "absolute peace," resisted being drawn into that unfolding war. The story of how and why that changed, of how a president (Woodrow Wilson) who ran for reelection on the slogan "He kept us out of war" could just over two months after his January 1917 inauguration ask Congress for a War Resolution against Germany, is multi-layered and outside the purview of this chapter and project. But in any case, by mid-1917, the United States was fully committed to its participation in The Great War, and one of the wartime images through which Americans were pushed to join and support that war effort was a longstanding figure given new, even more overtly celebratory patriotic emphasis in this fraught moment: the symbolic character of Uncle Sam.

The precise origins of Uncle Sam seem lost in history, but the figure began to be used as a representation of the United States during or just after the War of 1812. He appears, for example, in the 1816 political allegory *The Adventures of Uncle Sam, in Search After His Lost Honor*. But while he continued to pop up in various patriotic images and publications over the next century, it was with his iconic role in Great War recruitment and propaganda efforts that Uncle Sam became the figure who remains familiar and central to celebratory patriotisms to this day. That depiction was drawn by cartoonist and illustrator James Montgomery Flagg (1877–1960), who apparently based Sam's face on a self-portrait (aged slightly) and created other iconic elements such as the top hat with stars and the red, white, and blue outfit. Flagg's Uncle Sam debuted on the cover of the July 16th, 1916 issue of *Leslie's Weekly* magazine with the caption "What Are You Doing for Preparedness?," and then over the next two years became closely associated with the recruitment poster that read "I Want YOU for U.S. Army." More than four million copies of that poster were printed in 1917 and 1918, becoming the single most dominant celebratory patriotic image of America during this crucial, contested wartime moment.

That new image of Uncle Sam didn't just construct a particularly iconic vision of celebratory patriotism—it also directly implicated all Americans in that vision, implying (if not outright stating) that such celebratory patriotism was their collective obligation. Historian Christopher Capozzola analyzes that process at length in his book *Uncle Sam Wants YOU: World War I and the Making of the Modern American Citizen* (2008). As Capozzola argues in his introduction, "During World War I, when Americans discussed their relationship to the state, they used terms such as *duty, sacrifice,* and *obligation.* The language was everywhere" (Capozzola's emphasis). And he links those demands to other idealized and mythic patriotisms, writing, "When Uncle Sam jabbed his finger at the American public, he pointed out their rights, and he also pointed out who was or wasn't an American. But mostly . . . he pointed at people because he wanted them to do something." From Roosevelt's strenuous life to Antin's Americanizing education to Flagg's Uncle Sam, these Progressive era celebratory patriotisms all modeled an idealized nation to which Americans could—and in these visions should—contribute their own perspectives and efforts.

As Capozzola's phrase "who was or wasn't an American" suggests, however, not all Americans were offered the same chance to participate in those celebratory patriotic efforts, or to be defined as part of the imagined national community at all. Indeed, a number of evolving Progressive Era myths, each in some way extending back to the Gilded Age, coalesced during and after the war. These visions of the United States both demanded allegiance to a particular set of idealized and circumscribed national images and sought to identify, discriminate against, and ultimately exclude American communities that threatened those myths.

Many of those myths targeted the era's blossoming labor movement. Although the labor movement had by this time won a number of significant victories, including the eight-hour workday, laws against child labor, numerous health and safety regulations, and the 1913 formation of a federal Department of Labor, the prejudiced and xenophobic associations of labor activists with "anarchists" and other "foreign radicals"—and the concurrent attacks on them as fundamentally outside of American identity—that defined Gilded Age histories such as the Haymarket trial endured into the Progressive Era. Moreover, with the onset of World War I those associations became interconnected with wartime suspicions of outside agitators and foreign spies, many of them linked to the same European nations with whom the U.S. was at war. Through this lens the labor movement came to be seen not just as un-American, but as overtly anti-American and even treasonous. For example, during the war, executives of U.S. Steel, the mega-corporation formed in 1901 when financier J. P. Morgan merged Andrew Carnegie's steel company with two other sizable firms, amplified these anti-labor exclusions in two key ways: calling union organizers in their Chicago mills "German propagandists" and requiring steelworkers in those and other mills to sign a "Pledge of Patriotism" in which they pledged not to strike and agreed to other limitations of their activities.

After the war, those exclusionary anti-labor views not only endured but developed further into a more comprehensive strategy on behalf of corporations and their government allies. Known tellingly as the "American Plan," that strategy was initially formulated by a group of Midwestern corporations at a 1921 meeting in Chicago, then adopted more generally by the National Association of Manufacturers (NAM). This plan went far further than rhetoric or worker pledges, although those continued, or even than employers refusing to negotiate with unions or do business with unionized vendors, although those tactics were utilized as well. Instead, the plan called for overt violence against union organizers and striking workers, much of it perpetrated by armed "patrols" that the NAM would pay to import into unionized cities and target union gatherings and labor actions. Between those coordinated campaigns and violent actions and a series of labor injunctions from sympathetic courts, these anti-union forces succeeded in reducing the number of workers involved in labor actions from more than four million in 1919 to less than three hundred thousand in 1929.

Moreover, the era's attacks on unions as profoundly anti-American extended far beyond corporate employers and their direct allies. In a February 10th, 1920 speech at Baltimore's Mount Vernon Place Methodist Episcopal Church, the prominent Methodist Bishop William A. Quayle argued that "the very existence of our republican form of government is seriously threatened" by "organized labor." He went further still, claiming that "Labor's threat is a challenge against all we have and are in government, and as such it is our duty as American citizens to accept the challenge and in our strength rise up and crush the foe to our most cherished ideals. Our government is for all the people, not for any one class or faction." Labor's proposed policies, Quayle concluded, "will, if continued and advanced in their logical conclusion, banish political liberty from the land." In Quayle's remarks we see the mythic patriotic logic that underlay a phrase like "American plan," the explicit marshalling of "cherished ideals" like "republican government" and "liberty" in order to portray labor unions and activists as not only outside of that foundational and ongoing national project, but working actively to undermine and destroy it.

While the labor movement became a particular target of such exclusionary attacks, it was far from the only American community identified as un- and anti-American in the era. In his December 7th, 1915 State of the Union address, President Woodrow Wilson painted a wide swath of immigrant communities with that brush in order to request a Congressional Espionage Act: "There are citizens of the United States, . . . born under other flags but welcome under our generous naturalization laws to the full freedom and opportunity of America, who poured the poison of disloyalty into the very arteries of our national life . . . I urge you to enact such laws at the earliest possible moment and feel that in so doing I am urging you to do nothing less than save the honor and self-respect of the nation." Congress debated the idea for much of its next two sessions, and on June 15th, 1917, at the same moment when the first American soldiers were setting sail for France and the war, passed the Espionage Act, which made various forms of military and political subversion a crime and gave the Postmaster General the authority to refuse to mail publications determined to be in violation of those criteria. The Sedition Act, passed on May 16th, 1918 as a series of amendments to the Espionage Age, made clearer still the association of any criticism of the government with these crimes, banning "any disloyal, profane, scurrilous, or abusive language about the form of government of the United States . . . or the flag of the United States." That last clause is especially striking: Francis Bellamy had never intended the Pledge of Allegiance to be a legal requirement; but the Sedition Act made the expression of any negative sentiments about the flag a crime, which comes quite close to requiring that Americans indeed pledge allegiance to the flag.

Even a brief glimpse at applications of these laws during World War I reflects the breadth of perspectives that could be and were defined as seditious. A silent film entitled *The Spirit of '76* (1917) was seized by the government for portraying the English (now America's wartime allies) too harshly, and the film's producer, a Jewish American immigrant from Germany named Robert Goldstein, was sentenced to ten years in prison; at the sentencing Judge Benjamin Bledsoe told Goldstein, "Count yourself lucky that you didn't commit treason in a country lacking America's right to a trial by jury. You'd already be dead." The Postmaster General refused to mail copies of *The Jeffersonian*, a newsletter published by the Southern populist and anti-war activist Tom Watson; when Watson fought back in court a federal judge called the publication and its pacifist sentiments "poison," echoing Wilson's "poison of disloyalty" phrase." And eight members of the religious organization the Watch Tower Bible and Tract Society were convicted under the Espionage Act, based on charges stemming largely from the following sentence in their anti-war book *The Finished Mystery*: "And yet under the guise of patriotism civil governments of the earth demand of peace-loving men the sacrifice of themselves and their loved ones and the butchery of their fellows, and hail it as a duty demanded by the laws of heaven." Clearly, even the concept of patriotism itself was seen as immune to challenge or criticism under these mythic visions of the nation at war.

Although that war ended with the November 1918 Armistice, the governmental assaults on American communities under the guise of these exclusionary laws continued through 1919 and into 1920. Those efforts were due in large part to one figure, Wilson's newly confirmed Attorney General A. Mitchell Palmer (1872–1936), along with Palmer's deputy J. Edgar Hoover, whom Palmer appointed to run a new branch known as the General Intelligence Division (GID). Ironically, one of Palmer's first actions after taking office on March 5th, 1919 was to release nearly 10,000 German Americans who had been imprisoned during the war; their arrests were the direct result of a private organization called the American Protective League (APL), which surveilled and raided German American homes and businesses under the auspices of the Espionage and Sedition Acts. Palmer opposed the APL and stated that "its operation in any community constitutes a grave menace." Yet over the course of 1919, influenced in part by a series of April and June bombings by Italian supporters of the anarchist leader Luigi Galleani and in part by the Wilson administration's continued emphasis on advancing anti-immigrant and anti-union sentiments, Palmer became convinced by similarly extreme fears that, as he told the House Appropriations Committee in June, "on a certain day . . . [radicals] would rise up and destroy the government at one fell swoop."

Beginning with a July 1919 raid on an anarchist group in Buffalo, over the next six months Palmer, Hoover, and their colleagues conducted a series of raids on numerous communities, many of them closely associated with the labor movement. Indeed, the most prominent Palmer Raids (as they came to be known) targeted labor organizations directly: the November 7th, 1919 raids against Union of Russian Workers organizations in 12 cities; actions against striking United Mine Workers and their labor activist allies throughout November and December; and the largest group of raids, those conducted on and after January 2nd, 1920, which principally targeted the Communist Labor Party and affiliate organizations. After those latter raids, Palmer and Hoover tellingly sought to deport as many as 3,500 of the 10,000 Americans arrested; the Acting Secretary of Labor Louis Freeland Post canceled many of the warrants, but Palmer and company succeeded in deporting more than 550 resident aliens. In June 1920 testimony before the Congressional Rules Committee, Palmer attacked Post and revealed the mythic patriotism underlying these raids and deportations, claiming that Post's "tender solicitude for social revolution and perverted sympathy for the criminal anarchists . . . set at large among the people the very public enemies whom it was the desire and intention of the Congress to be rid of."

The fear-mongering inherent in Palmer's phrase "set at large among the public" reflects how the raids and their contexts became part of the larger phenomenon known as the Red Scare. Throughout 1919 and 1920, in multiple political and cultural settings, fearful and xenophobic images were deployed against a number of American communities. During the January 1919 Seattle general strike, a local newspaper warned that "This is America—not Russia," and Mayor Ole Hanson went further, arguing, "The time has come for the people in Seattle to show their Americanism. . . . The anarchists in this community shall not rule its affairs." Hanson would later expand upon those ideas in a pamphlet entitled *Americanism versus Bolshevism* (1920). Also in January, members of the Senate Committee on the Judiciary heard testimony on the "Bolshevik" threat and influence in the U.S., with Minnesota Senator Knute Nelson arguing that these foreign radicals "have really rendered a service to the various classes of progressives and reformers that we have here in this country." During the September 1919 Boston police strike, President Wilson called the labor action "a crime against civilization," and an editorial in the *Ohio State Journal* opined that "When a policeman strikes, he should be debarred not only from resuming his office, but from citizenship as well." And even the movies got into the act: through anti-radical films like *Dangerous Hours* (1920), in which the hero is seduced by a Bolshevik femme fatale who harbors a "wild dream of planting the scarlet seed of terrorism in American soil" and through extreme publicity campaigns like that for the film *Bolshevism on Trial* (1919), in which red flags were hung near theaters and actors in military uniforms tore them down.

While the worst excesses of the Red Scare had ended by the close of 1920, its mythic and xenophobic sentiments were also part of another trend that continued well into the 1920s: the extension of exclusionary immigration laws to include more and more immigrant communities. The first national immigration laws, those around the 1882 Chinese Exclusion Act, had made exclusion the defining element of federal immigration policy, and that trend continued with two 1907 laws: the Immigration Act of 1907, which introduced numerous new categories of immigrants restricted from entering the U.S., and the so-called Gentleman's Agreement, through which the Roosevelt administration effectively barred Japanese immigration to the U.S. The Immigration Act of 1917, passed by Congress on February 5th over President Wilson's December 1916 veto, went significantly further still: creating an "Asiatic Barred Zone" which restricted immigration from every South Asian nation other than the Philippines, which was an occupied American territory at the time, and adding numerous additional categories of restricted arrivals, including such controversial ones as "political radicals," "illiterates" (the act was the first to institute a literacy test for all arrivals), and "paupers" (the act was likewise the first to require a head tax for all arrivals).

Those restrictions clearly reflected exclusionary attitudes toward particular communities of immigrants, but it was with two 1920s laws that federal immigration policy fully endorsed the discriminatory attitudes implied by these earlier acts. The 1921 Emergency Quota Act, also known as the Johnson Quota Act because it was sponsored by Washington Representative Albert Johnson, was the first to establish both numerical limits on arrivals and a quota system to determine those limits, a combination that came to be known as the National Origins Formula. As its name suggests, the Emergency Quota Act was intended to be temporary, but it became a direct inspiration for the more permanent Immigration Act of 1924, also known as the Johnson-Reed Act, as it was again authored by Representative Johnson and co-sponsored by Pennsylvania Senator David Reed. In arguing for the necessity of both these exclusionary laws, Johnson cited the threat posed by "a stream of alien blood, with all its inherited misconceptions respecting the relationships of the governing power to the governed," making clear both the xenophobic prejudice and the mythic vision of American identity and ideals at the heart of these immigration restrictions.

Making those underlying principles even clearer still was a 1924 speech from South Carolina Senator Ellison DuRant Smith, another sponsor of the Johnson-Reed Act. "It seems to me the point as to this measure," Smith argued, "is that the time has arrived when we should shut the door. . . . Thank God we have in America perhaps the largest percentage of any country in the world of the pure, unadulterated Anglo-Saxon stock . . . and it is for the preservation of that splendid stock that has characterized us that I would make this not an asylum for the oppressed of all countries, but a country to assimilate and perfect that splendid type of manhood that has made America the foremost Nation in her progress and in her power, and yet the youngest of all the nations." And in his concluding section Smith weds that exclusionary perspective to myths America's founding histories and ideals: "We do not want to tangle the skein of America's progress by those who imperfectly understand the genius of our Government and the opportunities that lie about us. Let up keep what we have, protect what we have, make what we have the realization of the dream of those who wrote the Constitution." Like the anti-labor forces, like the concepts of espionage and sedition that produced the Palmer Raids and the Red Scare, these anti-immigrant voices sought to define all these American communities as not only outside of our national community, but also as posing a direct threat to that nation's mythic ideals and very existence.

*   *   *

Those anti-immigrant exclusions would also seem to line up closely with, or at least occupy similar terrain to, another Progressive Era effort: the Americanization movement. While those who sought to "Americanize" immigrants did not oppose their presence in the United States as blatantly or fully as did xenophobes like Johnson and Smith, they nonetheless demanded that all immigrants transform into a mythic form of American identity if they were to remain in the country. And as cultural critic Horace Kallen noted in his 1915 *Nation* magazine article "Democracy vs. the Melting Pot," "Americanization" had a very particular meaning: "The general notion, 'Americanization,' appears to denote the adoption of English speech, of American clothes and manners, of the American attitude in politics. It connotes the fusion of the various bloods, and a transmutation by 'the miracle of assimilation' of Jews, Slavs, Poles, Frenchmen, Germans, Hindus, Scandinavians into beings similar in background, tradition, outlook, and spirit to the descendants of the British colonists, the Anglo-Saxon stock." That is, the Americanization movement too often emphasized the same mythic definition of American identity as would Senator Smith when he argued for "that Anglo-Saxon stock that has characterized us."

Yet without ignoring that mythic definition, it's important to add that some proponents of the Americanization movement also expressed and embodied a more active patriotic perspective, one that saw both their work with immigrants and the experiences of immigrant Americans themselves as constituting inspiring elements of an overarching American community. One of those advocates was none other than Mary Antin, whose second book, *They Who Knock at Our Gates: A Complete Gospel of Immigration* (1914), celebrated immigrant communities just as fully as her first had celebrated American ideals. She does so in part by linking immigration to "The Law of the Fathers" (her first chapter title), the Declaration of Independence and the Constitution, and thus locating these evolving American communities alongside that idealized national and Revolutionary story. And she then weds those parallels to an argument that the process of Americanizing immigrants will likewise help all Americans better remember and recover those national ideals. In her concluding paragraphs she quotes the social worker and education reformer Grace Abbott, an advocate for the Americanization movement, to make that case: "I felt then, as I have felt many times when I have met some newcomer who has expected a literal fulfillment of our democratic ideals, that fortunately for America we had great numbers who were coming to remind us of the 'promise of American life,' and insisting that it should not be forgotten."

Abbott did a great deal of her reform work while living in Hull House, the Chicago settlement house founded by the reformer Jane Addams (1860–1935). Addams likewise envisioned Hull House and the settlement house movement it helped initiate as a vehicle through which immigrants could become Americanized—but also, and most importantly, as a space for active patriotic work that embodied the best of the nation, not only from these immigrant communities but from all those who worked for and with them. In her memoir of the movement, *Twenty Years at Hull House* (1912), Addams focuses precisely on the difficult, demanding, and vital work that the house and movement required, noting in the preface that "Because Settlements have multiplied so easily in the United States I hoped that a simple statement of an earlier effort, including the stress and storm, might be of value in their interpretation and possibly clear them of a certain charge of superficiality." And after tracing that work across a number of stages and subjects, her book ends with a chapter on Hull House's most important purpose, "Socialized Education," and a final line which links that goal directly to an active patriotic aim: "The educational activities of a Settlement, as well its philanthropic, civic, and social undertakings, are but differing manifestations of the attempt to socialize democracy, as is the very existence of the Settlement itself." For Antin, Abbott, and Addams, then, the Americanization movement was as much about moving the nation closer to its collective ideals as about helping immigrants become part of it.

Addams was also an important voice in a number of other Progressive Era political and social movements, including the Anti-Imperialist League formed to protest the U.S. occupation of the Philippines and the women's suffrage movement. The suffrage movement achieved its primary goal during this period, with the 1919 passage and 1920 ratification of the 19th Amendment granting American women the right to vote. But it was two prior 1910s moments that exemplified the movement's active patriotic advocacy for that civil right and national ideal. First there was the Women's Suffrage Procession, in which nearly 10,000 activists (the largest gathering in the movement's history) marched down Pennsylvania Avenue on March 3rd, 1913, the day before Wilson's inauguration. Organized by Alice Paul and Lucy Burns as a "march in a spirit of protest against the present political organization of society, from which women are excluded," the procession was met with vocal and violent resistance, not only from the gathered mob but also from many of the police who were tasked with protecting the marchers. According to a witness quoted in the *Washington Post*, two ambulances "came and went constantly for six hours, always impeded and at times actually opposed, so that doctor and driver literally had to fight their way to give succor to the injured." But the marchers persevered and completed their route, drawing national attention to their active patriotic efforts and cause and moving the collective conversations a good bit closer to support for that Constitutional amendment.

The movement's active patriotic perseverance in the face of extreme and violent resistance was embodied even more fully by the Silent Sentinels. Beginning on January 10th, 1917, for the next two and a half years suffrage activists protested in Washington, first outside the White House and then later in Lafayette Square. They did so silently, holding signs that both called out the Wilson administration with phrases like "Mr. President, you say liberty is the fundamental demand of the human spirit" and expressed their own determination: "We shall fight for the things which we have always carried nearest our hearts—for democracy, for the right of those who submit to authority to have a voice in their own governments." Many of the protesters were arrested on such spurious charges as obstructing traffic and disturbing the peace, and those arrests brought with them the worst of the carceral state: after her October 20th, 1917 arrest, Alice Paul was sentenced to seven months in prison and placed in solitary confinement at Virginia's brutal Occuquan Workhouse; and after a November 14th, 1917 mass arrest, the workhouse's superintendent ordered more than 40 guards to beat and torture the activists in what became known as the "Night of Terror." But as illustrated by Paul's prison hunger strike, the activists challenged these horrors with renewed commitment to their cause; a physician said of Paul during that strike that she had "a spirit like Joan of Arc, and it is useless to try to change it. She will die but she will never give up." None of them did, and the Silent Sentinels only ended their vigil on June 4th, 1919, when both the House and Senate passed the 19th Amendment and sent it to the states for ratification.

The 19th Amendment was far from the only Progressive Era legislative civil rights victory achieved through active patriotic protest and activism, and another telling such moment was the June 2nd, 1924 passage of the Indian Citizenship Act. Native Americans, long defined as legal "wards" of the U.S. government, had been purposefully excluded from the extensions of citizenship and civil rights in such documents as the 14th Amendment and the 1870 Naturalization Act. But the active patriotic service of Native American soldiers during World War I helped shift national conversations in favor of citizenship and inclusion. As theologian and photographer Joseph K. Dixon (a longstanding ally) wrote, "The Indian, though a man without a country, the Indian who has suffered a thousand wrongs considered the white man's burden and from mountains, plains and divides, the Indian threw himself into the struggle to help throttle the unthinkable tyranny of the Hun. The Indian helped to free Belgium, helped to free all the small nations, helped to give victory to the Stars and Stripes. The Indian went to France to help avenge the ravages of autocracy. Now, shall we not redeem ourselves by redeeming all the tribes?" With the Indian Citizenship Act, also known as the Snyder Act after its sponsor Representative Homer P. Snyder of New York, did just that, granting immediate citizenship to all Native Americans while guaranteeing that the change would "not in any manner impair or otherwise affect the right of any Indian to tribal or other property," an important recognition of the complex and evolving concept of Native American sovereignty.

While allies like Snyder and Dixon played important roles in securing the act's passage, it was the active patriotic efforts of a Native American performer that helped garner widespread public support for the law. Nipo T. Strongheart (1891–1966), also known as George Mitchell Jr., was born to a Yakima mother and white father, and grew up between those two worlds, including time at the reservation boarding school at Fort Simcoe and performing alongside his father in Buffalo Bill Cody's Wild West shows. In his 20s he became more committed to social and political causes, joining the Society of American Indians in 1916 and a year later, after being turned down for service in Teddy Roosevelt's World War I volunteer corps, serving with the newly established YMCA War Work Council. For the Council Strongheart toured military bases throughout the Eastern United States, lecturing and performing about Native American histories and rights. After the war he expanded those performances into a tour of Lyceum and Chautauqua fairs across the United States, becoming one of the era's most recognized Native American figures and voices. He highlighted World War I service in those talks, arguing, "This is the only country on earth for them . . . and if they are willing to shed their blood for it, they should be good enough to share equally in the advantages that are given to every other race within our borders." He also circulated petitions in support of Native American citizenship and voting rights, and the hundreds of thousands of signatures he gathered became crucial evidence in support of the Indian Citizenship Act.

The World War I service and sacrifice of tens of thousands of Native American soldiers itself comprised an important and inspiring form of Progressive Era active patriotism and one that helped achieve the era's legal victories. But in his complementary cultural and political advocacy and activism, Nipo Strongheart offered a model for active patriotism on the home front, one that parallels the efforts of reformers and movements like Mary Antin, Jane Addams, and the settlement and suffrage movements. All of these figures and communities both embodied national ideals and helped push the United States closer to a realization of those ideals for all Americans.

In so doing, those active patriotic figures and movements did tend to endorse key elements of the era's patriotic celebrations, visions of the founding national ideals which they then sought to extend to additional American communities. That active patriotic extension represented an important corrective to celebratory and mythic images of America as already great, highlighting and seeking to overcome the gaps between the ideals and the realities for too many Americans. But it was also complemented by distinct and equally significant critical patriotic perspectives, a group of Progressive Era voices and communities that more fundamentally challenged celebratory and mythic views in order to make the case for an alternative vision of American identity, history, and possibility.

The anti-war and pacifist movement represented one striking and courageous such critical patriotic perspective. Although the initial U.S. entry into the war was hugely contested and controversial, once war was declared, patriotism came to be consistently and closely associated, as it so often is during wartime, with supporting that war effort. That was true of celebratory images like Uncle Sam, myths like corporate Pledges of Patriotism or the Sedition Act, and active patriotic efforts like the emphasis on Native American World War I service and sacrifice. Indeed, despite the aforementioned vociferous and sustained debates over entering the war, when it came time in April 1917 for Congress to vote on President Wilson's requested declaration of war, the resolution passed with overwhelming support, sailing through the Senate 82 to 6 and the House 373 to 50, reflecting the power of these wartime patriotic images and the challenge faced by anyone who sought to oppose them.

One of those no votes in the House was cast by Wyoming Representative Jeannette Pickering Rankin (1880–1973), the first American woman to hold federal elected office and a steadfast pacifist who would later become the only member of Congress to vote against declaring war on Japan in December 1941. In 1917 Rankin was far from alone, as women's organizations offered much of the period's most vocal pacifist and anti-war sentiments. Fanny Garrison Villard (1844–1928), a longtime activist for suffrage, racial equality, and civil rights, organized an August 1914 Women's Peace Parade, a protest march of around 1,500 women in New York City. Jane Addams organized and was elected president of the Women's Peace Party, which held a convention on January 9th–10th, 1915, to approve a platform and plan of action. That platform opened with a direct echo of the U.S. Constitution's Preamble: "We, women of the United States, assembled in behalf of World Peace." And it featured as one its central demands a criticism of "militarism in our own country," foreshadowing directly how the arguments would shift as the U.S. moved toward war. Once that American war effort began, many of these activists continued their fight, joining forces with the American Union Against Militarism (AUAM), an organization founded by lawyer Roger Nash Baldwin as a predecessor to his American Civil Liberties Union (ACLU), to oppose both military intervention and the conscription of American soldiers into that fight.

Other prominent Progressive Era figures and communities offered their own critical patriotic anti-war messages. In December 1915, Henry Ford chartered an ocean liner, the *Oscar II*, and organized a group of peace activists to sail with him to Europe in an attempt to negotiate a peaceful end to the war; among those who took part in what came to be known as the Peace Ship was suffrage activist Inez Milholland, one of the chief organizers of the 1913 Women's Suffrage Procession in Washington. Although the U.S. was not yet involved in the war, Ford saw the ship as bringing American ideals to bear on the conflict, arguing, "Whatever we decide to do, New York is the place for starting it." The Peace Ship could not achieve an end to the war, but once the U.S. became involved 18 months later, American anti-war activists continued to offer critical opposition to that militarism. Labor and radical organizations like the International Workers of the World (IWW) and the Socialist Party of the USA challenged the war effort, with Socialist Party Chairman Eugene Debs arrested in June 1918 (under the Sedition Act) for giving an anti-draft speech in Canton, Ohio. At his sentencing, Debs linked this anti-war activism to a broader critical patriotic perspective on a shared national and human community, telling the judge, "Your Honor, years ago I recognized my kinship with all living beings, and I made up my mind that I was not one bit better than the meanest on earth. I said then, and I say now, that while there is a lower class, I am in it, and while there is a criminal element, I am of it, and while there is a soul in prison, I am not free."

The challenge that anti-war figures like Debs presented to celebratory and mythic ideals of wartime patriotism did not go unnoticed. When offered the chance to pardon Debs, who had begun a ten-year prison sentence in April 1919, President Wilson wrote, "While the flower of American youth was pouring out its blood to vindicate the cause of civilization, this man, Debs, stood behind the lines sniping, attacking, and denouncing them. . . . This man was a traitor to his country and he will never be pardoned during my administration." Even if we leave aside the war's deeply contested nature—again, as late as his 1916 presidential campaign Wilson was running as an anti-war candidate—Wilson's statement reflects precisely the value and necessity of such critical patriotic perspectives and efforts. They make certain that the equation of patriotism with sacrifice and death in war does not go unquestioned, and instead offer arguments that a crucial way to extend the legacy of founding American ideals of liberty, equality, and justice is to seek to keep Americans—in and out of the military—safe from the horrors and effects of war.

World War I was not the only threat to Americans in this period, and critical patriotic voices likewise sought to highlight other such threats and model collective national alternatives. The activist journalists and authors who came to be known as the muckrakers did so by addressing corruption, health and safety violations, and other ills in the nation's corporate and governmental settings. The journalist Upton Sinclair (1878–1968) spent seven weeks working undercover in Chicago's meat industry for a piece for the socialist newspaper *Appeal to Reason*, and turned the experience into his ground-breaking work *The Jungle*, published serially in the newspaper in 1905 and then as a book in 1906. Sinclair links the violations and corruptions in that corporate world to the challenges facing both working class and immigrant Americans; the majority of his characters are first-generation immigrants. And in his book's final chapter he envisions a successful campaign to unify those Chicago communities and work toward a better future: "And then will begin the rush that will never be checked, the tide that will never turn till it has reached its flood—that will be irresistible, overwhelming—the rallying of the outraged workingmen of Chicago to our standard! . . . Chicago will be ours! CHICAGO WILL BE OURS!" In a private letter to journalist William Allen White, Teddy Roosevelt called Sinclair's book "hysterical, unbalanced, and untruthful," but this balance of outraged critique and a radical vision for a new shared community became an enduring best-seller.

Another prominent and influential muckraking effort was the investigative journalism of Ida Tarbell (1857–1944). Tarbell was an iconoclastic activist who took part in many of the era's social and political debates, from the women's suffrage movement to America's entry into World War I. But she was best known for her investigative research into and writing about John D. Rockefeller's Standard Oil Company, which took shape across multiple serialized articles between 1902 and 1903 in *McClure's Magazine* (for which Tarbell worked as an editor for many years) and was published in book form as *The Rise of the Standard Oil Company* (1904). Tarbell was careful to ground that project in detailed work with a voluminous collection of primary documents, as well as extended interviews with Standard Oil executives among many other groups. But she came nonetheless to an impassioned and convincing perspective on the negative effects of both Rockefeller and a monopoly like Standard Oil on American society, writing in her book's conclusion that "our national life is on every side distinctly poorer, uglier, meaner, for the kind of influence he exercises." And her work contributed directly to a significant shift in those national conversations: the breaking up of Standard Oil under the auspices of the Sherman Antitrust Act.

Finally, the 1909–1910 founding of the National Association for the Advancement of Colored People (NAACP) comprised its own impressive and inspiring form of critical patriotism. The organization was founded over the course of two meetings at New York's Henry Street Settlement House (part of the settlement movement): at the first, on May 30th, 1909, a group featuring W.E.B. Du Bois, Ida B. Wells, and many others formed an organization called the National Negro Committee, a direct offshoot of a prior African American activist society known as the Niagara Movement; and a year later, on May 30th, 1910, they chose the name NAACP, elected officers, and established a mission. The first clause of that mission, "To promote equality of rights and to eradicate caste or race prejudice among the citizens of the United States," expressed both sides of a critical patriotic perspective: recognizing the presence of such prejudice as a defining American attribute; and committing to challenging and eliminating that negative element as part of a patriotic effort to bring the nation closer to its ideals of rights and equality. As Du Bois put it in his first (November 10th, 1910) editorial for *The Crisis*, the NAACP magazine that he founded and edited, "its editorial page will stand for the rights of men, irrespective of color or race, for the highest ideals of American democracy, and for reasonable but earnest and persistent attempts to gain these rights and realize these ideals."

One of the NAACP's most prominent early efforts illustrated its critical patriotic challenge to the era's mythic patriotisms. Director D. W. Griffith's film *The Birth of a Nation* (1915), an adaptation of Thomas W. Dixon's Clansmen novels that portrayed the Ku Klux Klan as American heroes helping liberate the white South from threatening African Americans and their allies, was being hailed as the first blockbuster film. Woodrow Wilson, whose mythic views of Reconstruction from his 1902 multi-volume *History of the American People* are quoted three times in the film, even arranged a special White House screening. In response to this mythic and racist vision of American history and identity, the NAACP organized a nationwide protest campaign, featuring marches and boycotts of theaters that showed the film. Throughout the Progressive Era mythic patriotisms defined numerous American communities as outside of the nation's identity and celebrations, but those communities fought back, offering active and critical patriotic challenges that exemplified an inclusive United States at the dawn of the 20th century.

Chapter Six

The Depression and World War II

Beyond the Greatest Generation

In the mid-1930s, two of the most prominent sports stories in American history together reflected the vital role of celebratory patriotism during the Great Depression. In 1933, boxer James Walter Braddock, who fought under the name James J. Braddock, was in desperate straits, depending on odd jobs and federal assistance programs to feed his family; just two years later, on June 13th, 1935, after a string of comeback wins against highly touted opponents, the 30-year-old Braddock fought at Madison Square Garden and defeated by unanimous decision the World Heavyweight Champion, Max Baer. Just over a year after that, at the August 1st–16th 1936 Berlin Summer Olympics, track and field athlete Jesse Owens achieved his own stunning success: Owens, a 22-year-old college athlete competing in his first international event, won four gold medals, becoming the most awarded athlete at that Olympics. In a period when the United States remained in the economic and social throes of the Depression, these athletic achievements became symbols of American perseverance and success, of an idealized national identity even in the most difficult of times. Moreover, because Owens achieved his success in Nazi Germany, directly challenging Adolf Hitler's theories of Aryan supremacy, his story likewise foreshadowed American celebratory patriotism in its World War II conflicts with that German state and leader.

Yet the aftermath and broader stories for these two sports figures, and particularly for Owens, reveal very different sides of America during this era. Braddock, nicknamed "Cinderella Man" by author and sportswriter Damon Runyan, became a national celebrity and icon; he retired from boxing shortly after and went on to serve as a 1st Lieutenant during World War II, training soldiers in hand-to-hand combat on the Pacific island of Saipan. Owens, on the other hand, came home to the same segregated and racist nation where as a collegiate athlete, despite setting three world records and tying another in a 45-minute span at a May 25th, 1935 meet, he had been unable to receive a scholarship and forced to eat and stay in "blacks-only" establishments when the team traveled. Such discriminatory realities continued to affect Owens after his Olympic triumphs: after he accepted a few endorsements the U.S. athletic association, he immediately withdrew his amateur status, ending his collegiate career; over the next few years he would have to race against amateurs and horses in order to make ends meet. Moreover, President Roosevelt never invited Owens to the White House nor publicly congratulated him; as Owens put it, refuting claims that Hitler had refused to shake his hand in Berlin, "Some people say Hitler snubbed me. But I tell you, Hitler did not snub me. I am not knocking the President. Remember, I am not a politician, but remember that the President did not send me a message of congratulations because, people said, he was too busy."

During the Great Depression and World War II, celebratory patriotic stories such as those of Braddock's and Owens' athletic triumphs served a vital role, framing the nation's perseverance through and victories over these profoundly challenging times; those stories have endured and grown into the "Greatest Generation" frame often applied to this period. Yet as Owens experienced, those celebrations could also be folded into exclusionary myths, perspectives embodied in such efforts as nationalist propaganda, the wartime policy of Japanese Internment, and the McCarthy hearings that dominated the immediate post-war period. But the era also featured striking examples of active patriotic communities, groups like the Depression era "Bonus Army" and the war's African American, Japanese American, and Native American soldiers who embodied a shared commitment to extending the nation's ideals. And cultural movements and works like the Harlem Renaissance, the political authors of the 1930s and '40s, and the autobiographical fiction of Filipino American immigrant and migrant laborer Carlos Bulosan expressed critical patriotic perspectives, highlighting the era's divisions and darker sides in order to imagine a more truly great future United States.

The prominence of athletic figures and achievements like Braddock and Owens aligns with a core element of much of the nation's celebratory patriotism during both the Great Depression and World War II: a view of these historical moments as epic conflicts in which Americans of all types, and especially "ordinary" Americans outside of the political and social elites on whom past celebrations had often focused, were engaged and through their battles with which they proved not only their own worth, but also and especially the enduring presence and value of national ideals. Those stories, and the forms of governmental, professional, personal, and cultural expressions in which they were created, constituted much of both the celebratory patriotism constructed within this period and the way that it has been expanded in the decades since into the overarching and enduring national ideal of the "Greatest Generation."

Much of the celebratory patriotism expressed during the Great Depression was closely tied to the President Franklin Roosevelt administration's New Deal programs, and in particular the literal and figurative constructions of American communities and identities comprised by the Works Progress Administration (WPA), which was formed in May 1935 and renamed in 1939 the Works Projects Administration. As Roosevelt reflected on the WPA's goals and effects, and especially on the Americans it employed, in the December 1942 letter through which he ended the program, "by almost immeasurable kinds and quantities of service the Work Projects Administration has reached a creative hand into every county in this Nation. It has added to the national wealth, has repaired the wastage of depression, and has strengthened the country to bear the burden of war. By employing eight millions of Americans, with thirty millions of dependents, it has brought to these people renewed hope and courage." And in his own celebratory take on the WPA, the book *American-Made: The Enduring Legacy of the WPA* (2008), author Nick Taylor expands on that view: "These ordinary men and women proved to be extraordinary beyond all expectation. They were golden threads woven in the national fabric. In this, they shamed the political philosophy that discounted their value and rewarded the one that placed its faith in them, thus fulfilling the founding vision of a government by and for its people. All its people."

A couple specific WPA programs and works can help illustrate that overarching, celebratory patriotic emphasis. One of the WPA's largest sections was Federal Project Number One, which sought to support and create cultural and historical works, and one of that section's divisions was the Federal Theatre Project. Its national director, Vassar Professor Hallie Flanagan, noted in her initial October 1935 mission statement that the project was intended not only to employ "theatre workers now on the public rolls," but for a more "far reaching purpose": "the establishment of theatres so vital to community life that they will continue to function after the program of this Federal Project is completed." The project staged numerous new works as well as revivals around the country between 1935 and its June 1939 conclusion, but collective celebrations were certainly a key through-line, as exemplified by the Illinois Theatre Project's Big Tent Theatre's 1936 production of *Abraham Lincoln: The Great Commoner*. Based in part on author Franklin W. Hart's 1926 biography, *Abraham Lincoln, The Great Commoner, The Sublime Emancipator*, the 1936's production's shortening of the title to Hart's first phrase emphasizes in particular that "everyman" vision of Lincoln, connecting him to the WPA's overarching goals of work and support for "ordinary" Americans—

and doing so in a state that would within 15 years of this production call itself "The Land of Lincoln," to drive home Flanagan's goal of theatre reflecting and amplifying "community life."

Another Federal Project Number One division, the Federal Art Project, likewise created and emphasized celebratory images through many of its distinct media and forms. This project, which ran from August 1935 through April 1943, was directed by the Icelandic American immigrant, curator, and author Holger Cahill, who saw the Federal Art Project as a crucial effort to return art to "its honorable place as a vital necessity of everyday life." Nearly 10,000 artists were commissioned to produce works in virtually every medium and form imaginable, but some of the most impressive, and some of the most overtly celebratory, were the project's murals. Perhaps the most famous such muralist was the Mexican artist Diego Rivera, whose overtly political Marxist works reflected a more critical form of artistic commentary. But while many of the project's other murals likewise celebrated workers, they generally did so more in the uncontroversial spirit of Vera Bock's famous poster "Work Pays America! Prosperity," which features two idealized workers atop a map of the United States. Exemplifying such celebratory murals were two by artist Seymour Fogel displayed at the Washington, DC headquarters of the Department of Health and Human Services, "Wealth of the Nation" and "Security of the People." Both feature a handful of figures taking part in everyday activities (at work and at home, respectively), but because of the mural's size as well as the figures' idealized proportions, these Americans became larger than life, the celebratory goals of the Federal Art Project and all the Federal Project Number one divisions writ literally and figuratively large.

Another Federal Art Project poster, Albert M. Bender's "A Young Man's Opportunity for Work, Play, Study, & Health" (1935), celebrated one of the New Deal's most popular programs, the Civilian Conservation Corps (CCC). In his March 1933 letter to Congress proposing this program, which would offer both local and national conservation and infrastructure work to unmarried young men between 18 and 25, Roosevelt explicitly linked it to celebratory images of both work and the American future, writing, "I call your attention to the fact that this type of work is of definite, practical value, not only through the prevention of great present financial loss but also as a means of creating future national wealth." The CCC camps, which were directly modeled on military camps including barracks and officers' quarters, presented themselves as helping both these specific communities of workers and the nation as a whole win the battle against the Depression's threats; as a North Carolina camp put it in its newsletter, *Happy Days*, "This is a training station; we're going to leave morally and physically fit to lick 'Old Man

Depression.'" And when the United States entered World War II, the camps and the CCC (which ran until 1942) directly transitioned into military training facilities, making even clearer the parallels between the celebratory patriotic projects of these Depression era programs and those of the nation at war.

Before turning to that wartime celebratory patriotism, it's worth noting one additional Depression era expression of that perspective: the period's numerous cultural celebrations of rural American communities. Some of the most prominent such cultural works were photographs, including John Vachon's and Walkers Evans's stunning portrait and landscape photography for the New Deal's Farm Security Administration (FSA) in the mid to late 1930s. Evans also worked with journalist and author James Agee on a 1936 project for *Fortune* magazine that combined Evans's photographs of rural Alabamans with Agee's written accounts of their stories; when *Fortune* opted not to run the story, the men turned it into a book, 1941's *Let Us Now Praise Famous Men*. The title refers to a passage from the religious text the Wisdom of Sirach, which includes two lines that together sum up Evans and Agee's goals in depicting these inspiring yet too easily forgotten Americans: "All these were honored in their generations, and were the glory of their times./ . . . And some there be which have no memorial; who perished, as though they had never been." And perhaps the most telling such Depression era cultural celebration is *The Wizard of Oz* (1939), in which despite the stunningly color-ful and frequently magical wonders Dorothy Gale experiences in Oz, made even more so when compared to the bleak black-and-white landscapes of Dust Bowl Kansas from which she comes, she never changes her mantra that "There's no place like home."

Not long after the United States emerged from the Depression, it found itself involved in another world war, and with that global military effort came the same kinds of celebratory patriotic efforts on the home front as during World War I, if with new developments for this 1940s conflict. One of those World War II evolutions in celebratory patriotism illustrated an extension of the De-pression era's emphasis on farming to the backyard of every American family: the Victory Garden. Through a recruitment campaign of posters and pamphlets featuring slogans like "Plant a Garden for Victory" and "Plant a Victory Gar-den: Our Food is Fighting," Roosevelt's Secretary of Agriculture Claude Wick-ard and his department encouraged millions of American homes and families to participate in this shared wartime effort: an estimated 20 million gardens were planted, a stunningly large number, as the total U.S. population on the 1940 census was 132 million; and by 1943 they supplied 40% of civilian needs for fruits and vegetables. Victory Gardens were also closely linked to the period's broader rationing efforts, which made every aspect of food into part of the col-lective war effort; as another poster argued, "Food is a Weapon: Don't Waste

It! Buy Wisely—Cook Carefully—Eat It All—Follow the National Wartime Nutrition Program." These programs worked to bring every American home and family into celebratory ideals of a unified nation fighting the war together.

Perhaps the most famous World War II posters and images presented a distinct but parallel way in which Americans on the home front could contribute to the collective war effort. The symbolic American worker known as Rosie the Riveter is most commonly associated with two celebratory images: J. Howard Miller's February 1943 "We Can Do It" poster, produced for the War Production Coordinating Committee and used as motivation for wartime workers; and Norman Rockwell's May 29th, 1943 *Saturday Evening Post* cover image of a riveter eating her lunch from a lunchbox labeled "Rosie" (with a copy of *Mein Kampf* under her feet). But the character was first created in the 1942 song "Rosie the Riveter," co-written by Redd Evans and John Jacob Loeb and recorded by a number of artists in the course of the war. The song's Rosie partly embodies a supportive home front, as her boyfriend Charlie is "a Marine" and she's "protecting Charlie, workin' overtime on the riveting machine." But it is also Rosie who truly exemplifies American ideals, not just because "she's making history, working for victory" but because "There's something true about—red, white, and blue about—Rosie the riveter." Like the Victory Gardens, this song and the iconic images that followed took a practical wartime home front reality—the need for new workers, including women and others who had in the years prior to the war been denied such opportunities—and transformed it into a celebratory patriotic story, one that has endured long after the war's conclusion.

"Rosie" was far from the only cultural text to contribute to the wartime celebratory patriotism, and the genre of film did so particularly consistently, with every year of the war seeing a number of film releases that depicted various military theatres, conflicts, and stories of perseverance and heroism. But perhaps the most celebratory World War II film was one set on the home front and focused on precisely the question of how cultural texts and figures can support the war effort. *Yankee Doodle Dandy* (1942) starred James Cagney as real-life Broadway composer and star George M. Cohan, who comes out of retirement to perform for President Roosevelt at the White House and receives a Congressional Medal of Honor in the process. Cohan always claimed that he was born on July 4th, although historical evidence indicates it might have been the 3rd, and the film makes prominent use of that mythic claim through the song "Yankee Doodle Boy," which features lines like, "I'm a Yankee Doodle dandy/A Yankee Doodle, do or die/A real-life nephew of my Uncle Sam/Born on the Fourth of July." Such lines bring together the nation's idealized origins, iconic symbols like Uncle Sam, and this patriotic artistic speaker to depict a truly unified United States.

Those celebratory patriotic images of an American community unified in its fights against and triumphs over first the Great Depression and then World War II's adversaries have endured over the decades since, and toward the end of the 20th century were given a particularly clear expression in journalist Tom Brokaw's book *The Greatest Generation* (1998). Brokaw builds on the period's celebratory views, including an emphasis on "ordinary" Americans who nonetheless rose to face and conquer extraordinary—and in Brokaw's argument genuinely unprecedented—challenges. As he puts it in his preface, "I began to reflect on the wonders of these ordinary people whose lives are laced with the markings of greatness. At every stage of their lives they were part of historic challenges and achievements of a magnitude the world had never before witnessed." While this Greatest Generation ideal built on the celebratory patriotisms I've traced in each chapter and time period, it also took that form of national celebration to a whole new level.

That celebratory patriotic emphasis on unity would seem to suggest, if not indeed depend upon, all Americans being part of those struggles and triumphs. But instead, many American communities were purposefully left out of those celebrations, and not only through political calculations like Roosevelt's decision to exclude African Americans from many New Deal programs in order to secure the support of the era's white supremacist Southern Democrats. Both the Depression and World War II likewise featured exclusionary myths, visions of the United States that defined particular communities as outside of their unifying definitions of the nation, often with divisive and destructive consequences for those excluded Americans.

Many of the Depression era's myths targeted communities of protest, Americans seeking to highlight and challenge the period's inequalities and injustices. For example, the World War I veterans who marched on Washington, D.C. in the spring of 1932 under the name of the Bonus Expeditionary Force or "Bonus Army" were extensively profiled by J. Edgar Hoover's newly christened Unites States Bureau of Investigation (USBI) as potential Communists and other forms of un- or anti-American radicals and subversives. The late July 1932 attack on the Bonus Army's Anacostia Flats camp by U.S. Army forces, while particularly striking for its brutal and thorough destruction of a protest community which by that time included numerous families and children among its sizable ranks, represented a logical endpoint of those exclusionary definitions of the community's identities and purposes.

Similar rhetorical and organized attacks targeted one of the Depression era's most extensive and vocal protest communities, the student movement. As historian Robert Cohen writes in his book, *When the Old Left Was Young: Student Radicals and America's First Mass Student Movement, 1929–1941* (1993), "no protest movement in Depression America was more unexpected than the student movement, nor more symbolic of the nation's transformation," as "at its peak in the late 1930s, the student movement's demonstrations involved hundreds of thousands of students annually—by some estimates, almost half of America's entire undergraduate population." But on most campuses, those student activists were met with significant official critique and pushback. In April 1932, for example, Reed Harris, the editor of the Columbia University student newspaper the *Spectator*, was expelled from the university because, as Dean Herbert Hawkes put it, his activist journalism represented "a climax to a long series of discourtesies, innuendoes, and misrepresentations" from student radicals on the campus. When Columbia students went on strike in protest, formed a group known as the Student League for Industrial Democracy, and led a campaign to abolish R.O.T.C. on campus, they drew further attention and challenge from national authorities such as J. Edgar Hoover's USBI, providing an early instance of what journalist Seth Rosenfeld has called Hoover's abiding "concern about alleged subversion within the education field" as well as his use of "dirty tricks to stifle dissent on campus."

Hoover and other Depression era proponents of such extreme anti-communist and anti-radical sentiments likewise feared that these outside influences could even take over U.S. government employees, leading to a key element of the influential and enduring 1939 law known as the Hatch Act. The Hatch Act originated with New Mexico Senator Carl Hatch's much more specific concerns that Democratic politicians were illicitly using WPA employees to help with their 1938 Congressional campaigns, a conflict of interest he sought to eliminate through this legislation. But the law as passed in August 1939, under the telling official title An Act to Prevent Pernicious Political Activities, included a quite distinct provision which revealed and amplified these broader, exclusionary fears: this section barred federal employees from membership in "any political organization which advocates the overthrow of our constitutional form of government." Hearkening back to the World War I era's legal connections between sedition and espionage, this law not only defined radical organizations and activisms as outside of the nation's political debates, but overtly linked them to fundamentally anti-American and treasonous purposes, a mythic vision of a United States where such perspectives were not only undesirable but illegal.

When the United States entered into World War II, those myths and fears of anti-American forces became folded into a wartime propaganda machine that was parallel to but even more extensive than what it had been during World War I. The increased availability and popularity of media such as film contributed to that greater breadth and range, as did the founding of a new federal agency, the Office of War Information (OWI). Some of that propaganda targeted the foreign nations with which the U.S. was at war, as exemplified by the anti-German and -Japanese editorial cartoons and animations of the illustrator Theodore Geisel, later known as the influential children's book author Dr. Seuss. Some propaganda amplified celebrations of the shared and collective war effort, including both the concept of Victory Gardens and the images of Rosie the Riveter. But a significant percentage of World War II propaganda was directed instead at divisive influences and seditious communities on the home front. A central theme of that latter type was that the enemy's spies could be anywhere and everywhere, as illustrated by a propaganda poster depicting a seemingly ordinary American woman with the caption, "WANTED! FOR MURDER. Her careless talk costs lives." Such messages, along with the ubiquitous phrase "Loose lips sink ships," did more than recommend wartime caution—they positioned Americans to constantly view each other as potentially hostile and treasonous.

Moreover, those propagandistic messages were often tied directly to parallel, and strikingly exclusionary, images of American ideals and identity. One poster, for example, featured a picture of an American eagle with the slogan, "Free Speech doesn't mean Careless Talk!" Echoing the Sedition Act's attempt to make certain forms of wartime speech illegal, this message depicted an overt limit to Constitutional ideals and guarantees, and more exactly suggested that Americans could lose those rights if they did not toe the line. Another prominent propaganda poster took those themes of speech and nation further still, wedding caricatured images of Hitler, Mussolini, and Tojo to the caption, "Don't Speak the Enemy's Language—Speak American." While the poster did not specify what exactly it would mean to "Speak American," the link to language certainly suggests an overt separation of "foreign languages" such as German, Italian, and Japanese from an implied "American language" of English—this despite the absence of any official language for the United States, and the presence of hundreds of thousands of Americans who spoke each of those languages. When intertwined with the fears of enemy spies and anti-American forces highlighted by many of these propagandistic texts, it's all too easy to imagine Americans who spoke those languages being viewed and defined as enemies of the United States.

Indeed, one of the era's and American history's most overtly exclusionary national policies depended on precisely such a myth of an American community's fundamentally foreign and hostile identity. Executive Order 9066, the February 19th, 1942 legal document through which the Roosevelt administration initiated the policy that came to be known as Japanese internment, opens with the rationale that "the successful prosecution of the war requires every possible protection against espionage and against sabotage." And in its conclusion the order connects those wartime home front fears to an exclusionary perspective on the Japanese American community, defining the policy's objective as "the conduct and control of alien enemies." Each of those last two words reflects a mythic definition of that Japanese American community, which as of 1940 numbered over 120,000 on the mainland and another 140,000 on the U.S. territory of Hawaii, with the majority in each setting born in the United States. Yet through that phrase "alien enemies" the executive order constructs imagined, interconnected images of foreignness and hostility and uses those elements to rationalize this exclusionary policy toward that sizeable, multi-generational American community.

Two of the era's many public voices offering support for that exclusionary policy reflect the layers of mythic patriotism upon which it depended. General John DeWitt, the commander of the wartime Western Defense Command, expressed a vision that entirely conflated Japanese Americans with the enemy nation upon whose destruction the war's success rested, testifying before Congress in early 1942 that "A Jap's a Jap. It makes no difference whether the Jap is a citizen or not. . . . I don't want any of them here. . . . We must worry about the Japanese all the time until he is wiped off the map." In a meeting with Karl Bendetsen, the Wartime Civil Control Administration official who would become the director of the internment program, DeWitt laid out the rationale behind such views, stating, "I have little confidence that the enemy aliens are law-abiding or loyal. . . . Particularly the Japanese. I have no confidence in their loyalty whatsoever." And in early 1943, when the Roosevelt administration was debating whether to change its policies and create Japanese American military regiments, DeWitt reiterated the absolute, unwavering certainty of his vision of this community as fundamentally anti-American, arguing, "there isn't such a thing as a loyal Japanese and it is just impossible to determine their loyalty by investigation—it just can't be done."

DeWitt's perspective might seem to be an extreme one, even within the era of Japanese internment. But more mainstream voices and texts likewise echoed those same mythic visions of the Japanese American community as ultimately outside of American identity. In a February 21st, 1942 *Los Angeles Times* editorial in support of internment, the editors wrote, "So, a Japanese American born of Japanese parents, nurtured upon Japanese traditions, living in a transplanted Japanese atmosphere and thoroughly inoculated with Japanese thoughts, Japanese ideas and Japanese ideals, notwithstanding his nominal brand of accidental citizenship almost inevitably and with the rarest exceptions grows up to be a Japanese, and not an American, in his thoughts, in his ideas and in his ideals, and himself is a potential and menacing, if not an actual, danger." After its initial clause recognizing the existence of Japanese American identity, this section of the editorial is particularly striking for its repetition of the word "Japanese," which is used seven times in this one sentence to create that overwhelming sense of this community's fundamental foreignness. That stark division, which culminates in "a Japanese, and not an American," becomes the grounding for the internment policy's essential argument, the belief that this community poses a danger to the United States.

Both that sense of danger and the policy based upon it were ostensibly tied to wartime contexts and concerns, and to what the Supreme Court called, in its 1944 *Korematsu v. United States* decision upholding internment's legality, "the military urgency of the situation." But these anti-Japanese myths, these exclusions of the community from a definition of American identity, extended well beyond the frames of internment and war. Perhaps the most troubling such extension was the acquittal of three white men accused of setting fire to a Japanese American family farm in Placer County, California on two different occasions in January 1945. Farmer Sumio Doi and his family had been released from internment earlier that month, but upon their return home were met with these repeated acts of racial terrorism. At the April 1945 trial, the arsonists' defense attorney more or less overtly admitted their guilt, arguing that their actions had been justified by a desire to keep the United States "a white man's country." And the entirely white jury apparently agreed with that mythic motivation, acquitting the men on all counts.

Both the Depression and World War II eras' fears of anti-American radicals, movements, and communities likewise extended into the post-war moment in an even more prominent and overarching way, with the emergence of the hugely influential mythic perspective expressed and embodied by Wisconsin Senator Joseph McCarthy. Despite McCarthy's central role in perpetuating and amplifying those myths, it's important to note that another vital source for that perspective, the tellingly named House Committee on Un-American Activities (HUAC), predated both McCarthy (who became a Senator in 1947) and the post-war period. HUAC, also known as the Dies Committee after its chair, Texas Representative Martin Dies Jr., was created as a special investigating committee in 1938, building upon and making more official the work of earlier Congressional committees such as the 1934–37 Special Committee on Un-American Activities to Investigate Nazi Propaganda and Certain Other Propaganda Activities. From the beginning, HUAC's investigations focused on fears of communism and targeted many of the period's most prominent American communities: student radicals, as illustrated by a 1939 investigation into the communist-affiliated American Youth Congress; New Deal artists, as illustrated by the 1938 subpoena of Federal Theatre Project director Hallie Flanagan to address communist influences on that project; and Japanese Americans, as illustrated by HUAC's infamous "Yellow Report" which made the case for internment based on a number of mythic arguments about Japanese loyalty to the empire.

When Senator McCarthy extended and amplified those investigations in the post-war period, he did so with the help of two interconnected mythic patriotic arguments. First, the World War II veteran McCarthy used propagandistic war stories to make the case for his own candidacy and governmental role. McCarthy had served as a Marine Corps intelligence officer and aviator between August 1942 and April 1945, and in the process received (or quite possibly gave himself) the nickname "Tail-Gunner Joe." When he ran for the Senate against incumbent Robert M. La Follette Jr., McCarthy criticized La Follette's lack of military service, although La Follette was 46 years old at the start of the war, and used the slogan "Congress needs a tail-gunner" to play up his own. He also created myths about his military service: an exaggerated number of aerial missions (32, rather than the actual number, 12) in order to qualify for a Distinguished Flying Cross; a broken leg that McCarthy referred to as a "war wound" but had in fact occurred during a shipboard celebration upon crossing the equator; and a letter of commendation that he claimed had been written by his commanding officer but turned out to have been written by McCarthy himself. None of these myths elide the reality of McCarthy's wartime experiences and service, but they reflect a willingness to create propaganda based on such real experiences in order to significantly bolster his own authority and arguments.

As he began making his overtly exclusionary arguments in early 1950, McCarthy did so through equally mythic images of a government and nation overrun by and fighting back against "enemies within." McCarthy used that phrase in a February 9th, 1950 speech to the Wheeling, West Virginia Republican Women's Club, an address in which he also produced "a list of names" of alleged "members of the Community Party . . . working and shaping policy in the State Department." As he turned that idea into the origin point for a four-year exclusionary crusade against "anti-American" forces and communities of all types, from communists and fellow travelers to leftist intellectuals and academics, artistic and cultural figures, homosexuals, and other "subversives," McCarthy linked that crusade to a mythic vision of an embattled American identity for which he was the consistent and chief champion. "McCarthyism is Americanism with its sleeves rolled," he argued in a 1952 speech during his successful reelection campaign, and he titled his book published later that year *McCarthyism: The Fight for America*.

While the celebratory patriotism of the "Greatest Generation" narrative depicted the battles of the Great Depression and World War II as collective efforts shared by all Americans, the period's myths instead envisioned a divided nation, one in which the defining battles positioned "loyal" Americans against dangerous anti-American forces and communities. As illustrated with particular clarity by both Japanese Internment and the McCarthy hearings, those exclusionary myths were more than just wartime propaganda, although during the war they certainly utilized that medium to support their perspective and implicate all Americans in these debates. They also and crucially connected to much broader myths of American identity, and had significant, lasting, and destructive effects on the American communities that they targeted.

Yet as has so often been the case, out of many of the same communities targeted by those myths—including Depression era protesters, anti-war activists, and Japanese Americans—came inspiring examples of active patriotism, of individuals and groups embodying, working for, and pushing the nation closer toward founding American ideals. These communities not only did not accept their absence from the national definition creation by the exclusionary myths, but through their actions revealed and modeled a distinct and more inclusive vision of America.

The protest community known as the Bonus Army came together in the first place because of a history of active patriotic service to the nation. The movement began with a group of World War I veterans, part of that war's Allied Expeditionary Force; hence their new name as the Bonus Expeditionary Force. After not being fully compensated at the time of their wartime service, WWI veterans had their payment once again deferred by the 1924 World War Adjusted Compensation Act, which paid them in Service Certificates that could not be redeemed until 1945. In May 1932, with the Depression nearing its lowest point, an Oregonian veteran named Walter Waters became determined to help his community receive this well-earned and long-overdue compensation, and began a march across the country to Washington to convince the federal government of their cause. In his 1933 book about the experience, *B.E.F.: The Whole Story of the Bonus Army*, co-written with journalist William C. White, Waters describes "the spontaneity which marked its rise and the great popular appeal which brought twenty thousand men [to] Washington in the first two weeks" as "something new in American life"; between 60,000 and 80,000 men and their families took part in the protest over its more than eight weeks of existence. He notes the United States Bureau of Investigation's attacks on the Bonus Army as "inspired, sponsored, and supported by Communists," calling these "slurs on honest, American ex-service men [that] must be corrected." Instead, Waters depicts the protests as very much in the spirit of the Revolution, arguing that "the event disclosed itself to thousands of American citizens who had never before thought particularly about it that the men whom they elect to represent them too often forget who it was that put them in power."

On July 28th, 1932, the Bonus Army's Anacostia Flats camp, also called by its participants a Hooverville to link it to those widespread Depression era communities of solidarity and resistance, met its tragic and violent end. But while the USBI's investigations and the U.S. Army's destruction of the camp reveal how mythic patriotism framed and responded to this community, the Bonus Army's active patriotic efforts and effects remain an essential part of the story as well. Those efforts produced an inspiringly organized and successful camp, one which featured streets and sanitation, daily parades and visiting dignitaries (such as Eleanor Roosevelt), and civic requirements for inhabitants. They inspired one of the period's most famous military leaders, the retired World War I Major General and most decorated Marine in U.S. history Smedley D. Butler, who gave a stirring speech to and in support of the Bonus Army, ending with a vision of their protests as part of an ongoing patriotic battle: "It's time you woke up—it's time you realized there's another war on. It's your war this time. Now get in there and fight." And despite the camp's destruction, the Bonus Army's patriotic efforts achieved significant short- and long-term goals: with the 1936 Adjusted Compensation Payment Act Congress finally paid the Service Certificates in full, and the Bonus Army was frequently invoked as a key inspiration for the post-World War II G.I. Bill, which supported that war's veterans far more fully and meaningfully than been the case for the World War I vets.

Just a few years after he addressed the Bonus Army, Butler became a leading voice for the nation's evolving anti-war, anti-fascism, and anti-imperialism movements. He began giving speeches to Veterans of Foreign Wars (VFW) organizations and other veterans' groups, making the same case he had made to the Bonus Army: that resisting these forces was the next stage in their ongoing, patriotic battle for the nation's and world's future. In 1935 he published a book, *War is a Racket*, which argued that far from advancing the nation's interests, a military leader such as himself too often served as "a racketeer; a gangster for capitalism." Although such anti-capitalist ideas comprised precisely the sort of radical perspective often defined in this era as un- and even anti-American, Butler not only argued the opposite, but in his November 1934 testimony before the House Special Committee on Un-American Activities helped expose an alleged conspiracy by business leaders to overthrow the Roosevelt administration and replace it with a fascist dictatorship. The scope of this alleged coup, known as the Business Plot, has never been entirely confirmed, but in the committee's report it acknowledged that there "was no question that these attempts were discussed, were planned, and might have been placed in execution," and that "your committee was able to verify all the pertinent statements made by General Butler, with the exception of the direct statement about the creation of the organization." In any case, Butler's principled, vocal, and successful opposition to these genuinely seditious forces illustrated one more layer to his ongoing active patriotic efforts throughout the decade.

As World War II began, and more exactly as the United States became involved in that global conflict, it grew more difficult for anti-war figures and communities to voice their perspectives, much less take action based on them, without being defined as anti-American or treasonous. But some continued to find ways to do so, and one of the most courageous such anti-war actions was undertaken by Montana Representative Jeannette Rankin. Rankin, the first woman to hold federal elected office, was one of a group in Congress who voted against Woodrow Wilson's World War I declaration of war, certainly not the majority stance but nonetheless part of a sizeable anti-war movement in that contested moment. After the Japanese bombed Pearl Harbor on December 7th, 1941, on the other hand, there were very few political or public figures willing to speak out in opposition to declaring war on a nation that had so blatantly and aggressively attacked the United States. But Rankin did so, becoming the only member of Congress to vote against the December 8th Declaration of War. While her lifelong pacifism was certainly a key factor in that striking choice, so too was her desire to highlight and challenge national inequalities, making the moment a distinctly active patriotic one as well. As Rankin put it when Congressional peers (some of whom hissed when she cast her vote) pushed her to change her vote to make it a unanimous declaration, "As a woman, I can't go to war, and I refuse to send anyone else."

While resisting the push for war thus comprised one way to offer active patriotic challenges to the era's myths, military service comprised another, particularly for members of American communities that had themselves all too consistently been the target of mythic perspectives. There were for example the Navajo code talkers, a community of military radio operators (some as young as 15 or 16 years old) recruited with the help of World War I veteran Philip Johnston, who had grown up on a Navajo reservation. The code talkers' work proved vital in the Pacific theater; as Marine signal officer Major Howard Connor later noted, "Were it not for the Navajos, the Marines would never have taken Iwo Jima." There were also the African American servicemen who comprised units like the renowned Tuskegee Airmen and the 761st Tank Battalion, a regiment known as the Black Panthers which General George Patton later called "one of the most effective tank battalions" in World War II. Although exclusionary attitudes kept the U.S. armed forces racially segregated throughout the war, these units and communities nonetheless exemplified the unified, active patriotic efforts without which the Allies could never have triumphed.

The war's most overt and inspiring active patriotic challenge to exclusionary myths came from Japanese American soldiers, however. I wrote about that community at length in my book *We the People*, and here I want to focus on a specific example of their patriotic perspective and service: the Varsity Victory Volunteers (VVV) in Hawaii. This group of Japanese American college students joined the Hawaii Territorial Guard (HTG) after the bombing of Pearl Harbor, but were expelled from the HTG due to their heritage. They challenged that decision, writing a letter to Territorial Governor Delos Emmons in which they argued, "Hawaii is our home; the United States, our country. We know but one loyalty and that is to the Stars and Stripes. We wish to do our part as loyal Americans in every way possible and we hereby offer ourselves for whatever service you may see fit to use us." Emmons accepted their request and the VVV (as they called themselves) became an integral part of the U.S. armed forces in both Hawaii and throughout the war effort, achieving the striking effects traced by historian Gwenfread Allen: "What followed afterward . . . was the natural result of the trend which was started in the early months of the war when a group of young men . . . demonstrated to a suspicious and skeptical community that the Americans of Japanese ancestry were every bit as American and every bit as loyal to this country and to her ideals as any other group of Americans."

Most of the VVV would go on to volunteer for the full Japanese American regiments formed after the U.S. military, inspired by the VVV's example, changed its exclusionary policy in early 1943; many thousands of soldiers likewise volunteered out of the internment camps. The largest such regiment, the 442nd Regimental Combat Team, would become by war's end the most decorated unit in American military history. Awarding them their third Presidential Citation in July 1946, President Truman noted, "You fought the enemy abroad and prejudice at home and you won." And indeed, like the Bonus Army and anti-war activists, these and other World War II soldiers not only exemplified active patriotic service, but did so in direct resistance to myths that sought to define them as outside of and even opposed to the United States.

Despite presenting such significant challenges to exclusionary myths, the active patriotic service of Americans like the VVV could nonetheless still be folded into overarching celebratory narratives like that of the "Greatest Generation." While it is indeed the case that all Depression and World War II era Americans played vital roles in those national and global battles, without collective memories of which our sense of that generation would risk replicating exclusionary myths, it's also important to remember and engage with Americans who offered critical patriotic perspectives in this period. In particular, a number of cultural and literary figures used their voices and texts both to highlight what was too often left out of national celebrations and to argue for alternative visions of the national community and ideals.

During the Depression, socially and politically radical artists and authors responded to that era's fraught and destructive histories by making the case for genuine resistance to and even revolution against the nation's hierarchies and power structures. Perhaps the most striking such artistic work was Mexican artist Diego Rivera's mural *Man at the Crossroads* (1933). Rivera was commissioned by John D. Rockefeller Jr. and his wife Abby Aldrich Rockefeller (a longtime patron of Rivera's) to paint a mural in the lobby of the main building of the newly completed Rockefeller Center in New York City, and the result was *Man at the Crossroads*, which contrasted communism with capitalism on either side of that titular figure, a symbolic representation of mankind's choices and future at this pivotal moment. When the *New York World-Telegram* newspaper called the mural "anti-capitalist propaganda," Rivera pushed back, adding images of Vladimir Lenin and a May Day parade; Rockefeller asked him to remove those images but Rivera refused, and Rockefeller had the mural plastered over and eventually removed entirely. In his May 1933 poem "I Paint What I See," the journalist and author E. B. White celebrated Rivera's artistic act of critical resistance, writing, *"I paint what I paint, I paint what I see,/I paint what I think,' said Rivera,/'And the thing that is dearest in life to me/In a bourgeois hall is Integrity'"* (White's italics).

A trio of groundbreaking American novelists and works likewise depicted what they saw and thought of the nation in this contested period, and wedded those often critical perspectives to patriotic visions of a more ideal collective future. John Dos Passos pulled together three historical novels— *The 42nd Parallel* (1930), *1919* (1932), and *The Big Money (1936)*—into *U.S.A.* (1938), a project which used experimental forms and structures such as "Newsreels" of historical events and biographies of prominent figures alongside conventional narrative sections to link his core group of fictional characters (representing American types such as World War I veterans, labor activists, Hollywood stars, and advertising executives) to overarching cultural and historical themes. In the concluding lines of a prologue written specifically for that combinatory edition, Dos Passos illustrates both the critical and patriotic sides of his vision of the titular nation, writing, "U.S.A. is a set of bigmouthed officials with too many bank accounts. U.S.A. is a lot of men in their uniforms buried in Arlington Cemetery. U.S.A is the letters at the end of an address when you are away from home. But mostly U.S.A. is the speech of the people." Although his characters consistently face the limits of America's hierarchies and oppressions, their persistent fights for their own and a collective future embody Dos Passos's determined belief in "the people" as exemplifying the nation's ideals.

Tom Joad, one of the protagonists of John Steinbeck's Depression era epic novel *The Grapes of Wrath* (1939), expresses a similar and even more impassioned belief in the people as the best of a collective community. Steinbeck's titular allusion to Julia Ward Howe's Civil War anthem is a telling one, as much of his novel depicts the Depression's divisions and destructions, both those experienced by the Joad family as they flee Dust Bowl Oklahoma for the mythic promise of California and the broader social and cultural horrors highlighted in the inter-chapters which frame the Joads' story. "I want to put a tag of shame on the greedy bastards who are responsible for this," Steinbeck noted of his goals for the novel, and much of it reflects that critical perspective potently and successfully. But in his closing speech in the novel, delivered to his mother before he sets out for a life of protest and activism, Tom Joad expresses a critically patriotic vision of the community he hopes to join and strengthen: "a fella ain't got a soul of his own, but on'y a piece of a big one—an' then—Then I'll be all aroun' in the dark. I'll be ever'where—wherever you look. Wherever they's a fight so hungry people can eat, I'll be there. Wherever they's a cop beatin' up a guy, I'll be there. . . . An' when our folks eat the stuff they raise an' live in the houses they build—why, I'll be there." In that moving speech, as in the novel's stunning final image—of Tom's sister, young Rose of Sharon Joad, who has just delivered a stillborn child, breastfeeding a starving stranger—Steinbeck offers a critically patriotic vision of an America worth fighting for and saving.

While the Joads experienced some of the worst of the period's oppressions and destructions, the Filipino immigrant, migrant laborer, and author Carlos Bulosan (1913–1956) experienced those and much more besides. Bulosan immigrated to the United States in 1930 at the age of 16, and for the next decade worked as a migrant laborer throughout the Western U.S., witnessing not only the economic and social hierarchies and divisions that Steinbeck depicts, but the era's exclusionary prejudice and violence targeting Filipino Americans, including constant police brutality, outbreaks of racial terrorism such as the 1930 Watsonville (California) massacre, and legal discriminations such as the 1934 Tydings–McDuffie Act and 1935 Filipino Repatriation Act. As I trace in my book *We the People*, those anti-Filipino exclusions were a defining element of early 20th century America, and reflect the ways in which the Depression's myths affected immigrant and minority communities with special force.

Bulosan documents all those exclusions and horrors in depth and with graphic detail in his first book, the autobiographical novel *America is in the Heart* (1946). But from its title on, that stunning work offers a critical patriotic perspective, one that refuses to turn away from all that Bulosan has experienced and witnessed, yet likewise refuses to abandon his fundamental belief in America's community and ideals. In the book's final lines, he expresses that vision of the nation with particular clarity and power: "It was something that grew out of the sacrifices and loneliness of my friends, of my brothers in America and my family in the Philippines—something that grew out of our desire to know America, and to become a part of her great tradition, and to contribute something toward her final fulfillment. I knew that no man could destroy my faith in America that had sprung from all our hopes and aspirations, *ever*" (Bulosan's emphasis). That final "our" is to my mind intentionally ambiguous, encompassing not only Bulosan's family and cultural community, but all those Americans whose struggles and hopes constitute the idealized nation that he, like Dos Passos and Steinbeck, imagines and contributes to.

Throughout this era, the artists and authors who took part in the community and movement known as the Harlem Renaissance contributed their own critical patriotic visions of American identity, and I'll end this chapter by highlighting two particularly critical patriotic Harlem Renaissance poems. In the opening four lines of his early sonnet "America" (1921), the Jamaican American poet, novelist, and journalist Claude McKay (1889–1948) comes up with pitch-perfect phrases through which to express that critically patriotic perspective: "Although she feeds me bread of bitterness,/And sinks into my throat her tiger's tooth,/Stealing my breath of life, I will confess/I love this cultured hell that tests my youth." And McKay goes on to depict himself as carrying forward the legacy of the American Revolution, writing that "as a rebel fronts a king in state,/I stand within her walls with not a shred/Of terror, malice, not a word of jeer." Portraying America's exclusionary power structure as a king is a deeply critical perspective on a nation founded on ideals of liberty and resistance to such tyranny. But McKay stands determined not just to challenge that power structure, but to embody an alternative America that can more genuinely live up to those ideals.

No single American text expresses both such critique and such patriotism more fully than a poem by McKay's Harlem Renaissance colleague and friend, Langston Hughes (1902–1967). The opening six stanzas of his magisterial poem "Let America Be America Again" (1936) both portray and challenge American ideals with clarity and power. Hughes alternates four-line stanzas that describe the nation's historic, mythologized ideals, "the dream it used to be" and "the dream the dreamers dreamed," with one-line, parenthetical responses from a critical African American perspective, challenges to those mythic patriotisms that include "(America never was America to me)" and "(There's never been equality for me, nor freedom in this 'homeland of the free.')"

Hughes moves from that bracing opening, through a series of stanzas which depict the American people in ways that parallel those of Dos Passos, Steinbeck, and Bulosan, up to culminating, critical patriotic images of a truly ideal, genuinely shared future: "O, let America be America again—/The land that never has been yet—/And yet must be—the land where *every* man is free" (Hughes's italics). And, finally, "O, yes,/I say it plain,/America never was America to me,/And yet I swear this oath—/America will be!"

Chapter Seven

The 1960s

Love It, Leave It, or Change It

In the summer of 1969, a pair of unique national celebrations reflected how American patriotism had evolved in the course of this tumultuous decade. On July 21st, the day after their Apollo 11 mission achieved the world's first successful moon landing, astronauts Neil Armstrong and Buzz Aldrin planted and saluted an American flag on the surface of the moon. A special NASA Committee on Symbolic Activities for the First Lunar Landing had been debating what to bring and leave behind on the moon since February, and had settled on an American flag. The action was meant to suggest not U.S. sovereignty over the moon but rather precise symbolism, a patriotic celebration of American achievement; to clarify that meaning, in November 1969 Congress included in an appropriations bill this statement: "The flag of the United States, and no other flag, shall be implanted or otherwise placed on the surface of the moon, or on the surface of any planet, by members of the crew of any spacecraft . . . as part of any mission . . . the funds for which are provided entirely by the Government of the United States. . . . This act is intended as a symbolic gesture of national pride in achievement and is not to be construed as a declaration of national appropriation by claim of sovereignty." Yet as we've seen throughout this book, symbolic, celebratory patriotism is a potent expression of collective identity and emphasis, and this lunar celebration echoed and extended the long history of those national ideals.

Just under a month later, on the morning of Monday August 18th, a very different collective celebration in Bethel, New York concluded with its own striking iteration of American patriotism. Woodstock, the music festival held on Max Yasgur's Bethel dairy farm (40 miles southwest of the town of Woodstock), had already over the prior three days become one of the decade's and nation's most iconic musical and cultural events. But the festival's final act, Jimi Hendrix with his newly re-named band Gypsy Sun and Rainbows, added an overtly American emphasis to their set, which had been pushed back from midnight Sunday to 9 A.M. Monday morning due to weather concerns: an extended, epic guitar rendition of "The Star-Spangled Banner." Hendrix, who had served in the U.S. Army's 101st Airborne Division for just over a year in the early 1960s (receiving an honorable discharge in June 1962), intended his anthem to offer in part a genuine, collective celebratory moment, later stating, "We're all Americans . . . it was like 'Go America!'" But at the same time, he used the musical elements of feedback and distortion to simulate bombs and explosions throughout his performance, rendering a version of the anthem that was clearly influenced by and reflective of the debates and divisions of its moment. As he put it, "We play it the way the air is in America today. The air is slightly static, see."

Hendrix's keen sense and performance of such static reflects deepening dissonances in the decade's competing visions of patriotism and national identity. The triumphs of the Space Program and initial preparations for the 1976 Bicentennial offered opportunities for celebratory patriotism, as in their more complex ways did the ongoing Cold War and the distinct but intertwined conflict in Vietnam. But the debates surrounding the latter conflict also produced phrases like "America: Love it or leave it," exclusions targeting anti-war protesters and other activists that were linked to broader myths such as the decade's ubiquitous cultural representations of Western and war stories. Those political and social protest movements themselves represented and expressed alternative, active forms of patriotism, embodiments of national ideals that challenged the decade's myths. And from the LGBT Rights and American Indian Movements to cultural figures like James Baldwin and Nina Simone, voices of critical patriotism offered visions of the nation that pushed back on the decade's celebrations and imagined a distinct path through the static and toward a more genuinely unified American future.

Two of the decade's most celebratory narratives can be highlighted through the same event: President John F. Kennedy's May 25th, 1961 address to a joint session of Congress. Kennedy had been inaugurated just a few months before, and was still in many ways the idealized figure whose presidency and administration would come to be defined in media coverage and popular consciousness, as well as in the administration's own propaganda, through such literally fantastic images as "Camelot." That specific Arthurian term and allusion would be most famously used to describe the administration by Kennedy's widow Jackie in a *Life* magazine interview given days after his November 1963 assassination, but it took hold as fully as it did because it reflected a number of foundational and ongoing images associated with the youthful, attractive Kennedy and his team. Moreover, Alan Jay Lerner and

Frederick Loewe's hit musical *Camelot* had debuted in October 1960, just a month before Kennedy would be elected president, and Lerner had been a Harvard classmate of Kennedy's. And after Kennedy's inauguration, it became public knowledge, through the administration's own statements as well as media coverage, that he frequently listened to the musical's original cast recording before bed, and that his favorite lines were from the final song, "Camelot (Reprise)," delivered by an aging King Arthur: "Don't let it be forgot/That once there was a spot,/For one brief, shining moment/That was known as Camelot."

Besides those legendary associations, Kennedy embodied mythic optimism and celebratory patriotism in other ways as well. At the time of his election, the 43-year-old Kennedy (1917–1963) was the youngest person ever elected to the presidency, succeeding the then-oldest man to have served as president (Dwight D. Eisenhower, who was inaugurated at 63 years old); Kennedy was also the first president born in the 20th century. Kennedy likewise wedded that representation of youth and a new generation of Americans to enduring celebratory ideals, as embodied most succinctly in his famous inaugural address line, "Ask not what your country can do for you—ask what you can do for your country." All those and other elements came together to create popular and enduring views of Kennedy and his administration as comprising an idealized form of the presidency and American government; those view complemented the stories which focused on his inspiring individual identity, such as journalist Ben Bradlee's 1964 book *That Special Grace*. And in the May 25th, 1961 address to Congress, one of his first prominent speeches as president, Kennedy developed a number of similarly idealized visions of the American future, collective goals which built on celebratory histories to imagine further progress.

Kennedy's address featured nine sections' worth of such goals, but it was Section IX: Space which drew much of the attention and helped initiate another of the decade's most prominent celebratory patriotisms. That section is best known for the pledge which led to the address's informal title as the "Moon Shot Speech": "I believe that this nation should commit itself to achieving the goal, before this decade is out, of landing a man on the moon and returning him safely to the Earth." But that emphasis on the goal of a moon landing takes up just one of the section's thirteen paragraphs, which focus far more fully on connecting space exploration and the accompanying scientific advancements to celebratory patriotism in an explicitly Cold War context. "If we are to win the battle that is now going on around the world between freedom and tyranny," Kennedy argues, "Now it is time to take longer strides—time for a great new American enterprise—time for this nation to take a clearly leading role in space achievement." Even the speech's moon-specific goals are linked to that frame, foreshadowing the July 1969 Apollo 11 flag-raising ceremony: Kennedy makes the case that, "in a very real sense, it will not be one man going to the moon—if we make this judgment affirmatively, it will be an entire nation."

Eighteen months later, Kennedy fleshed out both those arguments and their celebratory patriotic frames significantly further in a September 12th, 1962 speech at Rice University in Houston. He linked the goal of space exploration to a "capsule history of our progress," beginning as far back as William Bradford and the Plymouth Pilgrims, and then argued that "No nation which expects to be the leader of other nations can expect to stay behind in the race for space. . . . Those who came before us made certain that this country rode the first waves of the industrial revolutions, the first waves of modern invention, and the first wave of nuclear power, and this generation does not intend to founder in the backwash of the coming age of space. We mean to be a part of it—we mean to lead it . . . the vows of this Nation can only be fulfilled if we in this Nation are first, and, therefore, we intend to be first." And he once again defined the moon landing project specifically as an overtly national endeavor, praising his Rice University audience for "playing a part in putting a man on the moon as part of a great national effort of the United States of America."

That national effort was throughout the 1960s inextricably intertwined with overarching Cold War concerns, not only because of the Soviet Union's October 4th, 1957 successful launch of the Sputnik satellite which really began the space race, but also through Kennedy's consistent vision of American progress and achievements as directly driven by and contrasted with those of the U.S.S.R. In the Rice speech, for example, he noted of one such contested arena for progress that "Within these last 19 months at least 45 satellites have circled the earth. Some 40 of them were 'made in the United States of America' and they were far more sophisticated and supplied far more knowledge to the people of the world than those of the Soviet Union." The competition continued throughout the decade, and was still unfolding alongside the height of American achievement: two days before Apollo 11 arrived in lunar orbit, an unmanned Soviet spacecraft named Luna 15 entered the moon's atmosphere; the Soviet Union said only that its goals were to "conduct further scientific exploration of the Moon and space near the Moon," but it was clearly timed to coincide with the Apollo mission and perhaps gather lunar material before the U.S. astronauts could. The day after the Apollo astronauts planted their American flag, as they were en route back to Earth, Luna 15 crashed into the Moon's surface, an event reported to the astronauts by Mission Control, presumably to offer (since it was officially unrelated to their now-completed mission) one additional layer of patriotic celebration of their achievement.

Other, more overtly contested 1960s Cold War conflicts likewise offered opportunities for the creation and amplification of celebratory patriotisms. In his October 22nd, 1962 address to the American people during the Cuban Missile Crisis, for example, President Kennedy made the case for his administration's evolving response to that fraught moment by arguing that "The path we have chosen for the present is full of hazards, as all paths are—but it is the one most consistent with our character and courage as a nation and our commitments around the world. The cost of freedom is always high—and Americans have always paid it." Kennedy's successor, Lyndon B. Johnson, employed very similar language and frames in his August 4th, 1964 presidential address in the aftermath of the Gulf of Tonkin incident between the U.S. naval vessel *Maddox* and North Vietnamese forces, a highly contested encounter that Johnson framed as "open aggression on the high seas against the United States of America." He argued first that "the performance of commanders and crews in this engagement is in the highest tradition of the United States Navy," and then concluded his brief remarks with a recognition that "it is a solemn responsibility to have to order even limited military action by forces whose overall strength is as vast and as awesome as those of the United States of America." These and other Cold War episodes reflect the centrality of celebratory patriotic views of American ideals, past and present, to those evolving conflicts with the Soviet Union and its allies around the world.

As the decade moved toward its close, those celebratory patriotisms took on two distinct tones in conjunction with two unfolding national and international events. Representing a particularly idealized unifying tone were the preparations for the 1976 Bicentennial, which formally began with Congress's July 4th, 1966 creation of the American Revolution Bicentennial Commission (ARBC). While the ARBC initially sought to plan a single-city exposition (known as Expo '76) along the lines of the 1876 Centennial and 1893 World's Columbian Expositions, its emphasis gradually and thoroughly turned toward a vision of Americans celebrating the bicentennial across the nation, a shift that brought with it a slight name change to the American Revolution Bicentennial Administration (ARBA). One of the phrases found most consistently in their promotional materials, "What will you do for America's 200th birthday?," exemplifies that goal of connecting all Americans to these celebratory patriotic perspectives and efforts. And ARBA director and future Senator John W. Warner reiterated those interconnected goals of shared celebrations and patriotic unity, arguing that "the Bicentennial marks a major turning point for the United States and its people. Across the land, there is a renewed spirit of appreciation for the past and a dedication to improving the quality of life for all in the future. This spirit flows from the direct and active participation by millions of individuals in thousands of Bicentennial projects and events in their own communities." Or, as he also put it succinctly, "the success of the commemorations . . . will be judged on the number of participants, not the number of spectators."

In his own official Bicentennial message, President Gerald R. Ford framed the celebrations in similarly collective terms, noting that the occasion was "a time for celebration" but also an opportunity for all Americans to "pause and consider what our country means to us—and what it means to the world." Ford fleshed out those latter phrases with a series of idealized arguments about "what is unique about the American adventure," including an emphasis on the same idea of exploration that had driven Kennedy's vision of the space program: "The hallmark of the American adventure has been an eagerness to explore the unknown." Ford linked such explorations to a celebratory perspective on the Bicentennial's historic subject, noting that "Americans have also kept their faith in the wisdom and experience of the past, . . . our rich inheritance." And he defined these interconnected ideals as nothing less than "the foundation for American liberty," "the true meaning" of which was "embodied in our Declaration of Independence." In all these ways Ford's message pulled together the collective Bicentennial celebrations into a unifying vision of national ideals, past and present, on this historic anniversary.

In a telling sentence in his statement, John Warner did admit another part of the Bicentennial's contexts: that it "comes after a particularly difficult decade." One of the most divisive elements of that decade, the Vietnam War, had come to a definitive close just a year before the Bicentennial, with the July 1975 reunification of the nations of North and South Vietnam as a new country, the Socialist Republic of Vietnam. As has been the case with wars throughout American history, this one featured celebratory patriotic views through which Americans sought unity in response to this military conflict. But one of the most prominent such Vietnam era celebratory patriotisms, the ubiquitous phrase "Love it or leave it," represented a far more aggressive and divisive tone than did the Bicentennial preparations and celebrations. That phrase appeared on bumper stickers and billboards throughout this period, as well as in such cultural works as country artist Ernest Tubb's "It's America (Love it or Leave it)" (1970) and his country colleague Merle Haggard's "The Fightin' Side of Me" (1970), which begins, "I hear people talkin' bad,/About the way they have to live here in this country," and then argues, "They're running down a way of life/Our fightin' men have fought and died to keep/ If you don't love it, leave it." This phrase's version of celebratory patriotism was one overtly defined in opposition to criticisms of the nation, and indeed one that portrayed an idealized celebratory patriotism as a necessary element to being part of the United States at all.

The May 8th, 1970 "Hard Hat Riot" in New York City illustrated with stark clarity the effects of that aggressive celebratory stance. Hundreds of college and high school students had gathered at an early morning anti-war protest and memorial for the four Kent State University students who had been killed by National Guardsman on May 4th. Around noon, a group of around two hundred construction workers, many carrying American flags and signs with slogans like "America, love it or leave it" and "All the way, USA" attacked the protesters with clubs, steel-toed boots, and other weapons. Hours of violent clashes left nearly one hundred protesters injured and made clear the mythic logic behind and endpoint of the "love it or leave it" celebratory patriotic sentiment. If the space program, the Cold War, and the Bicentennial offered opportunities for unifying celebratory patriotism, the Hard Hat Riot illustrated the close connections between such celebratory views and the decade's painful national divisions.

That violent event also illustrates how easily and fully the decade's ostensibly unifying celebratory patriotisms could be and too often were transformed into mythic patriotisms instead, idealized stories of the nation that sought to literally and figuratively push out Americans whose perspectives or identities did not seem to comport with the myths. Conflicts over the Vietnam War like those surrounding the Hard Hat Riot provided a number of sources for these 1960s and early 1970s myths, but so too did broader cultural and social trends in the period, from the prevalence and popularity of Westerns and war stories to evolving perspectives on riots and crime in American cities.

Some of the period's most overtly mythic views were those which targeted members of the anti-war movement, along with the distinct but parallel social movement known as hippies, a group sometimes distinguished from anti-war protesters as hippies were thought to be uninterested in politics or protest. These mythic perspectives instead linked the two communities, defining them both as fundamentally outside of and even opposed to national values. Many of those myths were slipped into broader cultural conversations about these movements, as illustrated by a telling line from "The Flowering of the Hippies," an article by journalist Mark Harris published in the September 1967 issue of *The Atlantic*: "'Sorry, I've got to go panhandle,' I heard a hippie lady say, which was not only against the law but against the American creed, which holds that work is virtue, no matter what work you do." While it's not clear whether Harris agrees with that last sentiment or not—his portrayal of the movement is somewhat sympathetic but ultimately dismissive—it in any case offers a particular, mythic interpretation of "the American creed," of our founding national ideals. And this interpretation diverges significantly from an emphasis on "life, liberty, and the pursuit of happiness," all of which the hippie movement could be said to be directly in search of, in order to put this movement's goals at odds with those mythic ideals.

Arguments targeting the anti-war movement went even further in their mythic patriotic critiques. President Lyndon Johnson saw military service as perhaps the single most defining element of shared American patriotism, writing in a message to Congress on the subject of a Vietnam War draft that "we must continue to ask one form of service—military duty—of our young men. We would be an irresponsible Nation if we did not—and perhaps even an extinct one." Concurrently, Johnson saw much of the anti-war movement's efforts, and specifically its prominent collective actions like burning or discarding draft cards, as not a form of legitimate protest but instead as profoundly un-American, and he pushed Congress to clarify that such activities were also explicitly illegal. Congress did so with the 1965 Draft Card Mutilation Act, an amendment to the Selective Service Act; when anti-war protester David Paul O'Brien burned his card in opposition to this law and was arrested, the Supreme Court used similar arguments about national identity and security to uphold the law as constitutional. Writing for the 7–1 majority in that *United States v. O'Brien* (1968) decision, Chief Justice Earl Warren defined protests like O'Brien's as opposed to both the Constitution and American interests, arguing, "We think it clear that a government regulation is sufficiently justified if it is within the constitutional power of the Government [and] if it furthers an important or substantial government interest."

Complementing and extending such governmental and legal attacks on anti-war protesters were broader cultural myths that depicted the movement as fundamentally opposed to American ideals, ideals that were often, as in Johnson's statement, directly linked to military service. Perhaps the most telling, as well as the most constructed, of those myths is the story that protesters spit on returning Vietnam War veterans in airports and other public settings. In his book *The Spitting Image: Myth, Memory, and the Legacy of Vietnam* (1998), Vietnam vet and sociologist Jerry Lembcke traces at length the development and persistence of that myth, despite what Lembcke notes is a thoroughgoing absence of documentation or journalistic evidence for such actions from protesters. Indeed, the only consistent source for this myth is the kind of anecdotal evidence illustrated by Lembcke's first epigraph, from Vietnam vet Barry Streeter: "My flight came in at San Francisco airport and I was spat upon three times: by hippies, by a man in a leisure suit, and by a sweet little old lady who informed me I was an 'Army Asshole.'" While individual testimonies like Streeter's can't be discounted, they are not only the sole form of evidence for this myth, but are themselves countered by the testimonies of numerous other veterans, including Lembcke himself. Yet the spitting story has not only endured but become a central element to collective memories of the Vietnam War era and its anti-war movement, a testament to the power of such myths depicting protesters and veterans as contrasting and hostile forces within 1960s American society, rather than positioning them as potential allies, an idea for which Lembcke argues throughout his book.

Those myths of anti-war Americans reached their peak with the hostility directed at actress and activist Jane Fonda. Fonda had been involved with the anti-war movement since the late 1960s, and in 1970 along with author Fred Gardner and actor Donald Sutherland formed the group "Free the Army" (FTA), which toured the U.S. speaking to military members about their prospective wartime service. But it was after her July 1972 trip to North Vietnam to see first-hand the war's effects, and specifically after she was photographed sitting on an anti-aircraft gun in the course of those travels, that she became the target of sustained attacks that depicted her as nothing short of a traitor. Indeed, the Veterans of Foreign Wars (VFW) called for Fonda, now nicknamed "Hanoi Jane" by such antagonist voices, to be put on trial for treason, and some lawmakers took the request seriously; the Maryland state legislature, for example, debated whether to ban Fonda's films and the actress herself from their state. These attacks also associated Fonda with the spitting myth: at the time, as unsubstantiated rumors circulated that Fonda had spit upon U.S. prisoners of war during her time in North Vietnam, a charge that both she and POWs have thoroughly debunked; and in the decades since, as when veteran Michael Smith spit on Fonda during a 2005 book signing for her autobiography *My Life So Far* and told reporters, "she spit in our faces for 37 years. . . . There are a lot of veterans who would love to do what I did." These connections of Fonda's individual case to the broader myths of spitting protesters makes clear how much those latter myths depend on definitions of the anti-war movement as fundamentally un-American and even treasonous to the nation's identity and ideals.

Given those myths, it's worth noting one particularly striking detail of how Fonda has herself told the story of the anti-aircraft gun moment, linking it to her critical patriotism as an American. In a 2011 piece entitled "The Truth about My Trip to Hanoi," she writes, "The translator told me that the soldiers wanted to sing me a song. He translated as they sung. It was a song about the day 'Uncle Ho' declared their country's independence in Hanoi's Ba Dinh Square. I heard these words: 'All men are created equal; they are given certain rights; among these are life, Liberty and Happiness.' These are the words Ho pronounced at the historic ceremony. I began to cry and clap. 'These young men should not be our enemy. They celebrate the same words Americans do.'" This moment certainly represented its own form of mythic patriotism from the North Vietnamese, both about their newly independent nation's histories and about its fraught relationship with the United States.

But Fonda's effort to bridge the gap between the two competing views and nations reflects, as did all of her anti-war activism, a challenge not just to the ongoing Vietnam War, but to precisely the kinds of mythic patriotisms that depict such anti-war efforts as antithetical to—as spitting in the face of—the nation's ideals.

Beyond the specific context of these anti-war figures and moments, 1960s cultural works also helped create such mythic patriotisms. Not at all coincidentally, the deepening American involvement in the Vietnam War was accompanied by a rise in popular films about wartime heroism, most of them set during World War II: the epic star-studded *The Battle of the Bulge* (1965), the more intimate Frank Sinatra vehicle *Von Ryan's Express* (1965), and the gritty *The Dirty Dozen* (1967) illustrate the different layers of this mid- to late '60s filmmaking trend. Besides their World War II setting, what links such disparate films is an overarching emphasis on war's ability to bring out true patriotism and heroism from all involved, one exemplified by *The Dirty Dozen*'s story of a team of convicted, hardened criminals, many of them facing death sentences, turned war heroes. *The Dirty Dozen*'s final voiceover notes that for all the men who died in the culminating attack on a Nazi fortress (which is all but one of them), letters were sent to their next of kin which read, "They lost their lives in the line of duty," reflecting how such stories of wartime patriotism can turn even social outcasts into idealized heroes.

Perhaps the decade's most explicitly mythic war film was also one of the only ones to depict the Vietnam War: *The Green Berets* (1968). Although it originated with a 1965 novel by Robin Moore, the film adaptation truly took off after John Wayne, frustrated with the burgeoning anti-war movement, visited South Vietnam in 1966 and became determined to produce a film depicting the heroism of U.S. special forces. Wayne would co-direct as well as star in the film, turning down a lead role in *The Dirty Dozen* to do so and buying out the novelist Moore in order to make the film in precisely the ways he wanted to. He also obtained full cooperation and a great deal of military material from President Johnson and the Department of Defense, which in turn meant that the government had final script approval among other significant influences on the resulting film. The tagline in a theatrical poster for the film reflects its overt challenge to anti-war views: "So you don't believe in glory. And heroes are out of style. And they don't blow bugles anymore. So take another look—at the special forces in a special kind of hell—THE GREEN BERETS." And the film's most prominent character arc, the conversion of cynical anti-war journalist George Beckworth (David Janssen) into an impassioned advocate for the special forces who at one point even picks up a rifle and fights alongside them, illustrates quite clearly the mythic patriotic effects the film hoped to have on American audiences. "Out here," Wayne's

Colonel Mike Kirby famously tells Beckworth, "due process is a bullet," and we are meant to applaud this abandonment of founding, Constitutional American ideals.

The film's closing credits feature another such mythic patriotic cultural work, the popular 1966 song "The Ballad of the Green Berets." Performed by Special Forces Staff Sgt. Barry Sadler and co-written by Sadler and *Green Berets* novelist Robin Moore (who helped Sadler get a recording contract with RCA), "Ballad" was one of 1966's surprise smash hits, staying at #1 on *Billboard* magazine's Hot 100 chart for five weeks, becoming that magazine's number one single for the year, and forming part of Sadler's 12-song album *Ballads of the Green Berets*. Written in part to honor Specialist James Gabriel Jr., one of the first American soldiers killed in Vietnam when he was shot by the Viet Cong during an April 1962 training mission with the South Vietnamese army, "Ballad" depicts its title subjects as the literal embodiment of national ideals, as in its chorus's repeated lines: "Silver Wings upon their chest/These are men, America's best." And in the song's final verse and chorus, when it turns to the more specific story of a fallen Green Beret, it illustrates as well the ways such patriotic views are created and communicated to broader audiences, with that soldier's "last request" to his "young wife": "Put Silver Wings on my son's chest/Make him one of America's best." It's difficult to critique any tribute to a fallen soldier—but in that same concluding moment, that soldier is described as having "died for those oppressed," which is at best a limited and in many ways a mythic and inaccurate vision of America's involvement in the Vietnam War.

In his June 26th, 1968 zero-star review of *The Green Berets*, *Chicago Sun-Times* film critic Roger Ebert critiqued the film's similarly inaccurate portrayal of that war, writing, "At this moment in our history, locked in the longest and one of the most controversial wars we have ever fought, what we certainly do not need is a movie depicting Vietnam in terms of cowboys and Indians." That last phrase is a particularly telling one, and not just because by 1968 John Wayne was best known for his roles in three decades of iconic Westerns and certainly brought much of that genre experience to his directing work on *The Green Berets*; when the film's Hungarian American composer Miklós Rózsa initially turned down the job, stating "I don't do Westerns," the producers replied, "It's not a Western, it's an 'Eastern.'" The parallels between *Green Berets* and the genre of the Western also help us recognize that genre's resurgent 1960s role and contributions to the decade's myths of American history and identity.

John Wayne himself starred in half a dozen of the decade's hundreds of Western films, including the controversial historical epic *The Alamo* (1960) which, like *The Green Berets*, he developed and financed himself in order to make it reflect his perspective on American history as closely as possible. Of that group, his 1961 film *The Comancheros*, on which Wayne took over as director when Michael Curtiz became ill, particularly reflects the genre's simplistic and too-often exclusionary depiction of Native Americans. Wayne's Texas Ranger pursues wanted fugitive Paul Regret (Stuart Whitman) from Louisiana into the Texas Republic of 1843, where they eventually team up to fight against a much more dangerous force: the titular criminal gang, one of whose chief crimes is smuggling guns and whiskey to the region's Comanche nation. The gang's and film's name alone reflects the way in which association and alliance with that Native American community is enough to deem this group the villains, despite one of the film's heroes being a fugitive who has killed a man in a duel and the other (Wayne's Captain Jake Cutter) being a member of a paramilitary organization that has throughout its histories been consistently associated with exclusionary violence against Mexican Americans and Native Americans. Eventually Cutter and Regret find themselves fighting directly against the Comanches, but those culminating physical battles only reinforce the rhetorical exclusion that the name and title have already constructed.

Some of the decade's most influential Westerns were Italian director Sergio Leone's trilogy of groundbreaking "Spaghetti Westerns" starring Clint Eastwood. Eastwood had risen to prominence through his heroic role as Rowdy Yates in the more conventional television Western *Rawhide* (1959–1965), one of the period's many popular such TV Westerns. His characters in Leone's films—*A Fistful of Dollars* (1964), *For a Few Dollars More* (1965), and *The Good, the Bad and the Ugly* (1966)—were far more complex and anti-heroic than Rowdy, reflecting some of the decade's evolving debates about heroism and violence. Yet these films construct their own exclusionary myths, and not simply those toward Mexican and Native Americans, although that element remains present. In the Civil War-set *The Good, The Bad and the Ugly*, for example, the chief villain (Lee Van Cleef's Angel Eyes) is a sadistic Union Army officer working within a system of horrific Union prisons, and the two heroes (Eastwood's bounty hunter Blondie and Eli Wallach's bandit Tuco) are first depicted pretending to be Confederate soldiers and throughout the film are searching for Confederate gold. Leone argued that these elements were intended to "show the absurdity of war . . . the Civil War which the characters encounter. In my frame of reference, it is useless, stupid: it does not involve a 'good cause.'" But even if we elide the war's actual causes, the film goes further still in its mythic portrayals of that conflict and era, depicting the Union side as far more villainous, as indeed the "bad" in the titular trio.

Five years after *Good*, Eastwood would star in *Dirty Harry* (1971), the first of five films featuring iconic police inspector and action hero Harry Callahan (a role initially offered to none other than John Wayne). Harry's targets, in that first film and throughout the series, are a combination of dangerous, psychopathic criminals and official and governmental bureaucrats whose concerns about rules and civil rights make it more difficult for Callahan to stop those criminals. In *Dirty Harry*, for example, Callahan's initial arrest of the villain Scorpio is thrown out because he used torture and other illegal methods to gain information, but Callahan continues to use these "dirty," and in the film's portrayal entirely justified, methods to get his man. But besides the film's dismissal of those Constitutional American rights and values, it and the entire Dirty Harry series also reflect another of the era's myths: fears of rising crime, especially in the nation's urban communities.

Those fears were driven in part by the decade's frequent, prominent urban riots, from those in Watts, California in 1965 to those in many cities across the spring and summer of 1968. While the contexts and causes of those riots were inextricably linked to the civil rights movement, they were often framed in media and popular culture perspectives alongside these myths of rising crime rates and increasingly unsafe urban communities. From ubiquitous cultural depictions of muggings as a scourge of urban life to the re-christening of neighborhoods with extreme names like Boston's Combat Zone, these images all formed part of an overarching myth of "decivilization" (as social psychologist Steven Pinker has termed it). Whether through attacks on anti-American protesters or fears of disintegrating cities and communities, these 1960s mythic patriotisms contrasted a nation seemingly falling apart with the idealized America that they portrayed and sought to preserve.

Yet in contrast to those mythic fears, every prominent 1960s social movement could also and, I would argue, more accurately be described as active patriotism on behalf of the national community, as part of what John Warner in his Bicentennial statement called "a dedication to improving the quality of life for all in the future." Here I'll focus briefly on examples from three of those active patriotic activist efforts: the anti-war, civil rights, and Chicano Rights movements, each of which directly challenged those exclusionary myths and offered an alternative, inclusive vision of American history and ideals.

Exemplifying the active patriotism of the anti-war movement is an organization whose very existence challenges myths such as the image of spitting, anti-veteran protesters: Vietnam Veterans Against the War (VVAW). Founded by six veterans who met at the April 15th, 1967 "Spring Mobilization to End the War" protest in New York, the VVAW became a vital force in raising awareness about the war's realities for both American soldiers and the Vietnamese. As the VVAW's own history summarizes its active patriotic origins and goals, "We believe that service to our country and communities did not end when we were discharged. We remain committed to the struggle for peace and for social and economic justice for all people. We will continue to oppose senseless military adventures and to teach the real lessons of the Vietnam War. We will do all we can to prevent another generation from being put through a similar tragedy and we will continue to demand dignity and respect for veterans of all eras. This is real patriotism and we remain true to our mission."

In April 1971, the VVAW organized one of its most prominent efforts, a four-day protest in Washington, DC named "Operation Dewey Canyon III" in ironic tribute to two U.S. military invasions of both North Vietnam and, more controversially and perhaps illegally, the neighboring nation of Laos. This "limited incursion into the country of Congress" featured a number of significant actions and moments, but it was at an April 19th Memorial Service at Arlington National Cemetery that Reverend Jackson H. Day, a former 4th Infantry Chaplain, articulated the event's and organization's active and critical patriotic perspective most clearly. Quoting a survivor of the My Lai massacre who noted that "always before, the Americans brought medicine and candy," Day added, "I believe there is something in all of us that would wave a flag for the dream of an America that brings medicine and candy, but we are gathered here today, waving no flags, in the ruins of that dream." Yet if the Vietnam War all too consistently laid bare the ruins and failures of our national ideals, the VVAW itself embodied the continued legacy of those ideals, and more exactly an active patriotic effort to fight for those ideals on the home front.

While VVAW was initially somewhat specific in time and focus, the era's civil rights movement spanned nearly two decades and featured countless activisms and battles across numerous issues and arenas, as well as a wide variety of voices and perspectives. Here I'll highlight two particular efforts and communities that exemplify distinct sides to the movement's active patriotic perspectives and goals. One of the movement's central goals was to give African Americans the same rights that had been defined as core American principles since the Revolution; that goal was potently illustrated by the push for voting rights, which had been legally promised to African American men since the 15th Amendment in 1870 and women since the 19th in 1920 but had in practice consistently been denied. In his prominent early speech "Give Us the Ballot," delivered at the May 17th, 1957 Prayer Pilgrimage for Freedom demonstration in Washington, Martin Luther King Jr. both expressed that goal clearly and linked it to an active patriotic vision of African American and American identity. He opens by noting that "The denial of this sacred right is a tragic betrayal of the highest mandates of our democratic tradition." In the speech's most famous section, he lists a series of politically and socially progressive results (for all Americans) that will follow if you "Give us the ballot." And he concludes with an overarching, idealized vision of how such fights for African American rights constitute as well active patriotism on behalf of the nation's future: "when the history books are written in the future, the historians will have to look back and say, 'There lived a great people . . . a people who injected new meaning into the veins of civilization; a people which stood up with dignity and honor and saved Western civilization in her darkest hour; a people that gave new integrity and a new dimension of love to our civilization.'"

Since voting represents one of the most consistent ways all citizens can participate in and help shape American democracy and society, arguments and fights for voting rights comprise a clear and logical example of active patriotic efforts. My second such example from the civil rights movement, the Black Panthers, is perhaps a less obvious one, at least when it comes to U.S. patriotism; the Panthers were linked to the era's Black Nationalist movement, which at its extremes argued for African American separation from American communities and identity. But in many of their programs the Panthers unquestionably modeled an active patriotic vision of African American rights and goals. Take their famous founding emphasis on guns, for example: not only did the Panthers argue that this reflected another extension of a Constitutional right long denied to African Americans, the 2nd Amendment's "right to bear arms"; but they also carried those guns as part of "citizen patrols," an aggressive but fundamentally civic vision of Americans protecting their own neighborhoods and communities (the organization's full name was originally the Black Panther Party for Self-Defense). As the Panthers grew they extended their civic efforts to many other social settings and issues, as embodied by the Free Breakfast for Children Program, begun in Oakland in January 1969 and then developed throughout the country. This program reflected the Panthers' evolving desire not just to protect American communities in the present, but to help them move into a collective future more successfully; in their outreach efforts to local businesses and families, the Panthers emphasized that the program would help children "grow and intellectually develop because children can't learn on empty stomachs." And the breakfast program comprises one of the Panthers' most enduring active patriotic legacies, as it was a direct inspiration for the longstanding program throughout American public schools that offers free breakfast (and often lunch as well) to children in need.

The Black Panthers specifically and the civil rights movement more generally helped inspire a number of other, parallel organizations and efforts on behalf of historically oppressed and under-represented American communities. All these parallel movements likewise fought to extend founding American principles and rights to their communities and thus to all Americans. A particularly striking example of that active patriotic goal was the Mexican American Legal Defense and Educational Fund (MALDEF), part of the era's broader Chicano Rights Movement. MALDEF was founded in San Antonio, Texas in 1968, by a group of lawyers and community activists seeking "to create a legal organization to serve the Latino community." It received a Ford Foundation Grant with the direct support of two longstanding, active patriotic civil rights organizations: the NAACP, and specifically its Legal Defense and Educational Fund (LDF); and the League of United Latin American Citizens (LULAC), which was founded in 1929 by a group of Hispanic American World War I veterans. In the words of the organization's founding and enduring mission, MALDEF's "commitment is to protect and defend the rights of all Latinos living in the United States and the constitutional rights of all Americans."

In its more than 50 years of existence, MALDEF has fought for numerous rights, but its first significant legal victory was a particularly telling one. 192 Hispanic American students at Hidalgo, Texas's Edcouch-Elsa High School had been expelled after they boycotted classes, a walkout and protest intended to force the local school board to hear their testimonies on anti-Latino discrimination and abuse in the public schools. MALDEF helped them bring their case to court, where a judge ruled that the expulsion had violated the students' constitutional right to protest. Both the walkout and the legal defense exemplified these 1960s active patriotic efforts, inspiring protests and battles that collectively sought to push America's schools, communities, government, and society closer to our founding ideals.

Active patriotic voices like those of the VVAW, King and the Black Panthers, and the Chicano Rights Movement certainly highlighted America's historical and ongoing problems as part of their arguments for moving the nation forward more successfully. But some of the era's social movements and activists made such critical perspectives on the gap between the nation's ideals and its realities even more central to their efforts and arguments. For these critical patriotisms, offered by voices as diverse as the American Indian Movement, the LGBT Rights Movement, and artists such as James Baldwin and Nina Simone, genuine progress would only be possible if Americans could honestly confront and challenge the nation's fundamental and enduring flaws and failures.

The American Indian Movement (AIM), founded in July 1968 in Minneapolis, dedicated much of its early actions and activism to highlighting the historical horrors experienced by Native Americans at the hands of the U.S. government, in an attempt to move the nation toward a more genuinely collective future. As they put it in their founding statement of purpose, "The American Indian Movement is attempting to connect the realities of the past with the promise of tomorrow." One of their signature efforts, the October 31st, 1972 Trail of Broken Treaties 20-point position paper and subsequent protest march across the country to Washington, DC, embodied both sides of that critical patriotic goal: highlighting the long history of lies, abuse, and destruction symbolized by such broken treaties; and doing so in search of "a new American majority, . . . which by conscience is committed toward prevailing upon the public will in ceasing wrongs and doing right." "For our part," AIM's Preamble to that proposal added, "we propose to produce a rational, reasoned manifesto for construction of an Indian future in America. If America has maintained faith with its original spirit, or may recognize it now, we should not be denied."

As with the civil rights movement's push for voting rights, however, AIM also focused on efforts intended to make it more possible for Native Americans to exercise their own active patriotic rights as American citizens. Their July 1968 statement of "Original Objectives" began with "our main objective": "to solicit and broaden opportunities for the urban Indian in order that he may enjoy his full rights as a citizen of these United States." Two of their specific objectives expanded upon that goal: "to establish a program to educate the Indian citizen in his responsibility to his community"; and "to encourage Indian Americans to become active in community affairs." They pursued those objectives in part through education, founding institutions like the St. Paul, Minnesota Red School House and the Minneapolis Heart of the Earth Survival School (HOTESS) that emphasized cultural and historical awareness in order to better prepare young Native Americans for navigating life in 20th century America. And when viewed in conjunction with these civic objectives, AIM's famous protest actions, such as the 1969–1971 occupation of Alcatraz Island and the 1972 sit-in at the Bureau of Indian Affairs headquarters in Washington, were more than just acts of civil disobedience to raise collective awareness of historical and ongoing oppressions. They were also models of Native American critical patriotism, of activists using their bodies, voices, and collective spirit to reflect what is possible when individuals and communities become active in local and national affairs.

Histories of the era's LGBT rights movement often define it as arising in response to a specific, contemporary atrocity and oppression: the June 28th, 1969 police raid on New York City's Stonewall Inn (a prominent Greenwich Village gay bar). But while that moment and the resulting riots did provide a significant spark for and attention to a nationwide LGBT rights movement, they were far from the decade's first such activisms. One of the earliest and most overtly critical patriotic 1960s LGBT rights protests took place outside

Philadelphia's Independence Hall on July 4th, 1965. Organized by a courageous group of activists called the Gay Pioneers, this first of what would
become known as the Annual Reminder Marches was very purposefully held
in that historically significant location on that nationally symbolic occasion;
as one of its participants, Reverend Robert Wood, put it, "We were picket-
ing for freedom and equal rights, and the Liberty Bell was a great symbol."
Another local LGBT rights activist, Cuban American immigrant Ada Bello,
expressed that critically patriotic perspective directly: "The marches were to
convey to everybody that we were just as entitled as any citizen to have our
rights respected."

A few months after that first Annual Reminder March, the San Francisco
priest and activist Adrian Ravarour founded Vanguard, a community organization inspired by the civil rights movement and dedicated to critical patriotic advocacy and activism for LGBT rights. The Reverend Larry Mamiya,
an ally of the organization through its relationship with the city's radical
Glide Memorial Methodist Church, describes those emphases and goals in
his memoir: "At that time, I did not know about the background of Adrian's
founding philosophy, which included Mohandas Gandhi and the Rev. Dr.
Martin Luther King, Jr. among others. . . . In retrospect, Vanguard can be
seen as the spearhead of a nonviolent social change movement of young gay
people, the first in the nation dedicated to bringing about social justice and
equal rights." A year later, Vanguard helped organize and support one of
the decade's most influential LGBT protests, the August 1966 Compton's
Cafeteria Riot, in which a group of transgender activists, drag queens, and
their allies fought back against the consistent discrimination and police harassment and brutality they faced in the city's Tenderloin district. In her book
Transgender History (2008), scholar Susan Stryker calls the riot "the first
known incident of collective militant queer resistance to police harassment in
U.S. history," and notes that the protests, coupled with a number of ongoing
Vanguard community service efforts in the neighborhood, pushed the city to
"begin addressing them as citizens rather than as a problem to be removed."

If such organizations and collective protests represented one crucial thread
of 1960s critical patriotic activism, individual artistic and cultural voices
expressed and embodied another vital form of critical patriotism. Perhaps no
American artist has better or more consistently articulated and advocated for
the importance of such a critical patriotic perspective than did the author and
civil rights activist James Baldwin (1924–1987). I used as the epigraph for
this book one of Baldwin's most succinct and striking expressions of critical patriotism, from his influential early essay collection *Notes on a Native
Son* (1955): "I love America more than any other country in the world, and,
exactly for this reason, I insist on the right to criticize her perpetually." In a

new preface for the 1984 edition of that collection, Baldwin links that critical patriotic perspective even more overtly to both his personal and professional goals and their complex but inescapable relationship to American history and national ideals: "I was trying to locate myself within a specific inheritance and to use that inheritance, precisely, to claim the birthright from which that inheritance had so brutally and specifically excluded me."

Baldwin would expand and amplify that critical patriotism in virtually every moment and stage of his multi-faceted career, but no single event better reflects that perspective than his October 26th, 1965 debate with the conservative journalist William F. Buckley Jr. at Cambridge University's Cambridge Union Society. The question they debated was "Is the American Dream at the expense of the American Negro?," and Baldwin took the affirmative position, if with all the nuance and thoughtfulness he brought to every topic and text. He describes his first youthful realizations about the gaps between national ideals and his own identity, noting that "it comes as a great shock to discover that the country which is your birthplace and to which you owe your life and your identity, has not, in its whole system of reality, evolved any place for you." He highlights the desperate need to collectively recognize those gaps, arguing, "What is crucial here is that unless we can manage to accept, establish some kind of dialogue between those people whom I pretend have paid for the American dream and those other people who have not achieved it, we will be in terrible trouble." And he concludes by envisioning what will happen if we cannot follow that critically patriotic perspective into a more genuinely shared future: "Until that moment, until the moment comes when we, the Americans, we, the American people, are able to accept the fact, that I have to accept, for example, that my ancestors are both white and Black. That on that continent we are trying to forge a new identity for which we need each other and that I am not a ward of America. I am not an object of missionary charity. I am one of the people who built the country—until this moment there is scarcely any hope for the American dream, because the people who are denied participation in it, by their very presence, will wreck it."

If Baldwin provided some of the civil rights movement's most important literary and oratorical critical patriotic texts, his contemporary Nina Simone (1933–2003) created some of its most compelling and effective musical expressions. No song of Simone's embodies her critical patriotic perspective on race and America more fully than her first such civil rights anthem, "Mississippi Goddam," included along with another civil rights track, "Old Jim Crow," on her 1964 album *Nina Simone in Concert*. Written in response to two horrific 1963 events, the June murder of civil rights leader Medgar Evers and the September bombing of a Birmingham church that killed four young black girls, "Mississippi Goddam" came to Simone, she would later reflect, "in a rush of fury, hatred, and determination." From its title on, the song levels its righteous anger at a wide range of subjects, from those white supremacist-dominated Southern states, to the ostensibly supportive voices that urge African Americans to "go slow," to the entire nation itself. "Oh but this whole country is full of lies/You're all gonna die and die like flies/I don't trust you any more," Simone rages. But she recognizes that such a fate would also affect her and all Americans: "Lord have mercy on this land of mine/ We're all gonna get it in due time."

Yet like all these examples of critical and active patriotism, Simone's song likewise envisions the possibility of a future in which America finally and genuinely moves closer to its ideals of "equality" (the final verse's last word). "Don't tell me/I'll tell you/Me and my people just about due," as she puts it succinctly and powerfully. Too often, it seemed that 1960s celebratory patriotisms depended less upon shared ideals and more upon exclusionary myths that defined the decade's activists and protesters as outside of and even opposed to the national project. But if we remember the words and actions of those figures and movements themselves, we see just how fully they defined themselves as active and critical patriots, carrying forward the legacies of both America's ideals and the battle to extend them to all Americans.

Chapter Eight

The 1980s

Morning and Mourning in America

Two 1980 American sports moments concisely illustrate the status of celebratory and critical forms of patriotism at the start of this new decade. On February 22nd, the U.S. men's ice hockey team stunned the four-time defending gold medalist Soviet Union team 4–3 in the semifinals of the medal round at the 1980 Winter Olympics in Lake Placid, New York. As the Soviet Union team was mostly comprised of professional players and the U.S. team nearly all amateurs, this result is considered one of the greatest upsets in sports history, prompting both TV play-by-play announcer Al Michaels' famous call, "Do you believe in miracles?" and the nickname "The Miracle on Ice." The U.S. team itself immediately linked their victory to one of the nation's most iconic celebratory patriotic texts, breaking out into a spontaneous rendition of "God Bless America" in the locker room after the game; that moment, like the victory overall, is impossible to separate from Cold War celebratory patriotic contexts and contrasts, differences from the Soviet Union that were often framed as religious and cultural as well as political. For its next (March 3rd) cover, *Sports Illustrated* amplified that patriotic view, presenting a picture of the American players celebrating and waving an American flag with no headline or caption; as the picture's German American photographer, Heinz Klutmeier, himself an immigrant from the Cold War-divided city of Berlin, put it, "It didn't need it. Everyone in America knew what happened."

Just over seven months later, on October 2nd, 1980, a far more somber sporting event took place in Las Vegas, as legendary boxer Muhammad Ali lost his controversial last U.S. fight against the current heavyweight champion Larry Holmes. Ali had attempted to retire from boxing in July 1979 but was in need of money and decided to return one last time, despite physical ailments such as trembling hands that foreshadowed his 1984 diagnosis with Parkinson's syndrome, a diagnosis that may well have been accelerated by the brutal beating he took in this fight. Ali's financial struggles, like the frustrating arc of his 1970s boxing career overall, cannot be separated from one striking, critical patriotic moment and its effects and aftermaths: in March 1966, while holding the heavyweight title, Ali refusal to be drafted into service in the Vietnam War, an act of resistance which led to a June 1967 criminal conviction for violating the Selective Service Act and his ban from the sport of boxing between March 1967 and October 1970. Civil rights leader Ralph Abernathy was one of many voices to link Ali's protest to the era's overarching critical patriotic efforts, calling him "a living example of soul power, the March on Washington in two fists." But Ali's longtime trainer and friend Angelo Dundee later noted the drastic effect the backlash against Ali's activism had on his career, arguing, "One thing must be taken into account when talking about Ali: he was robbed of his best years, his prime years."

The Miracle on Ice helped kick off a decade defined by a great deal of celebratory patriotic optimism, much of it linked to President Ronald Reagan's symbolic imagery but also reflected in a spate of blockbuster films and in the era's celebrations of wealth and excess. Those celebrations were accompanied by exclusionary visions that defined the decade's triumphs in direct contrast to myths of poverty, crime, cultural collapse, and the residual problems caused by 1960s radicalism like Ali's anti-war protest. But the 1980s likewise featured their own forms of radical protest, active patriotic efforts illustrated by Vietnam veteran organizations and Jesse Jackson's Rainbow Coalition as well as by the anti-nuclear and anti-apartheid movements. And from AIDS activists to foundational rap artists, other communities and figures expressed more overtly critical patriotic perspectives on the decade's darker realities, hoping both to raise awareness about those failures and to push the nation closer to its ideals.

While celebratory patriotisms can be created by any number of sources, the federal government in general and presidents in particular have played key roles in advancing such celebrations at the national level. From George Washington to Abraham Lincoln, Teddy Roosevelt to John F. Kennedy, American presidents have consistently expressed and frequently embodied these celebratory visions of the nation's identity and ideals. Roosevelt and Kennedy were the two youngest men to assume the office, Roosevelt after William McKinley's September 1901 assassination and Kennedy after the 1960 election, making them particularly striking embodiments of an optimistic vision of the nation's future. Ronald Reagan (1911–2004), on the other hand, was at the time the oldest president, as he was just two weeks shy of his 70th birthday when he was inaugurated in January 1981. But nonetheless, the former Hollywood actor, TV motivational speaker, General Electric spokesperson, and California governor became one of the most overtly celebratory patriotic presidents and political leaders in American history.

President Reagan began communicating that defining celebratory patriotic vision as early as his January 20th, 1981 First Inaugural Address. Ironically, that speech has become best known for a much more critical perspective on the federal government, one summed up by the line, "In this present crisis, government is not the solution to our problem; government is the problem." But while Reagan's speech does round off his anti-Carter administration presidential campaign with those critical sentiments about the government, he advances them in direct service of an overarching argument for America's foundational and enduring greatness. He explicitly ties that anti-government message to his version of American exceptionalism, arguing, "We are a nation that has a government—not the other way around. And this makes us special among the nations of the Earth." He uses the words of Revolutionary founder Joseph Warren to call for Americans to "renew ourselves here in our own land, . . . [to] again be the exemplar of freedom and a beacon of hope." He links that call to a literal as well as figurative vision of "the monument to a monumental man: George Washington, Father of our country," that he faces from his vantage point on the Capitol Building's West Front; as Reagan notes, this was the first time the inauguration had been held in that now iconic spot. And he concludes the address with one final celebratory patriotic statement, a reflection of Americans' faith in their own potential for continued and even amplified greatness, asking, "after all, why shouldn't we believe that? We are Americans."

Reagan would build on that celebratory patriotism in a number of ways over his two terms as president. He did so most directly in the period leading up to and after his reelection in 1984, as illustrated with particular clarity by the hugely influential "Morning in America" campaign ad. That ad's repeated phrase "It's morning again in America" both utilized ideas of the nation's past greatness and made the case for an even more striking present greatness, as did the superlatives in the line, "our country is prouder and stronger and better." Of course such emphases were partly a logical campaign strategy for an incumbent president, but they relied upon the power of those conjoined past and present national celebrations to speak to American audiences. And after he won reelection handily over his Democratic opponent Walter Mondale, Reagan chose as a central text for his January 20th, 1985 second inauguration, which was held inside the White House and shortened due to extreme cold, an iconic American cultural work which reinforced those celebratory images: the traditional Shaker song "Simple Gifts," popularized by composer Aaron Copland in the ballet *Appalachian Spring*. The song's single verse links idealized values precisely to a perfect setting where those values can be lived: "Tis the gift to be simple, 'tis the gift to be free/'Tis the gift to come down where we ought to be,/And when we find ourselves in the place just right,/'Twill be in the valley of love and delight."

Reagan likewise advanced celebratory patriotism as a central element to his administration's and America's ongoing Cold War relationship with the Soviet Union. He did so most overtly in the March 8th, 1983 speech to the National Association of Evangelicals in which he coined the phrase "evil empire" to describe the U.S.S.R. Although that speech does focus at length on depicting the Soviet Union in such stark terms, Reagan develops those images through direct, extended contrast with idealized views of the United States. He grounds those views in a passage from Alexis de Tocqueville's *Democracy in America*, quoting de Tocqueville's argument that when he visited the nation's churches he "understood the greatness and the genius of America. America is good. And if America ever ceases to be good, America will cease to be great." And Reagan links his own vision of that goodness not just to religion—although, not surprisingly given the occasion, the speech does advance one of the most overtly religious arguments ever made by a sitting president—but also to an equally celebratory view of American history: "whatever sad episodes exist in our past, any objective observer must hold a positive view of American history, a history that has been the story of hopes fulfilled and dreams made into reality. Especially in this century, America has kept alight the torch of freedom, but not just for ourselves, but for millions of others around the world."

In his final speech as president, his January 11th, 1989 televised Farewell Address, Reagan concludes with an even more direct argument about the need for such celebrations as part of "the resurgence of national pride that I called the new patriotism." He worries that while "our spirit is back, . . . we haven't reinstitutionalized it," and adds, "I'm warning of an eradication of the American memory that could result, ultimately, in an erosion of the American spirit. Let's start with some basics: more attention to American history and a greater emphasis on civic ritual." He defines those emphases as education in the broadest sense, addressing "children" to request that, "if your parents haven't been teaching you what it means to be an American, let 'em know and nail 'em on it. That would be a very American thing to do." And he finishes the speech and his presidency by offering his own interpretation of one of America's oldest civic and celebratory perspectives, John Winthrop's image of the Massachusetts Puritan community as "a shining city upon a hill." Reagan argues of that "shining city" that, "After two hundred years, two centuries, she still stands strong and true on the granite ridge, and her glow has held steady no matter what storm. And she's still a beacon, still a magnet for all who must have freedom, for all the pilgrims from all the lost places who are hurtling through the darkness, toward home."

President Reagan advanced particularly clear versions of such celebratory patriotisms throughout the 1980s, but American cultural works in the era both reflected and extended those celebrations as well. One particularly prominent space for such pop culture celebrations was the evolving genre of the blockbuster Hollywood film. Of the decade's ten highest-grossing such blockbusters, a number present similarly idealized images of unity and civic pride as the answer to outside threats against American communities or the nation as a whole. Examples of this type include *Top Gun* (1986; the decade's 10th highest-grossing film), in which elite Navy fighter pilots have to learn to work together to eliminate a Soviet threat; *Ghostbusters* (1984; the 6th highest), in which the title characters and eventually the entire city of New York band together to defeat an invasion of supernatural creatures, after which one of the Ghostbusters declares triumphantly, "I love this town!"; and *Superman II* (1980; the 9th highest), in which that quintessentially American superhero returns from a self-imposed exile in order to fight alien invaders from his home planet of Krypton who are explicitly threatening the United States. In *Superman II* the leader of those invaders, General Zod, takes over the White House, forcing the president to kneel before him in surrender and removing both the building's dome and the American flag atop it; at the end of the film, having defeated Zod and his allies, Superman returns the dome and flag to the White House and resumes his patriotic responsibilities, telling the president, "Sorry I've been away so long. I won't let you down again."

Perhaps the most overt such celebratory patriotic 1980s film was not quite a blockbuster but was certainly a surprise hit, more than doubling its $17 million budget and living on as a cult classic with a substantial fan following. John Milius's *Red Dawn* (1984) depicts the opening battle of World War III as Soviet troops and their Cuban and Nicaraguan allies invade a small Colorado town as part of their overall attack on the United States. The film follows a group of American teenagers who become a resistance force against this invasion, taking up arms in defense of their freedom and challenging this far larger and more professional army in a story that intentionally echoes the American Revolution in both its details and its overarching themes. Although most of the protagonists have sacrificed their lives by the film's conclusion, they have done so for a patriotic future, on two interconnected levels: to help two of their youngest members escape to the region known as "Free America," and to symbolize the larger, ongoing patriotic resistance that their efforts and sacrifices have helped inspire. The film's final image is of a future town memorial to these fallen heroes, placed next to an American flag suggesting that the war has turned in favor of the U.S., and reading, "In the early days of World War III, guerrillas—mostly children—placed the names of their lost upon this rock. They fought here alone and gave up their lives, so 'that this nation shall not perish from the earth.'"

While films like *Red Dawn* and these other blockbusters depicted difficult and painful struggles in support of their celebratory visions of America, the mantra for many of the decade's more pleasurable celebrations was provided by another movie character, the stockbroker Gordon Gekko from Oliver Stone's *Wall Street* (1987). Although Gekko's famous catchphrase "Greed is good," shortened from the film where he states "Greed, for lack of a better word, is good," was, like Gekko himself, intended by Stone to be viewed critically, the line and perspective caught on and became iconic. They did so not only because of Michael Douglas's charismatic and Oscar-winning performance as Gekko, but also and especially because of the decade's overarching celebrations of extreme wealth as emblematizing the American Dream. Gekko's line and the speech in which he delivers it were themselves based on an influential figure and moment from the decade: financier Ivan Boesky's 1986 commencement address to UC Berkeley's School of Business Administration, where he argued, "Greed is all right, by the way. I want you to know that. I think greed is healthy. You can be greedy and still feel good about yourself." Thanks to both the fictional and the actual lines, among other factors, the '80s came to be known as the "Decade of Greed."

While iconic 1980s figures like Gekko, Boesky, Donald Trump, and others offered prominent individual examples of these emphases, it was a broader social type, the yuppie, that reflected with particular clarity the decade's celebrations of wealth, class, and the American Dream. The term "yuppie" was first used by journalist Dan Rottenberg in a May 1980 article for *Chicago* magazine, and he defined it not just through the three concepts it brings together ("young, urban, and professional") but also through this community's desires: "The Yuppies seek neither comfort nor security, but stimulation." These were, Rottenberg noted, "the people after the protest generation," and they exemplified a generation and era in which collective activism was replaced by individual success in cultural images. That shift was embodied by the character Alex P. Keaton, played by young actor Michael J. Fox on the popular '80s sitcom *Family Ties* (1982–1989). Keaton, the son of '60s hippies who hope to keep those values alive in the '80s, rebels by becoming a yuppie obsessed with wealth and status. President Reagan called *Family Ties* his favorite television show, supposedly even offering to appear in an episode, and Fox would become a consistent yuppie icon, as illustrated as well as by his characters and arcs in films like *The Secret of My Success* (1987) and *Bright Lights, Big City* (1988).

Real estate mogul Donald Trump, whose 21st century versions of both celebratory and mythic patriotisms have so dominated our current moment, articulated and exemplified this materialistic and idealized 1980s view in his 1987 bestselling book *The Art of the Deal* (co-written with Tony Schwartz). "I play to people's fantasies," he and Schwartz write. "People may not always think big themselves, but they can still get very excited by those who do. That's why a little hyperbole never hurts. People want to believe that something is the biggest and the greatest and the most spectacular." While those hyperbolic superlatives have been part of American celebratory patriotism in every historical period I've traced, in the 1980s they were given renewed life by voices such as Trump's and Reagan's, as well as through the cultural works and forms that embodied and amplified those optimistic and materialistic perspectives.

There's no necessary reason why such celebratory patriotism can't include all Americans, and it's certainly worth considering how our national ideals, both overall and as they have evolved across our histories, can and should be defined in inclusive ways that make them available and meaningful for every American. But as I've traced in every chapter and for every period, much of the time our most prominent celebratory patriotisms have at least featured (if not indeed foregrounded) concurrent, mythic visions of the America they celebrate, myths that at best leave out a number of Americans and at worst depend on purposefully and actively contrasting their celebrations with perspectives and communities defined as un- and even anti-American.

   In the 1980s, some of the most consistent and destructive such mythic contrasts were those which portrayed poverty and impoverished Americans as not just outside of the celebratory ideals of wealth and success, but also distinctly threatening to those ideals. One of the most prominent of the period's myths about poverty, the figure of the "welfare queen," was in fact central to Ronald Reagan's speeches about wealth, work, social programs, and American ideals. The phrase was first used by *Chicago Tribune* columnist George Bliss in a series of 1974 articles about Linda Taylor, a woman living in that city who was investigated and eventually convicted of defrauding welfare and other social programs; *Jet* magazine wrote about Taylor later that year and used the same phrase. But it was Reagan who brought the phrase to national prominence, beginning in his unsuccessful 1976 campaign for the Republican presidential nomination when he made stories of an unnamed "welfare queen" central to his stump speeches. "There's a woman in Chicago," he would begin, "She has 80 names, 30 addresses, 12 Social Security cards . . . " Reagan continued to utilize this figure, one loosely based on Taylor but turned into a mythic character through the absence of her name, the emphasis on exaggerated details such as his famous addition that she "drives a Cadillac," and the very repetition of the story, in both his 1980 campaign and numerous speeches attacking social programs and spending once he was president.

One of those presidential speeches, Reagan's August 1st, 1987 radio address to the nation on the topic of welfare reform, illustrates the broader myths which this famous figure and image foreshadowed. Reagan opens with a celebratory image of the nation: "Americans always have cared about the less fortunate." But in his second paragraph he pivots to his central themes: "More must be done to reduce poverty and dependency and, believe me, nothing is more important than welfare reform. It's now common knowledge that our welfare system has itself become a poverty trap—a creator and reinforcer of dependency." The phrase "poverty and dependency" is the crucial center of this myth, as it defines by direct association this community of Americans as not simply "less fortunate," but also and especially less active, less in control of their own social participation and success. To that end, Reagan also calls out Democratic proposals as designed to "discourage work," "make staying on welfare more attractive," and "keep [people] down in a state of dependency," another vision of those affected by such social programs as fundamentally outside of celebratory national ideals such as the importance of work and the mobility of the American Dream. As we've seen with longstanding images such as the "self-made man" and Horatio Alger's "rags to riches" stories, those emphases have consistently contributed to, and indeed in many ways principally constructed, idealized national myths, and Reagan here reflects an emerging critique of poverty as nothing less than a chosen, hostile alternative to those collective ideals.

In his prominent book *Losing Ground: American Social Policy, 1950–1980* (1984), sociologist Charles Murray turned such myths about poverty and society into an overarching argument about two competing strands of 20th century American history, and more exactly about how in his perspective the 1960s had begun to move the nation in the wrong direction. In an introduction to the book's 1994 10th anniversary edition Murray argues that, "one can be saddened by the plight of poor children and yet be opposed to new government social programs intended to relieve their plight—a combination that would have surprised no one throughout much of American history, but had been impermissible since the 1960s." He also claims that "it is now accepted that the social programs of the 1960s broadly failed; . . . and that the principles of personal responsibility, penalties for bad behavior, and rewards for good behavior have to be reintroduced into social policy"; those ideas would inform a great deal of the bipartisan mid-1990s push for "welfare reform." Much of Murray's book thus anticipates both Reagan's 1987 speech and his political perspectives on competing visions of government and policy, and *Losing Ground* came to be known as "the bible of the Reagan administration." But Murray's emphasis on the 1960s makes this a historical argument as well, one that depicts that decade and its Great Society social programs as representing a decisive and destructive turning point away from foundational American ideals, rather than, for example, as an extension of founding concepts like the Constitution's goal of "promot[ing] the general Welfare."

Murray's historical arguments also reflect another overarching 1980s myth: nostalgia for the 1950s as a unifying, idealized golden age prior to the debates and divisions of the 1960s. Historian J. Ronald Oakley's book *God's Country: America in the Fifties* (1986) traces that evolving 1980s perspective, highlighting contemporary visions of the '50s as "the personification of the American Dream." Oakley describes such images of the decade as "an ideal vision of a time that never existed," a national parallel to the psychological concept of a "nostalgia trap" that historian Stephanie Coontz introduces in her book *The Way We Never Were: American Families and the Nostalgia Trap* (1992). But even Oakley's thoughtful book is not immune to the pull of such nostalgia, particularly in its consistent contrasts of the '50s with the '60s, which Oakley depicts as "the dark years that followed" his focal decade. Even if we set aside the many specific ways in which 1960s social movements and historical trends began in the 1950s, this view of the two decades as contrasting reinforces images of celebratory and critical patriotisms as both entirely separate and fundamentally opposed to one another. That is, any visions of 1960s protests and conflicts as representing a change in American society—rather than as both a response to and an extension of ongoing issues, and indeed an amplification of battles that had defined the 1950s very fully as well—lends credence to myths which depict national identity and ideals as reflected best in times of unifying celebration. If and when such particularly celebratory periods seem to exist, they do so precisely by defining their moment's critical perspectives as not patriotic but instead divisive threats to the nation.

Published just after the 1980s, Coontz's book analyzes the decade's constructions of those nostalgic myths on a number of interconnected levels. Much of her focus is on '80s images of "the traditional family," a concept, Coontz notes, that, "like most visions of 'a golden age,' . . . evaporates on closer examination." She highlights how much of that particular nostalgia was created through 1950s sitcoms such as *Father Knows Best, Leave It to Beaver*, and *The Andy Griffith Show*, all of which were rerun frequently throughout the '80s, thanks to the advent of cable television. She links that idealized, exclusionary vision of "the traditional family" to a number of other familial myths in the period, including ones tied directly to poverty, dependency, and the "welfare queen" figure. And her overarching argument is that these nostalgic familial myths represent one telling example of a broader, defining American (and human) trend: that "as time passes, the actual complexity of our history . . . gets buried under the weight of the ideal image." This makes those idealized images especially and hugely influential—as she puts it in the concluding paragraphs of her introduction to a 2016 edition of the book, it remains "safe to say that many Americans will continue to interpret new developments in light of the historical myths discussed in this book."

In the 1980s, those nostalgic historical myths likewise helped create and amplify many other national myths. The various religious and political figures and communities that came together to form the Moral Majority and the Christian Coalition—a group that included Jerry Falwell Sr. and Liberty University, Pat Robertson and *The 700 Club*, Ralph Reed, and others—focused in particular on "the traditional family," but used that mythic ideal to advance a much broader form of mythic patriotism. The Moral Majority, which was first created in 1979 as a political action committee (PAC) supporting Ronald Reagan's presidential campaign, defined itself as "pro-traditional family," "pro-moral," and "pro-American," overtly linking national identity to those mythic social and religious ideals. Later in his life, Jimmy Carter would note the exclusionary goals of that organization and campaign, writing in an autobiography that the group "purchased $10 million in commercials on southern radio and TV to brand me as a traitor to the South and no longer a Christian." Throughout the '80s, the organization and its allies built on that origin point, continuing to advance a mythic vision of American identity and ideals that depended on defining various social and cultural forces as both outside of and treasonous to the nation.

The centerpiece of those 1980s efforts was the movement's opposition to the National Endowment for the Arts (NEA) and its support of controversial artists such as the photographers Andres Serrano and Robert Mapplethorpe. In an October 1989 fundraising letter attacking Mapplethorpe in particular, Pat Robertson called for allies in the battle to "turn back the tide of pornography, filth, and moral decay that is attacking every level of our society." In a May 1989 column for the *Washington Times*, commentator Pat Buchanan went further still in linking this cultural debate to patriotism, arguing that "A nation absorbs its values through its art. A corrupt culture will produce a corrupt people; America needs a cultural revolution." In that light, perhaps the most telling such artistic controversy was occasioned by Art Institute of Chicago student Dread Scott Tyler's 1989 installation "What is the Proper Way to Display an American Flag?" Tyler put an American flag on the floor and encouraged viewers to walk across it in order to leave comments about America in a ledger; the resulting, sustained outrage from conservative groups led the U.S. Senate to unanimously vote in favor of a resolution that Tyler had in so doing committed a federal crime. Artistic and cultural works have been part of American debates over patriotism in every time period; but in these 1980s culture wars, proponents of nostalgic, mythic patriotism made more critical artistic figures and their works direct targets of their exclusions.

Educational settings and debates became another arena in which these mythic patriotic voices advanced their exclusionary views. Often, those educational arguments seemed to offer purposefully unifying visions of America, as illustrated by the subtitle of professor E. D. Hirsch's book *Cultural Literacy: What Every American Needs to Know* (1987). But while Hirsch does indeed highlight an impressive variety of figures, texts, and topics in the course of his book, he does so in service of another overarching, nostalgic, mythic argument. "The decline of literacy and the decline of shared knowledge are closely related, interdependent facts," he argues, and "our children's lack of intergenerational information is a serious problem for the nation." He goes further still in connecting literacy to national identity, arguing that "a mastery of national culture is essential to mastery of the standard language in every modern nation." And in an American context, he explicitly contrasts that goal with the 1980s educational emphasis on multiculturalism; "however laudable it is," he concludes this section of his introduction, multiculturalism "should not be the primary focus of national education. It should not be allowed to supplant or interfere with our schools' responsibility to ensure our children's mastery of American literate culture."

Other prominent figures in this debate made a more aggressive critique of multiculturalism even more central to their mythic arguments about the need to return to an idealized vision of American education and literacy. One the most powerful such figures was William H. Bennett, who served first as President Reagan's Chair of the National Endowment for the Humanities (NEH) and then as his Secretary of Education; Bennett's *The Book of Virtues* (1992) developed at length his theory of "moral literacy" as a foundational American perspective that had been lost in an era of multicultural moral relativism and to which the nation's schools and society desperately needed to return. Making similar cases about higher education in particular were such books as Allan Bloom's *The Closing of the American Mind: How Higher Education Has Failed Democracy and Impoverished the Souls of Today's Students* (1987) and Dinesh D'Souza's *Illiberal Education: The Politics of Race and Sex on Campus* (1991). Bloom's reference to democracy reflects the celebratory patriotic undercurrent (and at times central current) of all these works, as illustrated as well by his lament against the "gradual stilling of the old political and religious echoes" in late 20th century educational settings and conversations. Through their nostalgic, mythic visions of education and the nation, these figures and books collectively critiqued multiculturalism and post-1960s America as having failed to live up to, much less carry forward and further instill, those founding ideals.

Such mythic perspectives on cultural and educational issues could certainly have tangible, destructive effects on individuals and communities: Dread Scott Tyler received numerous death threats and could have gone to jail, to note just one example. But it was another side to these nostalgic comparisons to the '50s and critiques of '80s society that had the most drastic such effects. Since at least the 1960s fears of a rise in crime, particularly in America's cities, had driven a variety of exclusionary and discriminatory national trends. Those fears continued to develop throughout the 1970s, as illustrated by cultural works like the hit film *Death Wish* (1974; based on Brian Garfield's 1972 novel of the same name), in which liberal architect Paul Kersey (Charles Bronson) sees his family brutalized by criminals and turns into a one-man vigilante anti-crime task force, wreaking havoc on New York City streets that have turned into a sort of urban Wild West. The film's tagline, "Vigilante, city style—judge, jury, and executioner," suggests the overt link between these urban settings and the need for this new form of justice, one violent enough to match those brutal new realities. *Los Angeles Times* reviewer Charles Champlin criticized the film as "despicable, . . . nasty and demagogic stuff, an appeal to brute emotions and against reason," and indeed *Death Wish* reflected precisely these irrational, growing fears of American cities overrun by dangerous criminals.

A decade after the film's release, a real-life New York vigilante divided the nation and reflected the power that these mythic perspectives could exert on American communities. Much like the fictional Paul Kersey, electrical engineer Bernard Goetz responded to an alleged prior attack by purchasing a gun and preparing to fight back; when he was accosted by four African American teenagers on the subway on the evening of December 22nd, 1984, he shot and gravely wounded them, leaving one paraplegic and creating a national firestorm. The New York media dubbed Goetz "The Subway Vigilante," and a great deal of both the media coverage and the broader public reaction seemed to side with Goetz, buying into his (and the film's) view of the city as having become a fundamentally dangerous space in which the constant threat of violence had to be met with its own parallel, justified violence. Although there was a strong racial component to that view, and Goetz was alleged to have expressed racist sentiments at earlier community meetings in his neighborhood, it's worth noting that any Americans could potentially share and express such exclusionary sentiments; illustrating that was the statement of Congress of Racial Equality (CORE) director Roy Innis, a longstanding civil rights leader who called Goetz "the avenger for all of us." The key words there are "all of us," a definition of a shared American community that explicitly locates the incident's four African American teenagers (Barry Allen, Troy Canty, Darrell Cabey, and James Ramseur) entirely outside of it.

That exclusionary vision, a definition of these urban Americans as not only outside of but essentially hostile to the national community, drove a number of other prominent, divisive 1980s trends as well: from the increasing "white flight" out of the nation's cities and the corresponding financial and political abandonment of those settings to the frustratingly slow (if not indeed nonexistent) collective response to the crack and AIDS epidemics decimating those urban spaces. Behind all those specific histories was a broader perspective that celebrated small-town and rural communities, along with the suburban ones that were growing exponentially throughout this period, as "the real America," and that both harkened back to the 1950s as a golden age for such communities and concurrently linked 1960s divisions and conflicts to America's cities. These cultural and historical myths were at the heart of many of the decade's most prominent celebratory patriotisms, and have continued to influence our national conversations into the 21st century.

It is not only particular settings and communities that have too often been left out of those celebratory patriotisms, however. As we've seen across all my chapters and time periods, the focus on celebration has likewise made it difficult—sometimes purposefully, sometimes unintentionally, but it's been a consistent effect in any case—to highlight more active and critical forms of patriotism, the kinds which are often captured in moments of collective service or protest. While those latter collective efforts are in many ways parallel, some of them emphasize the nation's ideals as particularly central to their perspectives and take action to express and embody those ideals; these efforts fall into the category I've called active patriotism.

Some of the most prominent examples of 1980s active patriotism came from the increasingly vocal community of Vietnam War veterans. The Vietnam Veterans of America (VVA), an organization founded in the summer of 1979 by veterans Bobby Muller and Stuart Feldman, became increasingly active throughout the 1980s, particularly after the November 13th, 1982 dedication of the Vietnam Veterans Memorial (known colloquially as The Wall) in Washington, DC. That initially controversial and eventually beloved memorial, designed by architect and sculptor Maya Lin after she won a 1981 contest, itself reflects a more active patriotic emphasis, a collective focus not on idealized mythologies of wartime heroism, but instead on the service and sacrifice of the hundreds of thousands of Americans who fought and tens of thousands who died in the war. As expressed by Vietnam Veterans Memorial Fund President Jan Scruggs, who had the original idea for a memorial on the National Mall in 1979, "it has helped people separate the warrior from the war, and it has helped a nation to heal." And it also helped further develop an interconnected community of veterans, as illustrated by a *New York Times* reporter's description of the dedication ceremony: "Bearded veterans wearing old fatigues can be seen reaching toward the names of remembered dead warriors, running their fingers across the letters."

One of the most active members of that veterans' community in the 1980s was author and activist Ron Kovic (1946–). Throughout the 1970s Kovic had become one of the best-known veteran peace activists, leading protests at the 1972 Republican National Convention, organizing a 1974 hunger strike inside California Senator Alan Cranston's office, and speaking at the 1976 Democratic National Convention. His autobiography *Born on the Fourth of July* (1976) linked those efforts to an overarching, active patriotic perspective, not just on his wartime service but also and especially on his ongoing commitment to political and social causes, a commitment Kovic maintained despite, as he notes in the introduction to a 2005 edition of the book, being "called a Communist and a traitor" for those efforts. Oliver Stone's 1989 film adaptation of *Born*, co-written by Kovic himself, extended that active patriotic story to a new medium and generation. But Kovic also continued to develop his own voice throughout the decade, both as a writer, as illustrated by his 1983 novel *Around the World in Eight Days* about a veteran seeking new purpose in his post-war life, and as a political activist. In the latter role, Kovic served as a delegate for groundbreaking presidential candidate Jesse Jackson at the 1988 Democratic National Convention in Atlanta; as he would later describe that ongoing political work, "I've had a very political life, I've met people across the political spectrum and I've tried to speak from my heart—and speak as freely as possible." As the Gulf War unfolded a few years later, Kovic was a consistent presence in the public protests and media conversations over that conflict, exemplifying the continued role of Vietnam veterans in those national debates.

Jesse Jackson's presidential campaign itself represented another influential form of 1980s active patriotic service. Jackson (1941–) had been involved in such service since his youthful work alongside Martin Luther King Jr. and the 1960s civil rights movement, and in 1971 had founded his own organization dedicating to advancing civil rights for all through African American activism, People United to Save Humanity (PUSH; "Save" was later changed to "Serve"). PUSH's collective goals became the inspiration for Jackson's more overtly political 1980s organization, the National Rainbow Coalition, the concept of which he first articulated in a July 18th, 1984 address of the same name at the Democratic National Convention in San Francisco. While sections of the speech highlighted Jackson's opposition to President Reagan's administration and policies, and others indicated the coalition's outreach to many different American communities including disabled veterans and small farmers, its central thread was the active patriotic argument described by

Jackson in these sentences: "We are often reminded that we live in a great nation—and we do. But it can be greater still. The Rainbow is mandating a new definition of greatness." Or, as he put it directly to "young America" in his conclusion, "Exercise the right to dream. You must face reality—that which is. But then dream of a reality that ought to be—that must be."

Other active patriotic protest movements in the decade fought for their own dream of a better future for both the nation and the world. Elsewhere in the speech Jackson implored his audience to "Choose the human race over the nuclear race," and the 1980s anti-nuclear movement, which focused on both nuclear weapons and nuclear power, did indeed comprise one of these communities of protest and activism. That movement was launched by a pair of sizeable 1979 gatherings focused on opposition to nuclear power: a May 6th march in Washington, DC that drew 65,000 attendees and a September 23rd demonstration in New York City that brought together nearly two hundred thousand protesters. But those were just a prelude to the June 12th, 1982 anti-nuclear weapon protest in New York City's Central Park, where an estimated one million people (the largest political demonstration in American history) came together to call for nuclear disarmament and an end to the Cold War arms race. That gathering helped create the concept of an International Day of Nuclear Disarmament, which was first celebrated one year later, on June 20th, 1983, with protests at 50 sites throughout the United States alongside many others around the world. More than 950 protesters were arrested at a single such site, California's Lawrence Livermore National Laboratory; activist Lanie Silver, quoted in a *New York Times* story on the arrests, summed up their active patriotic goals: "We have to speak up, we have to put our bodies on the line."

The decade's most physically demanding active patriotic anti-nuclear protest took place three years later, with 1986's Great Peace March for Global Nuclear Disarmament. After assembling in Los Angeles in February, more than a thousand peace activists began marching on March 1st; more than nine months later, six hundred marchers completed their 3,700 mile journey in Washington, DC on November 15th. The march was initially organized by longtime civil rights, anti-war, and anti-AIDS activist David Mixner and his organization People Reaching out for Peace (PRO-Peace), but PRO-Peace went bankrupt early in the march and the group became a distinct entity known as Peace City. Their statement of purpose highlighted the march's relationship to American historical and philosophical ideals: "The Great Peace March for Global Nuclear Disarmament is an abolitionist movement. We believe that great social change comes about when the will of the people becomes focused on a moral imperative. . . . It is the responsibility of a democratic government to implement the will of its people, and it is the will of the people of the United States and many other nations to end the nuclear arms race." Although this protest movement confronted a very specific late 20th century crisis, it did so consistently through the language, ideals, and legacy of American active patriotism from the Revolution onward.

The final active patriotic movement I'll highlight, the opposition to South Africa's apartheid regime, focused its efforts on changing a distinct culture and society from those of the United States. But the movement's 1980s iteration originated in direct response to a U.S. federal government action: the August 17th, 1984 U.S. abstention from a United Nations Security Council resolution condemning apartheid. It achieved its greatest success with another governmental action: the October 1986 Congressional passage, overriding President Reagan's veto, of the Comprehensive Anti-Apartheid Act, which placed sanctions on South Africa. And its leading figures emerged directly out of the activist movements of the 1960s, as illustrated by longtime California Congressman Ron Dellums, whose background included connections to both the Black Panthers and the anti-Vietnam War movement and who later reflected that "challenging apartheid in South Africa became a logical next place to go." As sociologist Neil Smelser describes that logic in a September 1985 *New York Times* article on the protests, "We have in the United States a sort of national motif of privilege versus equality," and "South Africa manifests this theme." Or, as former Equal Employment Opportunity Commission Director Eleanor Holmes Norton puts it in the same article, "We have had a spontaneous outpouring that comes from the concerns Americans have about racial oppression. More than outrage, you get empathy and understanding." Norton argues that "This issue has caught the imagination of Americans in a way that no other issue of the 1980's has," but in truth, apartheid became one of a number of causes in the decade to draw out active patriotic protests, collective efforts that embodied, expressed, and extended national ideals.

The U.S. government's support for South Africa's apartheid regime, like the nuclear arms race and the lack of attention to the plight of Vietnam veterans, represented without question a frustrating and divisive side to American society in the 1980s. But some of the decade's social and cultural issues went further still, revealing the oppressed American communities too often entirely excluded from the period's dominant visions of national identity. For these communities, like those afflicted by the AIDS epidemic and those living in America's abandoned urban spaces, active patriotic protest wasn't quite sufficient to express either their mourning or their righteous anger—they needed critical patriotic voices, perspectives on just how fully America was failing to live up to its ideals and just how far the nation still had to go if it were to truly become that iconic city on a hill.

As the HIV/AIDS epidemic ravaged the LGBT community in the mid-1980s and the federal government's unwillingness to even acknowledge this evolving public health crisis, much less fund and support research and treatment, transformed from ignorance to negligence to outright violence, community leaders created their own support systems that also comprised impassioned critiques of those national failures. Some, like the Gay Men's Health Crisis (GMHC) telephone hotline, established in a New York City apartment in January 1982, addressed and redressed unmet, practical needs, such as in that case offering the kinds of information, guidance, and solidarity entirely absent from the official responses. But others, like the NAMES Project AIDS Memorial Quilt, operated on a significantly more symbolic and national register. During a November 27th, 1985 candlelight march in San Francisco, AIDS activist Cleve Jones asked attendees to write the names of loved ones lost to the disease on signs that he then taped to the wall of the city's Federal Building; out of that origin point was born the idea of a mammoth, evolving patchwork quilt that could feature such names and tributes. Many of those lost to AIDS were not given traditional funerals, since funeral homes and cemeteries, as well as too often their own family members, stigmatized the illness; the quilt thus also became a way to both highlight those discriminatory practices and force these victims into collective consciousness. As NAMES Project Foundation Director Julie Rhoad has put it, "this is perhaps one of the most democratic memorials in existence, because it's literally made by the people for the people they love"; I would add that the quilt likewise offered, especially in its early years, a chance for those democratic voices to implicitly critique and explicitly counter the absence of their loves and lives from national conversations.

While the AIDS Memorial Quilt embodied that kind of critical patriotic challenge to national myths and absences, an activist organization like the AIDS Coalition to Unleash Power (ACT UP) expressed such challenges more directly still. ACT UP was founded in March 1987 by playwright and activist Larry Kramer when he asked the audience at one of his New York City speeches, "Do we want to start a new organization devoted to political action?" Within weeks, ACT UP was organizing protests of Wall Street in opposition to outrageously priced medications and treatments, and the New York City General Post Office in a Tax Day event to highlight government silence and inaction. In a March 23rd, 1987 *New York Times* op ed entitled "The F.D.A.'s Callous Response to AIDS," Kramer extended these critical patriotic protests to that arena, both criticizing the federal agency as "the single most incomprehensible bottleneck in American bureaucratic history —one that is actually prolonging this roll call of death" and ending with a demand for "humanitarianism from our President and Mayor—and heroism from the F.D.A." Righteous critique was certainly the organization's central goal; as historian David France puts it, "ACT UP's ethos was that they had united in anger." But as he adds, that anger was "coupled with intelligence," as when they organized a sit-in at the F.D.A. and then presented a multi-part proposal for researching and funding experimental treatments. This "inside-outside strategy," as ACT UP came to call it, embodied both levels of critical patriotism, and allowed the organization to influence the future just as fully as it engaged with the injustices of the present.

Larry Kramer would document those activist efforts and their '80s contexts in groundbreaking plays like *The Normal Heart* (1985) and *Just Say No, A Play about a Farce* (1988). But it's another dramatic work about the AIDS crisis, Tony Kushner's two-part play *Angels in America: A Gay Fantasia on National Themes* (1991–1993), that most fully models this critical patriotic perspective. Kushner embodies his critiques of American bigotry and hypocrisy in the character of Roy Cohn, the longtime "unofficial power broker" (as the play introduces him) who influenced Joseph McCarthy, Richard Nixon, Ronald Reagan, and Donald Trump, among many others. Kushner calls his Cohn "a work of dramatic fiction" based on a man "who was all too real," and he depicts through the character both the human story of a closeted gay man dying of AIDS and the mythic patriotic perspective of what the play's most consistent voice of conscience, the nurse and drag queen Belize, calls "an arrogant, sexual-political Stalinist-slash-racist flag-waving thug." When it comes to a character like Cohn, the answers to the collective, national "Great Questions" with which Kushner begins the play's second half—"Are we doomed? . . . Will the Past release us? . . . Can we Change? In Time?"—might thus seem largely dark and pessimistic. But Kushner's narrator demands instead a more optimistic possibility for what texts like *Angels* can symbolize and accomplish: "Show me the words that will reorder the world, or else keep silent." And in the play's final monologue, protagonist Prior Walter expresses that critical patriotic perspective overtly and potently: "This disease will be the end of many of us, but not nearly all, and the dead will be commemorated and will struggle on with the living, and we are not going away. . . . The world only spins forward. We will be citizens. The time has come."

These AIDS activists and artists were not the only New York-based community to advance influential critical patriotic views in the decade. Arising out of the 1970s experiences and collaborations of African American, Caribbean American, and Latinx individuals, neighborhoods, and communities in the Bronx, the musical and cultural genre that came to be known alternatively as rap and hip hop offered a vital new form of artistic, social, and political expression for urban Americans affected and abandoned by the myths of poverty and crime. Hip hop was first created by DJs, such as the Jamaican

American "Founder of Hip Hop" Clive Campbell (usually known by his stage name DJ Kool Herc), performing at neighborhood block parties, and so it often featured prominently a celebratory communal vibe and message. The song generally considered the first recorded hip hop track, The Sugarhill Gang's "Rapper's Delight" (1979), embodies those celebratory emphases. But from its earliest expressions the genre also offered striking examples of both the angry and the activist sides to a critical patriotic perspective, as illustrated respectively by two influential early 1980s tracks: Grandmaster Flash and The Furious Five's "The Message" (1982) and Brother D and Collective Effort's "How We Gonna Make the Black Nation Rise" (1980).

"The Message" features at its heart a darkly pessimistic perspective on what it means to be a young man growing up in these early 1980s urban settings, as expressed by the song's most-repeated lines, describing the city as "like a jungle" that "makes me wonder how I keep from going under." It ties that image to a deeply critical view of American identity and ideals, one captured by a trio of rhymes: "it's all about the money" with "ain't a damn thing funny" and "You got to have a con in this land of milk and honey." And the second-person final verse lays out in stark and stunning detail what it means to grow up in that setting, as exemplified by a series of images and rhymes in its opening lines: "You grow in the ghetto, living second-rate, and your eyes will sing a song of deep hate"; and "The place that you play and where you stay looks like one great big alleyway." The song's titular message seems mostly to be an attempt to force Flash's audiences—especially those who have abandoned and ignored these American communities—to acknowledge and engage with these destructive realities. But I would argue that the very act of writing and performing this song represents not just a way for the speaker to "keep from going under," but also a profoundly patriotic collective act, one that demands that shared reckoning in an effort to change both the conversation and, ideally but crucially, those realities.

"How We Gonna Make the Black Nation Rise" highlights many of the same experiences and realities, and adds other, equally destructive contemporary contexts with lines such as "The Ku Klux Klan is on the loose, training their kids in machine-gun use" and "The media is telling lies, the devil's taking off his disguise." Throughout the song Brother D pleads for audience awareness of and response to such conditions, alongside related ones like unemployment and pollution, rapping, "My people, people, people, can't you see what's really going on?" He implores his audience to "wake up," as the situation "hurts everybody, black or white." He links these contemporary struggles to a critical vision of history, rapping, "America was built, understand, by stolen labor on stolen land." He envisions a different collective possibility for this community, for those who resist and "dare to be free": "You gotta sacrifice for our righteous cause or remain a passive slave." And he ends with a particular clear expression of his patriotic perspective and goals, one linked to the song's titular question: "So while you dance and while you sing, all we wanna do is ask just one thing: Are you gonna help the Black Nation rise?" In response he offers his own culminating vision of "How we gonna make the Black Nation rise," arguing that "We gotta agitate, educate, and organize!" At this very early moment in hip hop history, both Grandmaster Flash and Brother D offer powerful examples of the genre's ability to express and embody such critical patriotic perspectives on America's 1980s failings—and, in "How We Gonna Make the Black Nation Rise?," Brother D imagines rap itself as a vehicle for moving the nation closer to its ideals.

Conclusion

Patriotism in the Age of Trump

On January 8th, 2020, with the possibility of war between the United States and Iran looming, a *Washington Post* story highlighted the heated debates over the role of journalism in such moments. The story's tagline summed up the core of those arguments: "Are you a journalist first or an American first? With conflict looming, an old question about patriotism is raised anew." Journalists who are critical of America's government or actions in times of war are, according to the longstanding perspective highlighted in this article, fundamentally unpatriotic and even un-American.

As that fraught recent moment also illustrates, such arguments are in no way limited to journalists. Doug Collins, a Republican Congressman from Georgia, was one of many conservatives to attack the patriotism of the entire Democratic Party in response to their critiques of the Trump administration's actions during this moment of potential foreign conflict, arguing that Democrats are "in love with terrorists." His use of the phrase "in love" is particularly telling: patriotism is often defined as the love of one's country, and such attacks imply, if they do not indeed state outright, that those who criticize the country are instead siding with—expressing an affinity for—the nation's enemies.

In the age of Trump, the presence and stakes of our debates over patriotism have, like the respective forms of celebratory, mythic, active, and critical patriotisms, never been clearer. In this conclusion I will briefly highlight a couple contemporary examples of each type (to complement those with which I began the introduction) and what they help us understand about patriotism and America, both in 2020 and throughout our history.

Trump himself uses and depends on celebratory patriotism more than any other president in American history. A search of his Twitter history alone

161

reveals hundreds of uses of the phrase "greatest country in the world" over his three-plus years as president, and a scan of his White House's official statements provides numerous additional examples within that overarching frame, such as the September 2019 brief entitled "President Donald J. Trump is Making America the Best Country in the World to Build and Buy Cars." Of course every national leader expresses celebratory perspectives on their nation, but no president has made greatness—and, indeed, unparalleled greatness—more central to his vision of America than has Trump. In so doing, he has illustrated and amplified the longstanding, close link between celebratory patriotism and ideas of American exceptionalism, definitions of the nation's idealized identity that emphasize not just its existence but also and especially its unique and unrivaled greatness. Our national celebrations have not always been so exaggerated nor so simplistic as Trump makes them, but they have consistently defined the nation as singularly great, an idealized view that this moment has forced us to recognize and reflect upon.

One limitation to such extreme celebrations is that they tend to view any more critical perspective on the nation as a direct, unpatriotic assault on America. The last two years have presented numerous case studies in that phenomenon with the outraged responses to the *New York Times Magazine*'s 1619 Project. In March 2020, journalist and entrepreneur Bob Woodson and his Woodson Center launched their own such celebratory patriotic response: entitled the 1776 Project, this effort is intended to "challenge those who assert America is forever defined by past failures." In contrast to that hyperbolic description of the 1619 Project's arguments, the 1776 project aims "to offer alternative perspectives that celebrate the progress America has made on delivering her promise of equality and opportunity." The key words there are "progress" and "promise"—while Woodson and his principal contributors are all African American and the project does genuinely reflect an inclusive vision of American identity, it nonetheless depends on a limited, mythic view of American history in which the nation's promised ideals have been consistently achieved through steady, successful progress. That argument, in other words, entirely equates patriotism with celebration, which illustrates why this perspective has such difficulty seeing criticism such as that offered by the 1619 Project as anything other than unpatriotic.

As we've seen throughout these chapters and time periods, such celebrations also lend themselves easily and all too frequently to mythic patriotisms, perspectives that emphasize precisely those figures and communities (often the more critical ones) that are defined as outside of the nation. Since he launched his 2016 presidential campaign with a speech attacking Mexican immigrants as a threat to the United States, Donald Trump has continually advanced such myths about the nation and those outside of it. He did so with particular clarity in his July 2019 responses to four freshman Democratic Congresswomen (known collectively as The Squad) who had been critical of his administration. Trump Tweeted that the four "come from countries whose governments are a complete and total catastrophe," and then suggested that they "go back and help fix the totally broken and crime infested places from which they came." Even if we leave aside the specific and blatant inaccuracies in his descriptions of the women's stories and identities, this overarching myth of "go back where you came from" equates criticism of America with "foreignness," turning any critical American into an excluded outsider by definition—and it is a sentiment which has been featured time and again in the rhetorical and violent hate crimes targeting Americans of color over the last few years.

One particular such recent hate crime exemplifies the close association of mythic patriotism with these xenophobic views. On May 26th, 2017, white supremacist domestic terrorist Jeremy Christian accosted two teenage girls (one African American and one Muslim American) on a Portland, Oregon commuter train, ordering them to "get out of his country"; when three men came to their defense, Christian stabbed the men, killing two and badly injuring the third. In his first court appearance, four days after the stabbings, Christian invoked in his defense precisely such an exclusionary vision of both patriotism and American identity and ideals, shouting, "Get out if you don't like free speech. You call it terrorism; I call it patriotism." While it's easy to dismiss Christian's final clause in that quote as part of the deranged rantings of a serial murderer, the larger truth is that mythic patriotisms have always (if usually a bit more implicitly) expressed a version of "Get out if you don't like" American ideals as the speaker would define them. "Love it or leave it" has returned, with renewed force and more overtly exclusionary intent, to our 21st century debates.

I can't imagine a more forceful, active patriotic rebuttal to that exclusionary myth than that embodied by the three men who challenged Christian on that Portland train. Before he passed away, young Taliesin Myrddin Namkai-Meche's final words were, "I want everyone on the train to know that I love them." The surviving man, Micah Fletcher, elaborated on that inclusive motivation for their courageous actions, arguing, "If you live here, move here, or if you want to call this city home, it is your home. And we must protect each other like that is the truth, no matter the consequences." That act of protection, of standing up for one's fellow Americans—physically in a case like this one, philosophically and rhetorically in many others—exemplifies one central kind of active patriotic service and sacrifice we've seen across all my chapters and time periods. Such acts and those who undertake them not

164   *Conclusion*

only advocate for but themselves represent American ideals, and moreover illustrate the vital importance, especially in contested moments like this one, of continuing to fight for those ideals.

Protests comprise another consistent form of active patriotism, of course, and much of the last few years in American society has been defined by sizeable and influential such public gatherings and activisms. Some of those protests are more individual, as with Colin Kaepernick's anthem protest; others are more collective, as with the millions of Americans who participated in the Women's March on January 21st, 2017, the day after Trump's inauguration. And some protests happen more quietly and formally, as with the many whistleblowers like Alexander Vindman and his colleagues who have stood up in opposition to various Trump administration actions and policies. As Vindman illustrates all too clearly, every whistleblower faces the very real possibility of reprisals, not only rhetorical but also professional, personal, and even, if not especially in this era of hate crimes and domestic terrorism, potentially violent. Yet they continue to stand up, protesting wrongs and embodying national ideals as active patriots do.

Sometimes the wrongs are substantive and defining enough that they require a more in-depth examination through a critical lens if the nation is to have a chance of moving closer to its ideals, however. That's the critical patriotic goal of the 1619 Project, which examines the histories and legacies of slavery as foundational to American history and identity. It's also the central subject of a contemporary writer like Ta-Nehisi Coates, who in acclaimed works like the autobiographical *Between the World and Me* (2015) makes the case that it is the struggle itself which should be our patriotic emphasis, rather than the uncertain possibility of hope for a better future. And it's at the heart of one of the great cultural works of the last few years, Gary Clark Jr.'s song "This Land" (2019), which originated when Clark was called the n-word (in front of his young son) by a racist neighbor while being accused of trespassing on the Texas property he had recently purchased. For much of the song he engages with such exclusionary attitudes and histories, singing in the chorus, "I remember when you used to tell me/'Nigger run, nigger run/Go back where you came from/We don't want, we don't want your kind/We think you's a dog born.'" But in response he offers an exemplary critical patriotic perspective on American identity: "Fuck you, I'm America's son/This is where I come from/This land is mine."

Such intimate, personal expressions comprise one vital form of critical patriotism, but so too do broader engagements with the gaps between national mythologies and the realities of our histories and stories. The 1619 Project offers a public scholarly model for engaging those questions; another recent song, The Killers' "Land of the Free" (2019), comprises a compelling pop cultural expression of such overarching critical patriotism. The song opens with a verse in which the speaker channels his father's idealized vision of the nation, a multi-generational immigrant story that seemingly embodies the titular image: "his mother Adeline's family came on a ship/Cut coal and planted a seed." But the remaining verses offer darkly ironic contrasts, depictions of how for far too many Americans, the nation is anything but that idealized land. The song's final lines express that critical patriotic perspective with particular clarity and power, and in relationship to one of the Trump era's most prominent national debates: "Down at the border, they're gonna put up a wall/Concrete and rebar steel beams/High enough to keep all those filthy hands off/Of our hopes and our dreams/People who just want the same things we do/In the land of the free." Those closing lines manage both to acknowledge the exclusion of so many from visions of America yet at the same time to challenge that exclusion, imagining a national story in which we are linked by what we share rather than divided from one another.

In June 2020, The Killers released a live acoustic version of "Land of the Free" with new verses, including one focused on the May 25th murder of George Floyd by Minneapolis police officer Derek Chauvin: "How many killings must a man watch in his home/'Til he sees the price on the tag?/Eight measured minutes and 46 seconds/Another boy in the bag, another stain on the flag." Floyd's was just one of a number of killings of African Americans in the spring and summer of 2020: some by police, such as the murder of Breonna Taylor by Louisville officers while she was sleeping in her home; and others by fellow citizens, like the lynching of Ahmaud Arbery by three Georgia men. This ongoing violence, and the discrimination and hatred that cause it, has indeed revealed America's flag to be as stained, its ideals as fraught and flawed, in the 21st century as they have been throughout our history.

In response to both Floyd's murder and all these ongoing histories, however, Americans in all fifty states undertook the most widespread mass protest in the nation's history. In their opposition not just to police brutality and systemic racism but also to mythic patriotisms such as those represented by memorials to divisive figures like Confederate leaders and Christopher Columbus, these protests have represented a potent expression of critical patriotism, an attempt both to highlight these wrongs and to imagine new possibilities for our civic and communal spaces. And the ubiquitous presence of masks among the protesters reflects another layer to their active patriotism, their desire to protect their fellow citizens from the ongoing threat of COVID-19 while still risking their own bodies and lives in service of their critical patriotic goals. These diverse communities of protesters, led by younger generations and inspired by the long history of active and critical patriotisms, have given voice to a profoundly different vision of America than that embodied by Trump and his movement.

Ultimately, I believe that is one of the most consistent goals of all active and critical patriotic efforts, and has certainly been my goal in tracing them throughout these chapters: to make clear that American patriotism has always been a contested space, containing multiple forms and perspectives. There certainly remains a significant place for a celebratory patriotic perspective, for national narratives that highlight our ideals and the best of who we are. It's vital, however, to acknowledge and resist the ease with which national celebrations can turn into mythic patriotisms, often precisely by defining criticism of the nation as un- and even anti-American. Such exclusionary definitions, of patriotism as of the nation itself, don't just leave out other perspectives and communities—they assume consensus when in fact there is debate, making it that much more difficult for alternative voices and views to be heard and included in our conversations and society.

We can't understand the age of Trump unless we trace the long history of those national narratives—of celebratory patriotism, and of how it can be transformed into mythic patriotism. That's why I have dedicated roughly two-thirds of each chapter to tracing those most prominent, interconnected, yet ultimately quite distinct forms. And once we better understand those particular historical perspectives, we can likewise become more open to the inspiring stories I've featured in my chapters' final thirds: alternative active and critical forms of patriotism, voices and communities working to engage with the gap between our ideals and realities and to push us toward a more perfect union. The legacies of those active and critical patriotisms likewise echo and extend into 2020 America, a moment when such patriotisms are more necessary and more crucial than ever.

A Note on Sources

INTRODUCTION:
COMPETING DEFINITIONS OF PATRIOTISM

For popular studies of American patriotism, see Jill Lepore, *This America: The Case for the Nation* (New York: Liveright Publishing, 2019); Jon Meachan and Tim McGraw, *Songs of America: Patriotism, Protest, and the Music that Made a Nation* (New York: Random House, 2019); Francesco Duina, *Broke and Patriotic: Why Poor Americans Love Their Country* (Stanford: Stanford University Press, 2018); Dan Rather and Elliot Kirschner, *What Unites Us: Reflections on Patriotism* (Chapel Hill: Algonquin Books, 2017); Michael Zezima, *50 American Revolutions You're Not Supposed to Know: Reclaiming American Patriotism* (New York: Disinformation Company, 2005); John Bodnar, ed., *Bonds of Affection: Americans Define Their Patriotism* (Princeton: Princeton University Press, 1996).

For academic studies, see Abram C. Van Engen, *City on a Hill: A History of American Exceptionalism* (New Haven: Yale University Press, 2020); Nichole R. Phillips, *Patriotism Black and White: The Color of American Exceptionalism* (Waco: Baylor University Press, 2018); Ben Railton, *History and Hope in American Literature: Models of Critical Patriotism* (Lanham, MD: Rowman & Littlefield, 2016); John D. Wilsey, *American Exceptionalism and Civil Religion: Reassessing the History of an Idea* (Downers Grove, IL: IVP Academic, 2015); Barry J. Balleck, *Allegiance to Liberty: The Changing Face of Patriots, Militias, and Political Violence in America* (Santa Barbara: Praeger, 2014); Teresa Bergman, *Exhibiting Patriotism: Creating and Contesting Interpretations of American Historic Sites* (Walnut Creek, CA: Left Coast Press, 2013); Terre Ryan, *This Ecstatic Nation: The American Landscape and the Aesthetics of Patriotism* (Amherst: University of Massachusetts Press, 2011); George McKenna, *The Puritan Origins of American Patriotism* (New Haven, CT: Yale University Press, 2007); George Kateb, *Patriotism and Other Mistakes* (New Haven, CT: Yale University Press, 2006); Vanessa B. Beasley, *You, the People: American National Identity in Presidential Rhetoric* (College Station: Texas A&M University Press, 2004); Anthony W. Marx, *Faith in Nation: Exclusionary Origins of Nationalism* (Oxford, UK: Oxford University Press, 2003); Deborah Harding, *Stars and Stripes: Patriotic Motifs in American Folk Art* (New York: Rizzoli, 2002); Walter Berns, *Making Patriots* (Chicago: University of Chicago Press, 2001); Michael Billig, *Banal Nationalism* (London, UK: Sage, 1995); John Bodnar, *Remaking America: Public Memory, Commemoration, and Patriotism in the Twentieth Century* (Princeton, NJ: Princeton University Press, 1992).

For the NFL protests, see Stephen Perry, *Pro Football and the Proliferation of Protest: Anthem Posture in a Divided America* (Lanham, MD: Lexington Books, 2019); Howard Bryant, *The Heritage: Black Athletes, a Divided America, and the Politics of Patriotism* (Boston: Beacon Press, 2018); Margaret Haerens, *The NFL National Anthem Protests* (Santa Barbara, CA: ABC-CLIO, 2018). For "America the Beautiful," see Lynn Sherr, *America the Beautiful: The Stirring True Story Behind Our Nation's Favorite Song* (New York: PublicAffairs, 2001). For "My Country, 'Tis of Thee," see Ace Collins, *Songs Sung Red, White, and Blue: The Stories Behind America's Best-Loved Patriotic Songs* (New York: HarperResource, 2003).

CHAPTER 1: THE REVOLUTION: DECLARING AND CONSTITUTING A NATION

For a recent biography of Patrick Henry, see Jon Kukla, *Patrick Henry: Champion of Liberty* (New York: Simon and Schuster, 2017). For overall studies of the Revolution and patriotism, see Tom Shachtman, *The Founding Fortunes: How the Wealthy Paid for and Profited from America's Revolution* (New York: St. Martin's Press, 2020); Jon Chandler, *War, Patriotism and Identity in Revolutionary North America* (Woodbridge, UK: Boydell Press, 2020); Richard Brookhiser, *Give Me Liberty: A History of America's Exceptional Idea* (New York: Basic Books, 2019); C. Bradley Thompson, *America's Revolutionary Mind: A Moral History of the American Revolution and the Declaration that Defined It* (New York: Encounter Books, 2019); Craig Bruce Smith, *American Honor: The Creation of the Nation's Ideals during the Revolutionary Era* (Chapel Hill: University of North Carolina Press, 2018); Steven F. Hayward, *Patriotism is Not Enough: Harry Jaffa, Walter Berns, and the Arguments that Redefined American Conservatism*

(New York: Encounter Books, 2017); Eric Nelson, *The Royalist Revolution: Monarchy and the American Founding* (Cambridge, MA: Harvard University Press, 2014); James P. Byrd, *Sacred Scripture, Sacred War: The Bible and the American Revolution* (New York: Oxford University Press, 2013); Ray Raphael, *Founding Myths: Stories that Hide Our Patriotic Past* (New York: New Press, 2004).

For the Declaration of Independence, see Christian Y. Dupont and Peter S. Onuf, eds., *Declaring Independence: The Origins and Influence of America's Founding Document* (Charlottesville, VA: University of Virginia Library, 2008); David Armitage, *The Declaration of Independence: A Global History* (Cambridge, MA: Harvard University Press, 2007); John E. Ferling, *A Leap in the Dark: The Struggle to Create the American Republic* (New York: Oxford University Press, 2003); Pauline Maier, *American Scripture: Making the Declaration of Independence* (New York: Alfred A. Knopf, 1997). For Benjamin Franklin, see Jonathan Dull, *Benjamin Franklin and the American Revolution* (Lincoln: University of Nebraska Press, 2010); Gordon Wood, *The Americanization of Benjamin Franklin* (New York: Penguin Press, 2004); Sheila L. Skemp, *Benjamin and William Franklin: Father and Son, Patriot and Loyalist* (Boston: Bedford Books, 1994). For Thomas Paine, see Craig Nelson, *Thomas Paine: Enlightenment, Revolution, and the Birth of Modern Nations* (New York: Viking, 2006); Harvey J. Kaye, *Thomas Paine and the Promise of America* (New York: Hill and Wang, 2005); Edward Larkin, *Thomas Paine and the Literature of Revolution* (Cambridge, UK: Cambridge University Press, 2005). For the Revolutionary poets, see Richard Buel, *Joel Barlow: American Citizen in a Revolutionary World* (Baltimore: Johns Hopkins University Press, 2011); Vincent Carretta, *Phillis Wheatley: Biography of a Genius in Bondage* (Athens, GA: University of Georgia Press, 2011); Henry Louis Gates Jr., *The Trials of Phillis Wheatley: America's First Black Poet and Her Encounters with the Founding Fathers* (New York: Basic Civitas Books, 2003); Emory Elliott, *Revolutionary Writers: Literature and Authority in the New Republic, 1725–1810* (New York: Oxford University Press, 1982); Richard Nickson, *Philip Freneau: Poet of the Revolution* (Trenton: New Jersey Historical Commission, 1980).

For Loyalists, see Gregg L. Frazer, *God against the Revolution: The Loyalist Clergy's Case against the American Revolution* (Lawrence: University Press of Kansas, 2018); Chaim M. Rosenberg, *The Loyalist Conscience: Principled Opposition to the American Revolution* (Jefferson, NC: McFarland, 2018); Rebecca Brannon, *From Revolution to Reunion: The Reintegration of the South Carolina Loyalists* (Columbia: University of South Carolina Press, 2016); Ruma Chopra, *Choosing Sides: Loyalists in Revolutionary America* (Lanham, MD: Rowman & Littlefield, 2013); Robert M. Calhoon, ed., *Tory Insurgents: The Loyalist Perception and Other Essays* (Columbia: University of South Carolina Press, 2010); Mary Louise Clifford, *From Slavery to Freetown: Black Loyalists After the American Revolution* (Jefferson, NC: McFarland, 1999). For women and the Revolution, see Barbara B. Oberg, ed., *Women in the American Revolution: Gender, Politics, and the Domestic World* (Charlottesville: University of Virginia Press, 2019); Nancy Rubin Stuart, *The Muse of the Revolution: The Secret Pen of Mercy Otis Warren and the Founding of a Nation* (Boston: Beacon Press, 2008); Carol Berkin, *Revolutionary Mothers: Women in the Struggle for America's Independence* (New York: Alfred A. Knopf, 2005); Mary Beth Norton, *Founding Mothers & Fathers: Gendered Power and the Forming of American Society* (New York: Alfred A. Knopf, 1996); Linda Kerber, *Women of the Republic: Intellect and Ideology in Revolutionary America* (Chapel Hill: University of North Carolina Press, 1980). For race and the Revolution, see Sean Wilentz, *No Property in Man: Slavery and Antislavery at the Nation's Founding* (Cambridge, MA: Harvard University Press, 2018); Robert G. Parkinson, *The Common Cause: Creating Race and Nation in the American Revolution* (Chapel Hill: University of North Carolina Press, 2016); Catherine Adams and Elizabeth H. Peck, *Love of Freedom: Black Women in Colonial and Revolutionary New England* (Oxford, UK: Oxford University Press, 2010); Gary B. Nash, *The Forgotten Fifth: African Americans in the Age of Revolution* (Cambridge, MA: Harvard University Press, 2006); Roger Wilkins, *Jefferson's Pillow: The Founding Fathers and the Dilemma of Black Patriotism* (Boston: Beacon Press, 2001); Patricia Bradley, *Slavery, Propaganda, and the American Revolution* (Jackson: University Press of Mississippi, 1998).

CHAPTER 2: THE EARLY REPUBLIC: YOUNG, EXPANDING, AND DIVIDED

For De Tocqueville, see Leo Damrosch, *Tocqueville's Discovery of America* (New York: Farrar, Straus and Giroux, 2010); Joshua Mitchell, *The Fragility of Freedom: Tocqueville on Religion, Democracy, and the American Future* (Chicago: University of Chicago Press, 1995). For overall studies of the era and patriotism, see Gerald Leonard and Saul Cornell, *The Partisan Republic: Democracy, Exclusion, and the Fall of the Founders' Constitution, 1780s–1830s* (Cambridge, UK: Cambridge University Press, 2019); Benjamin E. Park, *American Nationalisms: Imagining Union in the Age of Revolutions, 1783–1833* (Cambridge, UK: Cambridge University Press, 2018); Carol Berkin, *A Sovereign People: The Crises of the 1790s and the Birth of American Nationalism* (New York: Basic Books, 2017); J. Gerald Kennedy, *Strange*

Nation: Literary Nationalism and Cultural Conflict in the Age of Poe (New York: Oxford University Press, 2016); Jonathan J. Den Hartog, *Patriotism and Piety: Federalist Politics and Religious Struggle in the New American Nation* (Charlottesville: University of Virginia Press, 2014); Daniel Walker Howe, *What Hath God Wrought: The Transformation of America, 1815–1848* (Oxford, UK: Oxford University Press, 2007); Fred Somkin, *Unquiet Eagle: Memory and Desire in the Idea of American Freedom, 1815–1860* (Ithaca, NY: Cornell University Press, 1967).

For the War of 1812 and the anthem, see John R. Vile, *America's National Anthem: The "Star-Spangled Banner" in U.S. History, Culture, and Law* (Westport, CT: Greenwood Press, 2020); William Sterne Randall, *Unshackling America: How the War of 1812 Truly Ended the American Revolution* (New York: St. Martin's Press, 2017); Marc Ferris, *Star-Spangled Banner: The Unlikely Story of America's National Anthem* (Baltimore: Johns Hopkins University Press, 2014); Marc Leepson, *What So Proudly We Hailed: Francis Scott Key, a Life* (New York: St. Martin's Press, 2014); Troy Bickham, *The Weight of Vengeance: The United States, the British Empire, and the War of 1812* (Oxford, UK: Oxford University Press, 2012); Nicole Eustace, *1812: War and the Passions of Patriotism* (Philadelphia: University of Pennsylvania Press, 2012). For Revolutionary commemorations, see Adam Criblez, *Parading Patriotism: Independence Day Celebrations in the Urban Midwest, 1826–1876* (DeKalb, IL: NIU Press, 2013); Michael A. McDonnell, Clare Corbould, Frances M. Clarke, and W. Fitzhugh Brundag, eds., *Remembering the Revolution: Memory, History, and Nation Making from Independence to the Civil War* (Amherst: University of Massachusetts Press, 2013); Alfred Young, *The Shoemaker and the Tea Party: Memory and the American Revolution* (Boston: Beacon Press, 1999); Michael Kammen, *Mystic Chords of Memory: The Transformation of Tradition in American Culture* (New York: Alfred A. Knopf, 1991).

For expansion, see Levi Gahman, *Land, God and Guns: Settler Colonialism and Masculinity in the American Heartland* (London: Zed Books, 2020); Thomas Richards Jr., *Breakaway Americas: The Unmanifest Future of the Jacksonian United States* (Baltimore: Johns Hopkins University Press, 2020); Paul Frymer, *Building an American Empire: The Era of Territorial and Political Expansion* (Princeton, NJ: Princeton University Press, 2017); Meredith Mason Brown, *Frontiersman: Daniel Boone and the Making of America* (Baton Rouge: Louisiana State University Press, 2008); Jon Meacham, *American Lion: Andrew Jackson in the White House* (New York: Random House, 2008); Amy S. Greenerg, *Manifest Manhood and the Antebellum American Empire* (Cambridge, UK: Cambridge University Press, 2005); Robert Sampson, *John L. O'Sullivan and His Times* (Kent, OH: Kent State

University Press, 2003); Reginald Horsman, *Race and Manifest Destiny: The Origins of American Racial Anglo-Saxonism* (Cambridge, MA: Harvard University Press, 1981). For the Know Nothings, see Michael F. Holt, *The Rise of the Fall of the American Whig Party: Jacksonian Politics and the Onset of the Civil War* (New York: Oxford University Press, 1999); Tyler Anbinder, *Nativism and Slavery: The Northern Know Nothings and the Politics of the 1850s* (New York: Oxford University Press, 1992); John R. Mulkern, *The Know-Nothing Party in Massachusetts: The Rise and Fall of a People's Movement* (Boston: Northeastern University Press, 1990).

For the Young America movement, see Yonatan Eyal, *The Young America Movement and the Transformation of the Democratic Party 1828–1861* (Cambridge, UK: Cambridge University Press, 2007); Mark A. Lause, *Young America: Land, Labor, and the Republican Community* (Urbana: University of Illinois Press, 2005); Edward L. Widmer, *Young America: The Flowering of Democracy in New York City* (New York: Oxford University Press, 1999). For Transcendentalism, see Daniel S. Malachuk, *Two Cities: The Political Thought of American Transcendentalism* (Lawrence: University Press of Kansas, 2016); Philip F. Gura, *American Transcendentalism: A History* (New York: Hill and Wang, 2007); Alfred I. Tauber, *Henry David Thoreau and the Moral Agency of Knowing* (Berkeley: University of California Press, 2001); David S. Reynolds, *Walt Whitman's America: A Cultural Biography* (New York: Alfred A. Knopf, 1995). For my critical patriotic authors, see Drew Lopenzina, *Through an Indian's Looking Glass: A Cultural Biography of William Apess, Pequot* (Amherst: University of Massachusetts Press, 2017); Lucinda L. Damon-Bach and Victoria Clements, eds., *Catharine Maria Sedgwick: Critical Perspectives* (Boston: Northeastern University Press, 2003); Peter P. Hinks, *To Awaken My Afflicted Brethren: David Walker and the Problem of Antebellum Slave Resistance* (University Park: Pennsylvania State University Press, 1997).

CHAPTER 3: THE CIVIL WAR: TESTING WHETHER THE NATION COULD ENDURE

For overall studies of the war and patriotism, see Colin Woodard, *Union: The Struggle to Forge the Story of United States Nationhood* (New York: Viking, 2020); James A. Davis, *Maryland, My Maryland: Music and Patriotism during the American Civil War* (Lincoln: University of Nebraska Press, 2018); Alan Levine, Thomas W. Merrill, and James R. Stoner Jr., eds., *The Political Thought of the Civil War* (Lawrence: University Press of Kansas, 2018); Robert M. Sandow, ed., *Contested Loyalty: Debates over Patriotism in the Civil*

War North (New York: Fordham University Press, 2018); Melinda Lawson, *Patriot Fires: Forging a New American Nationalism in the Civil War North* (Lawrence: University Press of Kansas, 2002); Susan-Mary Grant, *North over South: Northern Nationalism and American Identity in the Antebellum Era* (Lawrence: University Press of Kansas, 2000); Marshall DeRosa, ed., *The Politics of Dissolution: Quest for a National Identity and the American Civil War* (New Brunswick, NJ: Transaction Publishers, 1998).

For Whitman, Melville, and Howe, see Christopher Sten and Tyler Hoffman, eds., *"This Mighty Convulsion": Whitman and Melville Write the Civil War* (Iowa City: University of Iowa Press, 2019); Lindsay Tuggle, *The Afterlives of Specimens: Science, Mourning, and Whitman's Civil War* (Iowa City: University of Iowa Press, 2017); Elaine Showalter, *The Civil Wars of Julia Ward Howe* (New York: Simon & Schuster, 2016); Garrett Peck, *Walt Whitman in Washington, D.C.: The Civil War and America's Great Poet* (Charleston, SC: History Press, 2015); Stanton Garner, *The Civil War World of Herman Melville* (Lawrence: University Press of Kansas, 1993). For the Confederacy, see Erik Mathisen, *The Loyal Republic: Traitors, Slaves, and the Remaking of Citizenship in Civil War America* (Chapel Hill: University of North Carolina Press, 2018); Philip D. Dillard, *Jefferson Davis's Final Campaign: Confederate Nationalism and the Fight to Arm Slaves* (Macon, GA: Mercer University Press, 2017); Gary W. Gallagher, *Becoming Confederates: Paths to a New National Loyalty* (Athens, GA: University of Georgia Press, 2013); Bruce C. Levine, *The Fall of the House of Dixie: The Civil War and the Social Revolution that Transformed the South* (New York: Random House, 2013); Andre M. Fleche, *The Revolution of 1861: The American Civil War in the Age of Nationalist Conflict* (Chapel Hill: University of North Carolina Press, 2012); Coleman Hutchison, *Apples and Ashes: Literature, Nationalism, and the Confederate States of America* (Athens, GA: University of Georgia Press, 2012); Anne Sarah Rubin, *A Shattered Nation: The Rise and Fall of the Confederacy, 1861–1868* (Chapel Hill: University of North Carolina Press, 2005). For the draft riots, see Barnet Schecter, *The Devil's Own Work: The Civil War Draft Riots and the Fight to Reconstruct America* (New York: Walker & Co., 2005). For the Dakota War, see John A. Haymond, *The Infamous Dakota War Trails of 1862: Revenge, Military Law and the Judgment of History* (Jefferson, NC: McFarland, 2016); Scott W. Berg, *38 Nooses: Lincoln, Little Crow, and the Beginning of the Frontier's End* (New York: Pantheon Books, 2012).

For the Gettysburg Address, see Martin P. Johnson, *Writing the Gettysburg Address* (Lawrence: University Press of Kansas, 2013); Carl F. Wieck, *Lincoln's Quest for Equality: The Road to Gettysburg* (DeKalb: Northern Illinois University Press, 2002); Garry Wills, *Lincoln at Gettysburg: The Words that*

Remade America (New York: Simon & Schuster, 1992). For the USCT, see Bob Luke and John David Smith, *Soldiering for Freedom: How the Union Army Recruited, Trained, and Deployed the U.S. Colored Troops* (Baltimore: Johns Hopkins University Press, 2014); John David Smith, *Lincoln and the U.S. Colored Troops* (Carbondale: Southern Illinois University Press, 2013); William A. Dobak, *Freedom by the Sword: The US Colored Troops, 1862–1867* (Washington, DC: U.S. Army Center of Military History, 2011). For immigrant soldiers, see Ben Railton, *The Chinese Exclusion Act: What It Can Teach Us about America* (New York: Palgrave Pivot, 2013); Allan Punzalan Isaac, *American Tropics: Articulating Filipino America* (Minneapolis: University of Minnesota Press, 2006). For nurses, see Robert C. Plumb, *The Better Angels: Five Women Who Changed Civil War America* (Lincoln, NE: Potomac Books, 2020); Daneen Wardrop, *Civil War Nurse Narratives, 1863–1870* (Iowa City: University of Iowa Press, 2015); Heather Butts, *African American Medicine in Washington, D.C.: Healing the Capital during the Civil War* (Charleston, SC: The History Press, 2014); Margaret Humphreys, *Marrow of Tragedy: The Health Crisis of the American Civil War* (Baltimore: Johns Hopkins University Press, 2013). For Douglass, see David W. Blight, *Frederick Douglass: Prophet of Freedom* (New York: Simon & Schuster, 2018); James Oakes, *The Radical and the Republican: Frederick Douglass, Abraham Lincoln, and the Triumph of Antislavery Politics* (New York: W.W. Norton, 2007). For Delany, see Tunde Adeleke, ed., *Martin R. Delany's Civil War and Reconstruction: A Primary Source Reader* (Jackson: University Press of Mississippi, 2020); Robert Steven Levine, *Martin Delany, Frederick Douglass, and the Politics of Representative Identity* (Chapel Hill: University of North Carolina Press, 1997). For Lucy Larcom, see Sylvia J. Cook, *Working Women, Literary Ladies: The Industrial Revolution and Female Aspiration* (Oxford, UK: Oxford University Press, 2008); Bernice Selden, *The Mill Girls: Lucy Larcom, Harriet Hanson Robinson, Sarah G. Bagley* (New York: Atheneum, 1983).

CHAPTER 4: THE GILDED AGE: WEALTH, EMPIRE, AND RESISTANCE

For the Statue of Liberty, see Yasmin Sabina Khan, *Enlightening the World: The Creation of the Statue of Liberty* (Ithaca, NY: Cornell University Press, 2010). For overall studies of Gilded Age patriotism, see Richard White, *The Republic for Which It Stands: The United States during Reconstruction and the Gilded Age, 1865–1896* (New York: Oxford University Press, 2017); Ben Railton, *Contesting the Past, Reconstructing the Nation: American Culture and Literature in the Gilded Age, 1876–1893* (Tuscaloosa: University of Alabama Press, 2007); Rebecca Edwards, *New Spirits: Americans in the Gilded Age, 1865–1905* (New York: Oxford University Press, 2006); Jonathan Hansen, *The Lost Promise of Patriotism: Debating American Identity, 1890–1920* (Chicago: University of Chicago Press, 2003); Alan Trachtenberg, *The Incorporation of America: Culture and Society in the Gilded Age* (New York: Hill and Wang, 1982).

For the Centennial, see Susanna W. Gold, *The Unfinished Exposition: Visualizing Myth, Memory, and the Shadow of the Civil War in Centennial America* (New York: Routledge, 2016); Linda P. Gross and Theresa R. Snyder, *Philadelphia's 1876 Centennial Exposition* (Charleston, SC: Arcadia, 2005); Bruno Giberti, *Designing the Centennial: A History of the 1876 International Exhibition in Philadelphia* (Lexington: University Press of Kentucky, 2002). For the Columbian Exposition, see David R. M. Beck, *Unfair Labor?: American Indians and the 1893 World's Columbian Exposition in Chicago* (Lincoln: University of Nebraska Press, 2019); Sarah Wadsworth and Wayne A. Wiegand, *Right Here I See My Own Books: The Woman's Building Library at the World's Columbian Exposition* (Amherst: University of Massachusetts Press, 2012); Wanda M. Corn, *Women Building History: Public Art at the 1893 Columbian Exposition* (Berkeley: University of California Press, 2011); Chaim M. Rosenberg, *America at the Fair: Chicago's 1893 World's Columbian Exposition* (Charleston, SC: Arcadia, 2008). For narratives of wealth and poverty, see Noam Maggor, *Brahmin Capitalism: Frontiers of Wealth and Populism in America's First Gilded Age* (Cambridge, MA: Harvard University Press, 2017); Samuel Bostaph, *Andrew Carnegie: An Economic Biography* (Lanham, MD: Lexington Books, 2015); Leon Fink, *The Long Gilded Age: American Capitalism and the Lessons of a New World Order* (Philadelphia: University of Pennsylvania Press, 2015); David Wagner, *Ordinary People: In and Out of Poverty in the Gilded Age* (Boulder: Paradigm Publishers, 2008); Jack Beatty, *Age of Betrayal: The Triumph of Money in America, 1865–1900* (New York: Alfred A. Knopf, 2007); Gary Scharnhorst and Jack Bates, *The Lost Life of Horatio Alger* (Bloomington: Indiana University Press, 1985).

For Haymarket, see Timothy Messer-Kruse, *The Trial of the Haymarket Anarchists: Terrorism and Justice in the Gilded Age* (New York: Palgrave Macmillan, 2011); James R. Green, *Death in the Haymarket: A Story of Chicago, the First Labor Movement and the Bombing that Divided Gilded Age America* (New York: Pantheon Books, 2006). For immigration restrictions, see Erika Lee, *America for Americans: A History of Xenophobia in the United States* (New York: Basic Books, 2019); Beth Lew-Williams, *The Chinese Must Go: Violence, Exclusion, and the Making of the Alien in America*

(Cambridge, MA: Harvard University Press, 2018); Ben Railton, *The Chinese Exclusion Act: What It Can Teach Us about America* (New York: Palgrave Pivot, 2013); Jonathan P. Spiro, *Defending the Master Race: Conservation, Eugenics, and the Legacy of Madison Grant* (Burlington: University of Vermont Press, 2009). For expansion and imperialism, see Sarah Miller-Davenport, *Gateway State: Hawai'i and the Cultural Transformation of American Empire* (Princeton, NJ: Princeton University Press, 2019); Daniel Immerwahr, *How to Hide an Empire: A History of the Greater United States* (New York: Farrar, Straus and Giroux, 2019); Daniel E. Bender, *Making the Empire Work: Labor and United States Imperialism* (New York: New York University Press, 2015); Brenda J. Child, *Boarding School Seasons: American Indian Families* (Lincoln: University of Nebraska Press, 1998); David Wallace Adams, *Education for Extinction: American Indians and the Boarding School Experience, 1875–1928* (Lawrence: University Press of Kansas, 1995); Richard J. Kerry, *The Star-Spangled Mirror: America's Image of Itself and the World* (Lanham, MD: Rowman & Littlefield, 1990).

For the Suffrage movement, see Ellen Carol DuBois, *Suffrage: Women's Long Battle for the Vote* (New York: Simon & Schuster, 2020); Angela Dodson, *Remember the Ladies: Celebrating Those Who Fought for Freedom at the Ballot Box* (New York: Center Street, 2017); and the sources listed under Chapter 5. For the Pledge of Allegiance, see Kevin M. Kruse, *One Nation Under God: How Corporate America Invented Christian America* (New York: Basic Books, 2015); John W. Baer, *The Pledge of Allegiance: A Revised History and Analysis, 1892–2007* (Annapolis, MD: Free State Press, 2007); Joel Westheimer, ed., *Pledging Allegiance: The Politics of Patriotism in America's Schools* (New York: Teachers College Press, 2007); Richard J. Ellis, *To the Flag: The Unlikely History of the Pledge of Allegiance* (Lawrence: University Press of Kansas, 2005). For August Spies, see Bruce C. Nelson, *Beyond the Martyrs: A Social History of Chicago's Anarchists, 1870–1900* (New Brunswick, NJ: Rutgers University Press, 1988). For Henry George, see Steven L. Piott, *American Reformers, 1870–1920: Progressives in Word and Deed* (Lanham, MD: Rowman & Littlefield, 2006). For Helen Hunt Jackson, see Valerie Sherer Mathes, *Helen Hunt Jackson and Her Indian Reform Legacy* (Austin: University of Texas Press, 1990). For Standing Bear, see Stephen Dando-Collins, *Standing Bear is a Person* (Cambridge, MA: Da Capo Press, 2004); Valerie Sherer Mathes and Richard Lowitt, *The Standing Bear Controversy: Prelude to Indian Reform* (Urbana: University of Illinois Press, 2003). For Ida B. Wells, see Mia Bay, *To Tell the Truth Freely: The Life of Ida B. Wells* (New York: Hill and Wang, 2009); P.J. Giddings, *Ida, A Sword among Lions: Ida B. Wells and the Campaign against Lynching* (New York: Amistad, 2008). For anti-imperialism, see Michael Patrick

Cullinane, *Liberty and American Anti-Imperialism, 1898–1909* (New York: Palgrave Macmillan, 2012); Richard Seymour, *American Insurgents: A Brief History of American Anti-Imperialism* (Chicago: Haymarket Books, 2012).

CHAPTER 5: THE PROGRESSIVE ERA: FROM ROOSEVELT AND REFORM TO WORLD WAR

For the transportation revolutions, see Heather B. Barrow, *Henry Ford's Plan for the American Suburb: Dearborn and Detroit* (DeKalb: Northern Illinois University Press, 2015); Victoria Saker Woeste, *Henry Ford's War on Jews and the Legal Battle against Hate Speech* (Palo Alto, CA: Stanford University Press, 2013); Steven Watts, *The People's Tycoon: Henry Ford and the American Century* (New York: Alfred A. Knopf, 2005); John D. Anderson, *Inventing Flight: The Wright Brothers and Their Predecessors* (Baltimore: Johns Hopkins University Press, 2004); Max Wallace, *The American Axis: Henry Ford, Charles Lindbergh, and the Rise of the Third Reich* (New York: St. Martin's Press, 2003). For overall studies of Progressive era patriotism, see T. J. Jackson Lears, *Rebirth of a Nation: The Remaking of Modern America, 1877–1920* (New York: HarperCollins, 2009); John Louis Recchiuti, *Civic Engagement: Social Science and Progressive-Era Reform in New York City* (Philadelphia: University of Pennsylvania Press, 2007); Robert Harrison, *Congress, Progressive Reform, and the New American State* (Cambridge, UK: Cambridge University Press, 2004); Alan Dawley, *Changing the World: American Progressives in War and Revolution* (Princeton, NJ: Princeton University Press, 2003); Lewis L. Gould, *America in the Progressive Era, 1890–1914* (Harlow, UK: Longman, 2001); Steven J. Diner, *A Very Different Age: Americans of the Progressive Era* (New York: Hill and Wang, 1998).

For Teddy Roosevelt, see William R. Nester, *Theodore Roosevelt and the Art of American Power: An American for All Time* (Lanham, MD: Lexington Books, 2019); Gregg Jones, *Honor in the Dust: Theodore Roosevelt, War in the Philippines, and the Rise and Fall of America's Imperial Dream* (New York: New American Library, 2012); Douglas Brinkley, *The Wilderness Warrior: Theodore Roosevelt and the Crusade for America* (New York: HarperCollins, 2009); Henry J. Hendrix, *Theodore Roosevelt's Naval Diplomacy: The US Navy and the Birth of the American Century* (Anapolis, MD: Naval Institute Press, 2009); Kathleen Dalton, *Theodore Roosevelt: A Strenuous Life* (New York: Alfred A. Knopf, 2002). For Mary Antin and Jewish immigration, see Melissa R. Klapper, *Jewish Girls Coming of Age in America, 1860-1920* (New York: New York University Press, 2005); Allan Mazur, *A Romance in Natural History: The Lives and Works of Amadeus Grabau and Mary Antin*

(Syracuse, NY: Garret, 2004); Hasia Diner, *A New Promised Land: A History of Jews in America* (Oxford, UK: Oxford University Press, 2003); and two volumes in *The Jewish People in America* series: Gerald Sorin, *A Time for Building: The Third Migration, 1880-1920* (Baltimore: Johns Hopkins University Press, 1992) and Henry L. Feingold, *A Time for Searching: Entering the Mainstream, 1920–1945* (Baltimore: Johns Hopkins University Press, 1992).

For World War I, propaganda, and the Red Scare, see Peter Stehman, *Patriotic Murder: A World War I Hate Crime for Uncle Sam* (Lincoln: University of Nebraska Press, 2018); Richard L. Pifer, *The Great War Comes to Wisconsin: Sacrifice, Patriotism, and Free Speech in a Time of Crisis* (Madison: Wisconsin Historical Society, 2017); Susan A. Brewer, *Why America Fights: Patriotism and War Propaganda from the Philippines to Iraq* (Oxford, UK: Oxford University Press, 2009); Christopher Capozzola, *Uncle Sam Wants YOU: World War I and the Making of the Modern American Citizen* (Oxford, UK: Oxford University Press, 2008); William H. Thomas Jr., *Unsafe for Democracy: World War I and the U.S. Justice Department's Covert Campaign to Suppress Dissent* (Madison: University of Wisconsin Press, 2008); Ann Hagedorn, *Savage Peace: Hope and Fear in America, 1919* (New York: Simon & Schuster, 2007); Regin Schmidt, *Red Scare: FBI and the Origins of Anticommunism in the United States, 1919–1943* (Copenhagen: Museum Tusculanum Press, 2000); Stephen M. Kohn, *American Political Prisoners: Prosecutions under the Espionage and Sedition Acts* (Westport, CT: Praeger, 1994). For immigration restrictions, see Aristide Zolberg, *A Nation by Design: Immigration Policy in the Fashioning of America* (Cambridge, MA: Harvard University Press, 2006); Mae M. Ngai, *Impossible Subjects: Illegal Aliens and the Making of Modern America* (Princeton, NJ: Princeton University Press, 2004); John Higham, *Strangers in the Land: Patterns of American Nativism, 1860–1925* (New York: Atheneum, 1963).

For Americanization and the Settlement movement, see Christina A. Ziegler-McPherson, *Americanization in the States: Immigrant Social Welfare Policy, Citizenship, and National Identity in the United States, 1908–1929* (Gainesville: University Press of Florida, 2009); Louise W. Knight, *Citizen: Jane Addams and the Struggle for Democracy* (Chicago: University of Chicago Press, 2005); Christopher M. Sterba, *Good Americans: Italian and Jewish Immigrants during the First World War* (New York: Oxford University Press, 2003); Frank Van Nuys, *Americanizing the West: Race, Immigrants, and Citizenship, 1890–1930* (Lawrence: University Press of Kansas, 2002). For the Suffrage movement, see Doris Stevens and Angela P. Dodson, *Jailed for Freedom: A First-Person Account of the Militant Fight for Women's Rights* (New York: Black Dog & Leventhal, 2020); Annessa Babic, *America's Changing*

Icons: Constructing Patriotic Women from World War I to the Present (Lanham, MD: Rowman & Littlefield, 2018); Angela P. Dodson, *Remember the Ladies: Celebrating Those Who Fought for Freedom at the Ballot Box* (New York: Center Street, 2017); Jean H. Baker, *Sisters: The Lives of America's Suffragists* (New York: Hill and Wang, 2005); Francesca Morgan, *Women and Patriotism in Jim Crow America* (Chapel Hill: University of North Carolina Press, 2005). For Native Americans, see Thomas Grillot, *First Americans: U.S. Patriotism in Indian Country after World War I* (New Haven, CT: Yale University Press, 2018); Paul C. Rosier, *Serving Their Country: American Indian Politics and Patriotism in the Twentieth Century* (Cambridge, MA: Harvard University Press, 2009); Lori Lynn Muntz, *Representing Indians: The Melodrama of Native Citizenship in United States Popular Culture of the 1920s* (Iowa City: University of Iowa PhD Dissertation, 2006).

For pacifism, see Kevin S. Giles, *One Woman Against War: The Jeannette Rankin Story* (Booklocker.com, 2016); Cynthia Wachtell, *War No More: The Antiwar Impulse in American Literature, 1861–1914* (Baton Rouge: Louisiana State University Press, 2010); Norma Smith, *Jeannette Rankin, America's Conscience* (Helena: Montana Historical Society Press, 2002); Barbara S. Kraft, *The Peace Ship: Henry Ford's Pacifist Adventure in the First World War* (New York: Macmillan, 1978). For muckrakers, see Steve Weinberg, *Taking on the Trust: The Epic Battle of Ida Tarbell and John D. Rockefeller* (New York: Norton, 2008); Kevin Mattson, *Upton Sinclair and the Other American Century* (Hoboken, NJ: John Wiley & Sons, 2006); Cecelia Tichi, *Exposés and Excess: Muckraking in America, 1900/2000* (Philadelphia: University of Pennsylvania Press, 2004); Judith and William Serrin, *Muckraking! The Journalism that Changed America* (New York: New Press, 2002). For the NAACP, see Dick Lehr, *The Birth of a Movement: How* Birth of a Nation *Ignited the Battle for Civil Rights* (New York: Perseus Books, 2017); Susan D. Carle, *Defining the Struggle: National Racial Justice Organizing, 1880–1915* (Oxford, UK: Oxford University Press, 2013); Manfred Berg, *The Ticket to Freedom: The NAACP and the Struggle for Black Political Integration* (Gainesville: University Press of Florida, 2005); Mark Robert Schneider, *We Return Fighting: The Civil Rights Movement in the Jazz Age* (Boston: Northeastern University Press, 2002).

CHAPTER 6: THE DEPRESSION AND WORLD WAR II: BEYOND THE GREATEST GENERATION

For the sports moments, see two books by Jeremy Schaap, *Triumph: The Untold Story of Jesse Owens and Hitler's Olympics* (Boston: Houghton

Mifflin, 2007) and *Cinderella Man: James J. Braddock, Max Baer, and the Greatest Upset in Boxing History* (Boston: Houghton Mifflin, 2005). See also Louis Moore, *I Fight for a Living: Boxing and the Battle for Black Manhood, 1880–1915* (Urbana: University of Illinois Press, 2017). For overall studies of the Depression, see Kenneth J. Bindas, *Modernity and the Great Depression: The Transformation of American Society, 1930–1941* (Lawrence: University Press of Kansas, 2017); Morris Dickstein, *Dancing in the Dark: A Cultural History of the Great Depression* (New York: Norton, 2009); David Welky, *Everything was Better in America: Print Culture in the Great Depression* (Urbana: University of Illinois Press, 2008); T. H. Watkins, *The Great Depression: America in the 1930s* (Boston: Little, Brown, 1993); For overall studies of World War II, see Blaine T. Browne, *Mighty Endeavor: The American Nation and World War II* (Lanham, MD: Rowman & Littlefield, 2019); James T. Sparrow, *Warfare State: World War II Americans and the Age of Big Government* (New York: Oxford University Press, 2011); Marilyn E. Hegarty, *Victory Girls, Khaki-Wackies, and Patriotutes: The Regulation of Female Sexuality during World War II* (New York: New York University Press, 2008); Robert B. Westbrook, *Why We Fought: Forging American Obligations in World War II* (Washington, DC: Smithsonian Books, 2004); Gerald L. Sittser, *A Cautious Patriotism: The American Churches and the Second World War* (Chapel Hill: University of North Carolina Press, 1997).

For the New Deal programs, see Julie Burrell, *The Civil Rights Theatre Movement in New York, 1939–1966: Staging Freedom* (New York: Palgrave Macmillan, 2019); Andrew Kelly, *Kentucky by Design: The Decorative Arts, American Culture and the Arts Programs of the WPA* (Lexington: University Press of Kentucky, 2015); Sharon Ann Musher, *Democratic Art: The New Deal's Influence on American Culture* (Chicago: University of Chicago Press, 2015); David A. Taylor, *Soul of a People: The WPA Writers' Project Uncovers Depression America* (Hoboken, NJ: Wiley, 2009); Nick Taylor, *American-Made: The Enduring Legacy of the WPA* (New York: Bantam Books, 2008); Jason Scott Smith, *Building New Deal Liberalism: The Political Economy of Public Works, 1933–1956* (New York: Cambridge University Press, 2006). For war propaganda, see Helen Fordham, *George Seldes' War for the Public Good: Weaponising a Free Press* (New York: Palgrave Macmillan, 2019); Cecelia Gowdy-Wygant, *Cultivating Victory: The Women's Land Army and the Victory Garden Movement* (Pittsburgh, PA: University of Pittsburgh Press, 2013); Donna B. Knaff, *Beyond Rosie the Riveter: Women of World War II in American Popular Graphic Art* (Lawrence: University Press of Kansas, 2012); Margaret Regis, *When Our Mothers Went to War: An Illustrated History of Women in World War II* (Bellingham, WA: NavPub, 2008); James J. Kimble, *Mobilizing the Home Front: War Bonds and Domestic Propaganda*

(College Station: Texas A&M University Press, 2006); Clayton Laurie, *The Propaganda Warriors: America's Crusade Against Nazi Germany* (Lawrence: University Press of Kansas, 1996). For the Greatest Generation, see Harvey J. Kaye, *The Fight for the Four Freedoms: What Made FDR and the Greatest Generation Truly Great* (New York: Simon & Schuster, 2014); Kenneth D. Rose, *Myth and the Greatest Generation* (New York: Routledge, 2008); David Kennedy, *Freedom from Fear: The American People in Depression and War, 1929–1945* (New York: Oxford University Press, 1999); Tom Brokaw, *The Greatest Generation* (New York: Random House, 1998).

For protests and the Depression, see Douglas M. Charles, *J. Edgar Hoover and the Anti-interventionists: FBI Political Surveillance and the Rise of the Domestic Security State, 1939–1945* (Columbus: Ohio State University Press, 2007); Robert Cohen, *When the Old Left Was Young: Student Radicals and America's First Mass Student Movement, 1929–1941* (New York: Oxford University Press, 1993). For Japanese internment, see Chertin M. Lyon, *Prisons and Patriots: Japanese American Wartime Citizenship, Civil Disobedience, and Historical Memory* (Philadelphia: Temple University Press, 2012); Greg Robinson, *A Tragedy of Democracy: Japanese Confinement in North America* (New York: Columbia University Press, 2009); Nacy Clark de Nevers, *The Colonel and the Pacifist: Karl Bendetsen, Perry Saito, and the Incarceration of Japanese Americans during World War II* (Salt Lake City: University of Utah Press, 2004). For McCarthyism, see Raymond Caballero, *McCarthyism vs. Clinton Jencks* (Norman: University of Oklahoma Press, 2019); Landon R. Y. Storrs, *The Second Red Scare and the Unmaking of the New Deal Left* (Princeton, NJ: Princeton University Press, 2013); Thomas Doherty, *Cold War, Cool Medium: Television, McCarthyism, and American Culture* (New York: Columbia University Press, 2003); Ted Morgan, *Reds: McCarthyism in Twentieth-Century America* (New York: Random House, 2003).

For the Bonus Army, see Michael J. Rawl, *Anacostia Flats: Eisenhower, MacArthur, Patton, and the Rout of the Bonus Marchers* (New York: PublishAmerica, 2006); Paul Dickson and Thomas B. Allen, *The Bonus Army: An American Epic* (New York: Walker & Co, 2005); Hans Schmidt, *Maverick Marine: General Smedley D. Butler and the Contradictions of American Military History* (Lexington: University Press of Kentucky, 1998). For diverse WWII soldiers, see Chris Dixon, *African Americans and the Pacific War, 1941–1945: Race, Nationality, and the Fight for Freedom* (Cambridge, UK: Cambridge University Press, 2018); James M. McCaffrey, *Going for Broke: Japanese American Soldiers in the War Against Nazi Germany* (Norman: University of Oklahoma Press, 2013); Linda Tamura, *Nisei Soldiers Break Their Silence: Coming Home to Hood River* (Seattle: University of

Washington Press, 2012); Maria Höhn and Martin Klimke, *A Breath of Freedom: The Civil Rights Struggle, African American GIs, and Germany* (New York: Palgrave Macmillan, 2010); Tom Holm, *Code Talkers and Warriors: Native Americans and World War II* (Broomall, UK: Chelsea House, 2007). For radical art, see Donald Pizer, *Toward a Modernist Style: John Dos Passos* (New York: Bloomsbury Academic, 2013); Chris Vials, *Realism for the Masses: Aesthetics, Popular Front Pluralism, and U.S. Culture, 1935–1947* (Jackson: University Press of Mississippi, 2009); Barbara A. Heavilin, *John Steinbeck's* The Grapes of Wrath: *A Reference Guide* (Westport, CT: Greenwood Press, 2002); Anthony Lee, *Painting on the Left: Rivera, Radical Politics, and San Francisco's Public Murals* (Berkeley: University of California Press, 1999). For the Harlem Renaissance, see Shannon King, *Whose Harlem Is This, Anyway?: Community Politics and Grassroots Activism during the New Negro Era* (New York: New York University Press, 2015); Vera M. Kutzinksi, *The Worlds of Langston Hughes: Modernism and Translation in the Americas* (Ithaca, NY: Cornell University Press, 2012); W. Jason Miller, *Langston Hughes and American Lynching Culture* (Gainesville: University Press of Florida, 2011); Winston James, *A Fierce Hatred of Injustice: Claude McKay's Jamaica and His Poetry of Rebellion* (London: Verso, 2001); Houston A. Baker, *Modernism and the Harlem Renaissance* (Chicago: University of Chicago Press, 1987).

CHAPTER 7: THE 1960S: LOVE IT, LEAVE IT, OR CHANGE IT

For overall studies of patriotism and the '60s, see Christopher B. Strain, *The Long Sixties: America, 1955–1973* (Chichester, UK: Wiley Blackwell, 2017); Victor Brooks, *Last Season of Innocence: The Teen Experience in the 1960s* (Lanham, MD: Rowman & Littlefield, 2012); Michael W. Flamm and David Steigerwald, *Debating the 1960s: Liberal, Conservative, and Radical Perspectives* (Lanham, MD: Rowman & Littlefield, 2008); Maurice Isserman and Michael Kazin, *America Divided: The Civil War of the 1960s* (New York: Oxford University Press, 2000); Richard M. Fried, *The Russians are Coming! The Russians are Coming!: Pageantry and Patriotism in Cold-War America* (New York: Oxford University Press, 1998); Tom Engenhardt, *The End of Victory Culture: Cold War America and the Disillusioning of a Generation* (New York: Basic Books, 1995); David Farber, *The Sixties: From Memory to History* (Chapel Hill: University of North Carolina Press, 1994).

For Kennedy and the space program, see Douglas Brinkley, *American Moonshot: John F. Kennedy and the Great Space Race* (New York: Harper-Collins, 2019); Scott D. Reich, *The Power of Citizenship: Why John F. Ken-

nedy Matters to a New Generation (Dallas: BenBella Books, 2013); Deborah Cadbury, *Space Race: The Epic Battle between America and the Soviet Union for Dominance of Space* (New York: HarperCollins, 2006); David Farber and Eric Foner, *The Age of Great Dreams: America in the 1960s* (New York: Hill and Wang, 1994); Walter A. McDougall, *The Heavens and the Earth: A Political History of the Space Age* (New York: Basic Books, 1985). For the Bicentennial, see Tammy S. Gordon, *The Spirit of 1976: Commerce, Community, and The Politics of Commemoration* (Amherst: University of Massachusetts Press, 2013); Christopher Capozzola, "'It Makes You Want to Believe in the Country': Celebrating the Bicentennial in the Age of Limits," in Beth Bailey & David Farber, eds., *America in the 70s* (Lawrence: University Press of Kansas, 2004).

For protesters, see Simon Hall, *American Patriotism, American Protest: Social Movements since the Sixties* (Philadelphia: University of Pennsylvania Press, 2011); Jerry Lembcke, *Hanoi Jane: War, Sex, and Fantasies of Betrayal* (Amherst: University of Massachusetts Press, 2010); Christoph Grunenberg and Jonathan Harris, *Summer of Love: Psychedelic Art, Social Crisis, and Counterculture in the 1960s* (Liverpool: Liverpool University Press, 2005); Mary Hershberger, *Jane Fonda's War: A Political Biography of an Antiwar Icon* (New York: New Press, 2005); Mary Susannah Robbins, *Against the Vietnam War: Writings by Activists* (Syracuse, NY: Syracuse University Press, 1999); Jerry Lembcke, *The Spitting Image: Myth, Memory, and the Legacy of Vietnam* (New York: New York University Press, 1998). For exclusionary cultural works, see Joe Street, *Dirty Harry's America: Clint Eastwood, Harry Callahan, and the Conservative Backlash* (Gainesville: University Press of Florida, 2016); Scott Eyman, *John Wayne: The Life and Legend* (New York: Simon & Schuster, 2014); Scott Simmon, *The Invention of the Western Film: A Cultural History of the Genre's First Half Century* (Cambridge, UK: Cambridge University Press, 2003); J. David Slocum, *Violence and American Cinema* (New York: Routledge, 2001); Garry Wills, *John Wayne's America: The Politics of Celebrity* (New York: Simon & Schuster, 1997); John H. Lenihan, *Showdown: Confronting Modern America in the Western Film* (Urbana: University of Illinois Press, 1980).

For VVAW, see David Cortright, *Soldiers in Revolt: GI Resistance during the Vietnam War* (Chicago: Haymarket Books, 2005); Gerald Nicosia, *Home to War: A History of the Vietnam Veterans' Movement* (New York: Crown Publishers, 2001); Andrew E. Hunt, *The Turning: A History of Vietnam Veterans Against the War* (New York: New York University Press, 1999); Charles DeBennedetti, *An American Ordeal: The Antiwar Movement of the Vietnam Era* (Syracuse, NY: Syracuse University Press, 1990). For the Civil Rights Movement, see Keisha N. Blain, *Set the World on Fire: Black Nation-*

alism Women and the Global Struggle for Freedom (Philadelphia: University of Pennsylvania Press, 2018); Sylvie Laurent, *King and the Other America: The Poor People's Campaign and the Quest for Economic Equality* (Oakland: University of California Press, 2018); Ari Berman, *Give Us the Ballot: The Modern Struggle for Voting Rights in America* (New York: Farrar, Straus and Giroux, 2015); Joshua Bloom and Waldo E. Martin Jr., *Black against Empire: The History and Politics of the Black Panther Party* (Berkeley: University of California Press, 2013); Cynthia E. Orozco, *No Mexicans, Women, or Dogs Allowed: The Rise of the Mexican American Civil Rights Movement* (Austin: University of Texas Press, 2009); Lorena Oropeza, *Raza Si, Guerra No: Chicano Protest and Patriotism during the Viet Nam War Era* (Berkeley: University of California Press, 2005).

For AIM, see Troy R. Johnson, *Red Power: The Native American Civil Rights Movement* (Chichester, UK: Chelsea House, 2007); Dennis Banks and Richard Erdoes, *Ojibwa Warrior: Dennis Banks and the Rise of the American Indian Movement* (Norman: University of Oklahoma Press, 2004); Joanne Nagel, *American Indian Ethnic Renewal: Red Power and the Resurgence of Identity and Culture* (New York: Oxford University Press, 1996); Kenneth S. Stern, *Loud Hawk: The United States versus the American Indian Movement* (Norman: University of Oklahoma Press, 1994). For the LGBTQ movement, see Katherine Crawford-Lackey, *Preservation and Place: Historic Preservation by and of LGBTQ Communities in the United States* (New York: Berghahn Books, 2019); Vern L. Bullough, ed., *Before Stonewall: Activists for Gay and Lesbian Rights in Historical Context* (New York: Harrington Park Press, 2002); John D'Emilio, *Sexual Politics, Sexual Communities: The Making of a Homosexual Minority in the United States, 1940–1970* (Chicago: University of Chicago Press, 1983). For Baldwin, see Douglas Field, *All Those Strangers: The Art and Lives of James Baldwin* (New York: Oxford University Press, 2015); Katharine Lawrence Balfour, *The Evidence of Things Not Said: James Baldwin and the Promise of American Democracy* (Ithaca, NY: Cornell University Press, 2001). For Simone, see Alan Light, *What Happened, Miss Simone?: A Biography* (New York: Crown Archetype, 2016); Nadine Cohodas, *Princess Noire: The Tumultuous Reign of Nina Simone* (Chapel Hill: University of North Carolina Press, 2010).

CHAPTER 8: THE 1980S:
MORNING AND MOURNING IN AMERICA

For the sports moments, see Barbara L. Tischler, *Muhammad Ali: A Man of Many Voices* (New York: Routledge, 2016); Wayne Coffey, *The Boys of*

Winter: The Untold Story of a Coach, a Dream, and the 1980 U.S. Olympic Hockey Team (New York: Crown Publishers, 2005). For overall studies of 1980s patriotism, see Bradford Martin, *The Other Eighties: A Secret History of America in the Age of Reagan* (New York: Hill and Wang, 2011); James Livingston, *The World Turned Inside Out: American Thought and Culture at the End of the 20th Century* (Lanham, MD: Rowman and Littlefield, 2010); Gil Troy and Vincent Cannato, eds., *Living in the Eighties* (Oxford, UK: Oxford University Press, 2009); Sean Wilentz, *The Age of Reagan: A History, 1974–2008* (New York: HarperCollins, 2008); Robert M. Collins, *Transforming America: Politics and Culture During the Reagan Years* (New York: Columbia University Press, 2007); John Ehrman, *The Eighties: America in the Age of Reagan* (New Haven, CT: Yale University Press, 2006).

For Reagan, see Steven F. Hayward, *The Age of Reagan: The Conservative Counterrevolution, 1980–1989* (New York: Crown Forum, 2009); James Mann, *The Rebellion of Ronald Reagan: A History of the End of the Cold War* (New York: Viking, 2009); John Patrick Diggins, *Ronald Reagan: Fate, Freedom, and the Making of History* (New York: W.W. Norton, 2008); Gil Troy, *Morning in America: How Ronald Reagan Invented the 1980s* (Princeton, NJ: Princeton University Press, 2007); Richard Reeves, *President Reagan: The Triumph of Imagination* (New York: Simon & Schuster, 2005); Garry Wills, *Reagan's America: Innocents at Home* (Garden City, NY: Doubleday, 1987). For wealth and poverty, see Lauren Greenfield, *Generation Wealth* (London: Phaidon, 2017); Jefferson Cowie, *Stayin' Alive: The 1970s and the Last Days of the Working Class* (New York: New Press, 2010); Lawrence R. Samuel, *Rich: The Rise and Fall of American Wealth Culture* (New York: AMACOM, 2009); David Haglund, "Reagan's Favorite Sitcom: How *Family Ties* Spawned a Conservative Hero," *Slate*, March 2, 2007; Vivyan Campbell Adair, *From Good Ma to Welfare Queen: A Genealogy of the Poor Woman in American Literature, Photography, and Culture* (New York: Garland, 2000); James Grant, *Money of the Mind: Borrowing and Lending in America from the Civil War to Michael Milken* (New York: Farrar, Straus and Giroux, 1992).

For nostalgia, see Stephanie Coontz, *The Way We Never Were: American Families and the Nostalgia Trap, Revised and Updated Edition* (New York: Basic Books, 2016); Natasha Zaretsky, *No Direction Home: The American Family and the Fear of National Decline, 1968–1980* (Chapel Hill: University of North Carolina Press, 2007); Philip Jenkins, *Decade of Nightmares: The End of the Sixties and the Making of Eighties America* (Oxford, UK: Oxford University Press, 2006); Van Gosse and Richard Moser, eds., *The World the Sixties Made: Politics and Culture in Recent America* (Philadelphia: Temple University Press, 2003). For the culture wars, see

Andrew Hartman, *A War for the Soul of America: A History of the Culture Wars* (Chicago: University of Chicago Press, 2015); Irene Tavis Thomson, *Culture Wars and Enduring American Dilemmas* (Ann Arbor: University of Michigan Press, 2010); Jonathan Zimmerman, *Whose America?: Culture Wars in the Public Schools* (Cambridge, MA: Harvard University Press, 2002); James Davison Hunter, *Culture Wars: The Struggle to Define America* (New York: Basic Books, 1991). For crime and cities, see Antero Pietila, *Not in My Neighborhood: How Bigotry Shaped a Great American City* (Chicago: Ivan R. Dee, 2010); Kevin Kruse, *White Flight: Atlanta and the Making of Modern Conservatism* (Princeton, NJ: Princeton University Press, 2005); Eric Avila, *Popular Culture in the Age of White Flight: Fear and Fantasy in Suburban Los Angeles* (Berkeley: University of California Press, 2004); Thomas Sugrue, *The Origins of the Urban Crisis: Race and Inequality in Postwar Detroit* (Princeton, NJ: Princeton University Press, 1996); George P. Fletcher, *A Crime of Self-Defense: Bernard Goetz and the Law on Trial* (Chicago: University of Chicago Press, 1988).

For the anti-nuclear movement, see Natasha Zaretsky, *Radiation Nation: Three Mile Island and the Political Transformation of the 1970s* (New York: Columbia University Press, 2018); Robert Surbrug, *Beyond Vietnam: The Politics of Protest in Massachusetts, 1974–1990* (Amherst: University of Massachusetts Press, 2009); Marco Giugni, *Social Protest and Policy Change: Ecology, Antinuclear, and Peace Movements in Comparative Perspective* (Lanham, MD: Rowman & Littlefield, 2004); Christian Peterson, *Ronald Reagan and Antinuclear Movements in the United States and Western Europe, 1981–1987* (Lewiston, NY: Edwin Mellen Press, 2003). For AIDS activism, see Jennifer Brier, *Infectious Ideas: U.S. Political Responses to the AIDS Crisis* (Chapel Hill, NC: University of North Carolina Press, 2009); Deborah B. Gould, *Moving Politics: Emotion and ACT UP's Fight against AIDS* (Chicago: University of Chicago Press, 2009); Ann Silversides, *AIDS Activist: Michael Lynch and the Politics of Community* (Toronto: Between the Lines, 2003); Michael P. Brown, *RePlacing Citizenship: AIDS Activism and Radical Democracy* (New York: Guilford Press, 1997). For hip hop, see Lakeyta M. Bonnette, *Pulse of the People: Political Rap Music and Black Politics* (Philadelphia: University of Pennsylvania Press, 2015); Jeffrey O. G. Ogbar, *Hip-Hop Revolution: The Culture and Politics of Rap* (Lawrence: University Press of Kansas, 2007); Jeff Chang, *Can't Stop Won't Stop: A History of the Hip-Hop Generation* (New York: St. Martin's Press, 2005); Charlie Ahearn and Jim Fricke, eds., *Yes Yes Y'all: The Experience Music Project Oral History of Hip Hop's First Decade* (Cambridge, MA: Da Capo Press, 2002); Robin D. G. Kelly, *Race Rebels: Culture, Politics, and the Black Working Class* (New York: Free Press, 1994).

CONCLUSION: PATRIOTISM IN THE AGE OF TRUMP

For Trump and patriotism, see Jack Pitney, *Un-American: The Fake Patriotism of Donald J. Trump* (Lanham, MD: Rowman & Littlefield, 2020); Rich Lowry, *The Case for Nationalism: How It Made Us Powerful, United, and Free* (New York: Broadside Books, 2019); Marc Benjamin Sable and Angel Jaramillo Torres, eds., *Trump and Political Philosophy: Patriotism, Cosmopolitanism, and Civic Virture* (New York: Palgrave Macmillan, 2018). For 21st century exclusions, see John E. Finn, *Fracturing the Founding: How the Alt-Right Corrupts the Constitution* (Lanham, MD: Rowman & Littlefield, 2019); Eric Klinenberg, *Antidemocracy in America: Truth, Power, and the Republic at Risk* (New York: Columbia University Press, 2019); Ben Railton, *We the People: The 500-Year Battle over Who is American* (Lanham, MD: Rowman & Littlefield, 2019); Alexandra Minna Stern, *Proud Boys and the White Ethnostate: How the Alt-Right is Warping the American Imagination* (Boston: Beacon Press, 2019); Sasha Polakow-Suransky, *Go Back to Where You Came From: The Backlash against Immigration and the Fate of Western Democracy* (New York: Nation Books, 2017).

For 21st century critical patriotism, see Kevin M. Gannon, *Radical Hope: A Teaching Manifesto* (Morgantown: West Virginia University Press, 2020); Amitai Etzioni, *Reclaiming Patriotism* (Charlottesville: University of Virginia Press, 2019); Dana R. Fisher, *American Resistance: From the Women's March to the Blue Wave* (New York: Columbia University Press, 2019); Eric Burin, ed., *Protesting on Bended Knee: Race, Dissent, and Patriotism in 21st Century America* (Grand Forks: Digital Press at the University of North Dakota, 2018); Samhita Mukhopadhyay and Kate Harding, eds., *Nasty Women: Feminism, Resistance, and Revolution in Trump's America* (New York: Picador, 2017). Also see the sources listed under the introduction.

Index